An Entrepreneur Gui
to Finding Your Flow

YOUR LIFE
YOUR LEGACY

BY ROGER HAMILTON

Published by Achievers International, (65) 6372 3383
Printed in Singapore by Kepmedia International Pte Ltd

ISBN 978-981-05-8381-1

1st published October 2006
2nd published May 2007

Foreword

*"Your work is to discover your work
and then with all your heart to give yourself to it."*
- Buddha

Imagine a race in which the runner takes off full of energy and enthusiasm. Intent on winning, for the first few moments he enjoys the breeze in his face and the feeling of progress. However, after a while he thinks ahead to the finish line, and wonders how far it is. Then he wonders exactly where it is. He realizes that he has no idea. In his excitement to get going, he never thought to get a map.

No matter how much energy and enthusiasm you may have, without certainty of where you are going and how you will get there, you will soon lose momentum. In such times, many of us seek motivation to keep us going. My approach has not been to seek motivation, but to seek certainty – to seek direction. Once you have clarity about your path, then your momentum along it will reach new levels.

Wealth Dynamics will give you this clarity. It identifies your own natural path to lasting wealth. It explains why it is that when you follow your natural path, you find your flow: you attract the resources you need to achieve your true potential. It explains why your life path leads to your life purpose. It is based on the life experiences, successes and failures of many who have run the race before us. It covers the journeys of those who we admire today for what they have achieved – the lives they have lived and the legacies they have left.

Wealth Dynamics is not just *one* path to wealth creation, but *every* path – of which *your* path is one. This book is about *your* life. It is about *your* legacy.

Roger HAMILTON

Chairman, XL Results Foundation

3

Contents

Part One: Running Your River
How your wealth profile leads you to your wealth path

Part Two: Finding Your Flow
Eight wealth profiles and thirty-eight wealth creators

Part Three: Leaving Your Legacy
How your life path leads you to your life purpose

INTRODUCTION

READING THIS BOOK

This book is divided into three parts. The first part, "Running Your River", explains the time-tested principles of Wealth Dynamics. Just as the laws of nature give us a technical understanding of what makes a river flow, the rules behind Wealth Dynamics give us a technical understanding of what makes wealth flow – why some struggle to create a trickle while others have carved a roaring river.

The second part, "Finding Your Flow", provides an insight into the lives of thirty-eight Wealth Creators whose rivers flow today. They are organized into the eight wealth profiles so that you can see just how different each profile is. We document failures as well as successes, underlining the perils of breaking the rules of your game or diverting from your flow. Each story adds another layer to your understanding of wealth creation.

Each of the thirty-eight Wealth Creators have been chosen for the different lessons we can learn from their journey. Each has found their flow. Each has created enormous attraction on their natural path. Their individual net worth ranges from $100 million to $50 billion. Each is living a purpose and leaving a legacy.

The third part, "Leaving Your Legacy", delves into the mechanics of Wealth Dynamics: how you can apply the profile distinctions to communicate, contribute, lead and live more effectively. It breaks down your path into a series of steps that take us on the magical road from path to purpose – from duty to destiny.

Tomorrow's future is built on the shoulders of today's Wealth Creators. In today's economies, there is unprecedented access to the daily global flow of money, talent and resources. When we take responsibility for mastering how to direct part of this flow, we can direct it towards making a difference.

> *"The power of money is the power to give it away -*
> *to make a difference."*
> - Narayana Murthy

PART ONE

Running
Your River

CHAPTER ONE

WHAT IS WEALTH?

*"I have enough money to last me the rest of my life,
unless I buy something."*
- Jackie Mason

THE WEALTH PARADOX

Evelyn Adams won the New Jersey lottery not once but twice, in 1985 and 1986. All $5.4 million of winnings has since evaporated – mostly into Atlantic City slot machines. Relegated to living in a trailer in a trailer park, Adams said, "I wish I had the chance to do it all over again. I'd be much smarter about it now."

William "Bud" Post won $16.2 million in the Pennsylvania lottery. He invested in a car and restaurant business. Within a year he found himself $1 million in debt and went on to declare bankruptcy. To make matters worse, his brother was arrested for hiring a hit man to assassinate him so he could claim the winnings for himself. "Bud" now lives on Social Security saying, "I wish it had never happened. It was a total nightmare."

While many of us deny that we would be quite as careless as Evelyn and Bud, why is it that so many of *us* continue to work so hard, earn so much and still have so little to show for it?

This book is not about '*making money',* as many of us lose the money we make. This book is about '*creating wealth'.* If you have not created wealth, any excess cash you have becomes a terribly temporary condition. Why? Because there is peculiar paradox that pops up as the cash rolls in.

We call this the wealth paradox: The more money you have, the more opportunities you have to lose it.

The Wealth Paradox:

"The more money you have, the more opportunities you have to lose it."

Losing money is not a problem when you don't have any to lose, but as you find yourself with excess income, many new opportunities open up. It is tempting to spend it or invest it in areas where you have little experience and little idea of the pitfalls ahead: your confidence exceeds your competence and the money disappears.

So why are we so busy trying to make money when, after we finally get it, we're likely to lose it anyway?

Even *more* frustrating, why is it that when we look at people who we consider wealthy, no matter how much their money or business gets taken away from them, it comes right back again?

The story of Donald Trump is legend. Trump built a property empire in the 1980's (largely on deals leveraged with a high level of debt). When the market turned in 1990, he was no longer able to make interest payments, resulting in $3.5 billion in business debt and a further $900 million in personal debt. This means that you and I were around $900 million wealthier than Donald Trump in 1990. However, in the following decade Trump reversed the situation and by 2005 he had a net worth of $2.7 billion listed on the Forbes 400 list of the richest Americans.

Most of the Wealth Creators in the following pages have faced challenges where they have lost a substantial amount of money, business or both – but they bounce back, again and again. The Wealth Paradox separates the temporary nature of money from the permanent nature of wealth. Whatever money you have, it will eventually fall – or rise – back to your level of wealth. This leads us to the definition of wealth.

THE DEFINITION OF WEALTH

As a result of the Wealth Paradox, we cannot simply equate wealth to money. So if wealth is not how much money you have, what is it?

Definition of Wealth:

"Wealth is not how much money you have. Wealth is what you're left with when you lose all your money."

True wealth lies in your power to give and receive at your full potential. Those who grow their wealth are continuously increasing their flow, attracting more and contributing more. Only when you live at your potential can you give at your potential. Growing wealth leads to a greater income – and a greater outcome.

To use a metaphor, wealth is like a garden. The most inspiring, lovingly nurtured garden gives the most pleasure and attracts the most butterflies. Wealth Creators don't build nets to catch butterflies. They grow an inspiring garden.

THE NET & THE GARDEN

Wealth is permanent, like the garden, while money is temporary, like the butterflies. Using the analogy of money being as tricky and transient as butterflies is quite useful. It allows us to draw a clear distinction between the strategies of those who are busy trying to make money compared to those who are building wealth.

The NET

You want to catch butterflies, so you decide to build a net. Surely, with a net you can catch them more easily! You read books on the subject and you practice skills in butterfly catching. You find that you are making improvements. Your net gets bigger and smarter and gradually you do catch more butterflies, but there is something wrong.

After many years of this strategy you still need to wake up every day and go out to catch more butterflies. You need to hold on to the butterflies you have caught or they will fly away just as quickly. The more butterflies you have, the more difficult they are to hold on to. You are constantly in fear that the butterflies will disappear or that someone with a bigger net will beat you at your own game.

When the butterflies disappear, you're left with nothing.

Many people have become experts at sales, marketing, management and customer service. Yet they still struggle to make money. We all know of people who have learnt the strategies of successful stock market traders, property investors and serial entrepreneurs yet are still left funding their losses. They carefully follow the strategies they learn and then remain baffled as to why they do not attract the same opportunities, resources and sheer luck as their role models. They are trying to make money without first building wealth.

They are trying to chase butterflies with a net.

The GARDEN

Successful Wealth Creators don't worry about building a net. They grow a garden. By focusing on creating an inspiring garden, you are growing something permanent around you. As the garden grows, the butterflies come. As time goes by, the effort required to manage the garden falls as the number of butterflies rises. In fact, the butterflies, birds and bees end up pollinating your garden for you. You don't fear butterflies leaving, as there are always more coming.

If anyone takes your butterflies, there will be more the next day.

Every successful Wealth Creator is focused entirely on building their wealth foundation rather than their moneymaking activities. They build a reputation, a powerful network, a knowledge base, a resource base and a track record. This is their garden, and it is built not around their expertise, but around their passion, their path and their purpose. Every day, they wake up to their garden, not to an empty net.

In a recent speech to a group of students, Warren Buffett said:

"I may have more money than you, but money doesn't make the difference. If there is any difference between you and me, it may simply be that I get up and have a chance to do what I love to do, every day. If you learn anything from me, this is the best advice I can give you."

ATTRACTING MORE BY MOVING LESS

Warren Buffett attracts billion dollar butterflies. He does it by letting people know that his investment company, Berkshire Hathaway, is interested in businesses between $5 billion and $20 billion in size, with consistent earning power, good return on equity, little debt, and good management. He promises confidentiality and quick response from himself and his Vice-Chairman, Charlie Munger. Consequently, he has described his acquisition strategy like this: "It's very scientific. Charlie and I just sit around and wait for the phone to ring. Sometimes it's a wrong number."

Each Wealth Creator has stopped chasing opportunities and chosen to build a wealth foundation around their specific passions and talents. As the American industrialist, Andrew Carnegie said: "The men who have succeeded are the men who have chosen one line and stuck to it." This does not mean sticking to a particular profession, industry or even country. It does mean sticking to your wealth profile. Warren Buffett attracts the deals that suit Berkshire Hathaway; Richard Branson attracts the businesses that suit Virgin, and Jack Welch - while CEO of General Electric - attracted the right people to join his leadership team.

Each different wealth profile has different values that result in different attractions – they are tending to different gardens. Welch used a similar metaphor when talking about his role at GE: "My main job was developing talent. I was a gardener providing water and other nourishment to our top 750 people. Of course, I had to pull out some weeds, too."

THE RIVER OF WEALTH

"Be still like a mountain and flow like a great river."
- Lao Tse

Does the garden metaphor resonate with you? Are you busy chasing butterflies with a net or are you growing a garden? The garden is the first step. Here is the second. You can water your garden with a bucket, or you can water it with a permanent river.

We can all relate to the idea of growing a garden. But running our own river? Every great Wealth Creator has created their own river. When we grow our river, we grow our flow. As we grow our flow, we grow our attraction. At first glance, the two metaphors are similar: as with the butterflies, the water in the river is temporary; as with the garden, the river is permanent.

There are, however, four important additions:

1. Water

Water, like money, flows. Money is already flowing around this planet at an unprecedented rate. Great Wealth Creators have achieved their wealth not by 'making money' but by 'creating flow'. They have learnt how to redirect some of this money flow through themselves and their enterprises. Wealth then, is largely about good plumbing. There are rules to this plumbing, and the structure of Wealth Dynamics is based on these rules.

2. Flow

Flow is about more than cash flow. It is about life flow. Each of us creates our greatest wealth when we are in our own personal flow. Those of us who build a river around this flow attract all the resources, people and opportunities in the same way that a leaf thrown in a river will naturally be attracted to the central current. When we are creating the *right* river, it *feels* right for us. When you find your flow, you begin to love life and live life fully.

3. Path

There are different paths to running a river, and we each have a natural path of least resistance. Wealth Dynamics classifies these paths into eight profiles. Each is a different game with different players and different rules. Until you follow your natural path, life feels like a struggle and you will find little attraction. Many of us are operating at a fraction of our true potential. Focus on your natural path and life soon changes from hard-to-get to easy-to-give.

4. Purpose

In a river, flow assumes exit as well as entry. Giving more opens the way to receiving more. With flow, a bigger income goes hand-in-hand with a bigger outcome. In the limited time we have on this planet, we choose our power to create and our power to contribute. When you live in your flow you maximize this power. You attract the resources to leave a lasting legacy. Your path leads to your purpose.

HE SAID, SHE SAID

When we look at the Wealth Creators carving the biggest rivers it doesn't take us long to notice that they appear to be taking entirely different approaches. Bill Gates, founder of Microsoft, is the wealthiest man in the world with a staff of close to sixty thousand. Warren Buffett, Chairman of Berkshire Hathaway, is the second wealthiest man with a team of fourteen. Richard Branson, founder of the Virgin Group, has become one of the UK's best known entrepreneurs with over two hundred companies (and two books). J.K. Rowlings, author of the Harry Potter series, has made a fortune in the last eight years with six books (and one company)...

Their advice differs as much as their paths. Meg Whitman, CEO of eBay and one of the wealthiest women in America, advocates always adapting to the customer's needs while Henry Ford, who took his Model T car to a phenomenal 48% market share famously said, "The customer can have (a car of) any color he wants, so long as it's black". Warren Buffett insists on a detailed understanding of any company he invests in, saying "Risk comes from not knowing what you are doing," whereas Ray Kroc, who built McDonald's so successfully, said "If you're not a risk taker, you should get the hell out of business."

Who do we listen to and whose principles should we follow? Should we be accessible at all times like Donald Trump or should we play hard to get like Tiger Woods? Should we venture into new countries like Branson or simply trade their currencies like George Soros (and save the airfare)? Making sense of the many approaches to wealth creation can be compared to making sense of the different games on ESPN. Each has different rules, different teams, and different strategies. Only by understanding the games can we listen to the soccer player say "Kick the ball, don't pick it up," and the basketball player say "Pick up the ball, don't kick it," and realize that they aren't contradicting each other. They are simply playing different games.

Success comes from knowing which game to play, and then playing that game – and only that game. Each of us has a game that is most suited to our own natural habits and talents. So how do we find out which game to play?

Wealth Dynamics takes the entire world of confusing, contradictory and convoluted information on wealth creation and puts it into a coherent and comprehensive system. It gives each of us clarity on our personal path of least resistance to wealth creation: what our strategy should be, who we need in our team, how we should apply ourselves, when we should take action and – more importantly - when we should not. This book, then, is more than a collection of stories or an explanation of some new wealth creation theory.

It is a journey into the universal flow of wealth that we are all a part of, and leads towards fresh insight into the true meaning of 'entrepreneurial spirit'.

CHAPTER TWO

ARE YOU FEELING LUCKY?

"Everything in life is luck."
- Donald Trump

GETTING LUCKY

You will find it very easy, when reading the stories of the billionaires and multi-millionaires in this book, to say, "They were lucky." The reason it's easy to say, is because it's true. The key to wealth is luck.

Luck is the phenomena that Swiss Psychiatrist, Carl Jung, termed synchronicity. Luck is intimately related to flow. As your flow grows, your luck grows. As your luck grows, your flow grows. Wealth Creators know how to grow their own luck.

Sam Walton, founder of Wal-Mart, was the richest man in the world in the 1980's, and his family remains the richest family in the world today. Sam fell into retailing at the age of 21 because his family's neighbor happened to be a retailer with 60 variety stores. Hugh Mattingly became one of Walton's first mentors, showing him the trade and offering him a job.

So did Walton have a plan for wealth? "I don't know about that kind of stuff. But I know this for sure: I loved retail from the very beginning, and I love it today." So did the success formula of a Wal-Mart in every town happen by chance? No, it was by necessity. As Walton was getting ready to start his first store, his wife Helen said, "I'll go with you any place you want so long as you don't ask me to live in a big city. Ten thousand people are enough for me."

"Everything existing in the universe is the fruit of chance and necessity."
- Democritus (460BC)

A friend of Walton's, Tom Bates, worked for a retail franchiser, Butler Brothers. So Walton asked Tom what he'd have that suited a small town, and at the age of 27 got started with a Butler Brothers franchise in Newport, Arkansas. By chance it was right across the street from a very successful competitor, John Dunham. "It was a real blessing for me to be so green and ignorant, because it was from that experience that I learned a lesson which has stuck with me all through the years: you can learn from everybody. I didn't just learn from reading every retail publication I could get my hands on; I probably learned the most from studying what John Dunham was doing across the street."

Then came the billion-dollar piece of bad luck - not because it cost a billion, but because it led to a billion. "In all my excitement at becoming Sam Walton, Merchant, I had neglected to include a clause in my lease which gave me an option to renew after the first five years." Seeing the success of the store, the landlord chose not to renew the lease and forced the sale of the outlet from Walton to his own son. With no other viable location in Newport, Walton loaded his family and belongings into a truck and started driving. They didn't stop until they came to a small town, Bentonville, population 3,000. There, at the age of 32, he started Walton's Five and Dime Store. Twelve years later, also in Bentonville, the first Wal-Mart opened; today Bentonville is the headquarters of Wal-Mart's $220 billion global empire. When Sam Walton died, he was the richest man in the world.

"I run on the road, long before I dance under the lights."
- Muhammad Ali

Three years ago, Steve Jobs, founder of Apple, was busy developing the iMac into a multimedia editing device. Jeff Robbin, a 28-year-old developer who had left Apple months before Jobs' return, had started a company to develop Soundjam, a jukebox program. Jobs bought the company as Robbin had impressed the team at Apple, and over the next year Jobs asked him to develop a jukebox for the Mac, which he did, naming it iTunes.

Jobs thought, if photo files can be portable in your camera, why can't music files be portable too? So next he asked Robbin if he could come up with a portable music player, and nine months later the iPod was launched. But it was only after the team was playing with the iPod prototypes that they came up with the idea of the Apple iTunes online music store. Less than 18 months after the rollout of the iPod, the online store opened in April 2003. They hoped to sell a million songs in the first six months, and ended up selling that many in the first six days.

The online music store was the critical bridge that opened up the entire PC-user market in a way that software alone had never managed to do for Apple. By the end of 2005, Apple had a 62% share of the online music market. Apple's iPod business alone is predicted to hit $6.2 billion in 2006 – around what Apple's entire revenue was when Jobs took over. Did Apple's share price triple in 2005 as a result of a plan, or as a result of sheer luck? Steve Jobs has now made a billion dollars by being lucky on three separate occasions. All three happened by luck, but none happened by accident.

Great entrepreneurs do not create success. They create the conditions for success to occur. Wealth Creators are luck creators.

HOW TO CREATE LUCK

"Give luck a chance to happen."
- Tom Kite, US Golfer

Once you begin following your path, luck happens as a result of the flow you grow. Here's a simple way to build that foundation – to build your luck.

The foundation of luck is built on four conditions:

Location, **U**nderstanding, **C**onnections, **K**nowledge

Think of a game of football. Think of David Beckham. Now, he's lucky! The 30-year-old English footballer earns over $80,000 per week kicking a ball and, together with his wife, Victoria, has a net worth of close to $100 million.

So what is it that makes a footballer lucky? As we watch the game, there's an opening and Beckham scores. We think *"That was lucky. Out of all the spots on the pitch, he was exactly at the right place at the right time!"…*

LOCATION – Who chooses where you place yourself each day? We each have an opportunity to be at the right place, at the right time. Many of us are so busy going to work every day, we're always at the wrong place, wrong time. Luck starts with choosing to be at the right place, right time.

UNDERSTANDING – At the critical moment, when the ball is in front of the goal, we may find ourselves at the right place, right time, but we have no understanding of the reason we are there: to kick the ball. Many of us are still spectators, watching the game. By the time we notice the ball, it's too late to kick. The players know the reason they are there is to kick the ball, so have already anticipated it, positioned themselves, and kicked it. Luck comes from playing the game, not watching it.

CONNECTIONS – Many of us have positioned ourselves in front of the goal, and understand we're there to kick the ball. We've started our business, our investments, but there's no ball coming. We wait, and wait, and the years tick by. Still, there's no ball coming. If this happens to you, try looking around to see if there's anyone else on the pitch. Many of us have not invested in our connections – the players who should be kicking us the ball. There's no one on the pitch!

Great Wealth Creators have million dollar balls being kicked to them every day as a result of the connections they have built. Connections, by the way, are not the same as a network. Many of us have big networks, but networks are full of spectators, not players playing our game. So there are still no opportunities coming our way.

KNOWLEDGE – There's no point having balls coming your way if you don't know how to kick them. There's no point having opportunities coming your way if you don't know what to do with them. Knowing how to kick the ball comes with playing the game. The more you play, the more you know. Which is why, the sooner you choose your game, and play it, the sooner your luck begins to flow.

"To know and not to do is not yet to know."
- Zen saying

We build these four conditions not by investing our money, but by investing our time. Some of us have been too busy going to work each day to have invested any time in building our luck, and we are no luckier today than we were five years ago.

As you read the lucky stories in this book, consider how each Wealth Creator invests their time and becomes luckier and luckier as a result. Wealth isn't about how much money you have. It's what you have left when you lose all your money. When you've kicked the ball, the luck remains, and another ball will be along in a moment.

SEVEN PHENOMENA OF FLOW

As we play our natural game, and attract others who are playing the same game, we come across seven phenomena which accelerate us. Each of us has experienced one or more of these at times when we were in the flow. When you sustain this flow, these seven phenomena become magnified. In the coming chapters, we look at the different games each of the eight different wealth profiles play. As they each follow their natural path, they come across these same seven phenomena, accelerating their flow:

1. **Critical Moments** – These are the moments when the game is won or lost. How you recognize these moments and react in these fractions of time will define your life.

2. **Learning Cycles** – Each game is in itself a learning cycle. The number of times you play and your cumulative learning will define your performance in future critical moments.

3. **Failing Forward** – There are two types of failure. One gives you the learning, the other ends the game. Knowing how to differentiate between the two allows you to continue to play.

4. **Opportunities** – There are two types of opportunities. One you create, one you attract. Knowing how to pass on one and how to attract the other is key to the level at which you play.

5. **The Strength of Certainty** – Our success in life has more to do with what we say no to than what we say yes to. Being certain of the game you play escalates your attraction.

6. **The Power of Perseverance** – Continuing to play the same game, through good times and bad times, gives a level of confidence to others to play with you. We fail when we quit.

7. **The Magic of Momentum** – Winning teams win and lose on momentum. Momentum comes from an ongoing combination of the previous six. Momentum is the ultimate attractor.

PHENOMENON #1

CRITICAL MOMENTS

"I never get the accountants in before I start up a business.
It's done on gut feeling."
- Richard Branson

In many sports, the game may last 60 minutes, 90 minutes or more. But the game is won or lost in a number of critical moments that usually amount to less than five minutes of the game. No matter how well you play for the rest of the time, it counts for little if you fumble during those defining moments. So too, in life we can count the critical moments when a shift in action or reaction would have entirely changed our outcome.

In 1980, IBM had what Andy Grove, the founder of Intel, calls a "strategic inflection point", when all the rules changed. Apple had started the PC revolution, and IBM had no PC. An IBM group launched "Project Chess", a revolutionary outsourcing initiative that would cobble together the pieces from third party suppliers to create an IBM PC. To source an operating system, a member of the team contacted Bill Gates, a young 25-year-old software programmer he had heard of.

Gates didn't have any operating system to speak of, and so referred IBM on to Gary Kildall, the founder of Digital Research. But when IBM got no response from him, they came back to Gates. This was a classic critical moment typical of those that all entrepreneurs come across. How Gates handled that call defined his future.

He agreed to find them a solution, and then visited Tim Paterson, from Seattle Computer Products, who had just created an operating system called QDOS (Quick and Dirty Operating System). Gates bought it for $56,000, immediately repackaged it as PC-DOS for IBM, and then repackaged it again as MS-DOS (employing Paterson to modify it) and marketed it to the other emerging PC manufacturers, setting the future foundation and fortune for Microsoft.

At critical moments, it is our instincts that count most. It is not intellectual learning that creates mastery, but physical learning from practice. You cannot master touchdowns by reading books on football. It is financial fitness (by mastering the game) not financial literacy (by mastering the rules) that defines our success. Otherwise the best footballers would be the referees. As Warren Buffett said, "If past history was all there was to the game, the richest people would be librarians."

When you play the same game again and again, you begin to anticipate and master the critical moments, which re-occur in different forms. You begin to look forward to increasing the number of critical moments and to testing your mastery.

When we are not following our path, it feels like hard work. Not only do we miss critical moments, they seem few and far between. That's the clue that tells you to change path. If it feels like hard work, you're already doing the wrong thing.

When we follow our path, the game comes naturally. The longer we play the game, the better we master it. The better we master it, the more we multiply our critical moments – in the same way that sportspeople in the flow suddenly find multiple scoring opportunities.

In the words of Donald Trump, "Money was never a big motivation for me, except as a way to keep score. The real excitement is playing the game."

PHENOMENON #2
LEARNING CYCLES

> *"Experience isn't interesting till it begins to repeat itself.*
> *In fact, till it does that, it hardly is experience."*
> - Elizabeth Bowen

When I was studying architecture at Cambridge, at the age of 19, I had the chance to meet one of the most successful architects in the world today. Something had been troubling me about my future architectural career, and I asked him a question:

"Why is it that all the most successful architects only appear to become successful in their 60's?"

He responded, "All mastery comes from learning cycles: starting it, trying it, completing it, learning from it, and then repeating the cycle. In architecture, a learning cycle can take five to seven years. So by the time you've gone through enough cycles to begin mastering it, you're already in your 60's."

"But I want to be successful faster," I said. "How can I do that?"

"Simple," he replied. "Don't be an architect."

I left architecture and started my first business – a publishing business – figuring that with a monthly publication I could have twelve learning cycles in my first year.

As you keep playing the same game, your learning cycles build on each other – in a way that they cannot if you keep switching games. As you increase your cycles, you increase your insight into the game.

FAILING FORWARD

*"Success is the ability to go from one failure to another
with no loss of enthusiasm."*
- Winston Churchill

Multiplying critical moments and learning cycles is a scary thought for many of us. While we know that failure is a necessary step on the path to success, it still sounds painful. Great entrepreneurs get over this by differentiating between two different types of failure: failure that steers us versus failure that sinks us.

Let's compare physical strength to financial strength for a moment. If you want to build your muscles, you go to the gym and exercise with weights that literally push your muscles to failure. You rest, recover, and gradually find your muscles strengthening. This is what we mean by failure that steers – and strengthens – you.

On the other hand, you might go into the gym and see someone lifting an 80 kilogram weight. Confident that you can do the same, you jump into position, attempt to lift the weight, and experience a failure that sinks you. Worse still, you might give yourself a physical injury that puts you out of action for a month.

Similarly, while some of us invest the appropriate time or money into multiple failures that steer us to greater financial learning, others step up to the plate with little training and put our life savings in one venture. We lose money we could not afford to lose, and experience a failure that sinks us. We give ourselves a financial injury that puts us out of action for years.

Successful Wealth Creators separate failures that can sink them from failures that steer them. Great entrepreneurs maximize the failures that steer them and avoid the failures that can sink them. As they play their game, failure becomes a calculated cost of learning, with the entrepreneur always remaining in the game. In Warren Buffet's words: "I don't look to jump over 7-foot bars: I look around for 1-foot bars that I can step over."

PHENOMENON #4
OPPORTUNITIES

"Business opportunities are like buses,
there's always another one coming."
- Richard Branson

As with failure, opportunities also come in two forms – and we are often focused on the wrong one.

Outbound opportunities are the ones that we come up with ourselves – a new idea, a new business concept, a venture to try. Many of us think this is where our wealth lies which is why we never get started.

Inbound opportunities are the ones that get passed to us by others. Without exception, each Wealth Creator in this book created the most wealth through inbound opportunities. And as they followed their path, they attracted inbound opportunities of a higher and higher quality.

Richard Branson has been a master at attracting inbound opportunities. When they arrive he checks whether kicking the ball will result in a failure that will steer him or a failure that will sink him. He finds out how much he might lose if it all goes wrong, and, if he decides to kick the ball, he "ring-fences" the new enterprise with its own structure, team and financing.

In 1984, as Branson was busy with Virgin Music, Randolph Fields, a US lawyer, approached him to finance an airline for the transatlantic route that had opened after Sir Freddie Laker's airline had collapsed in 1982. This was an inbound opportunity out of the blue.

Branson did his numbers and decided: "If I could lease the plane for one year and then have the chance to return the plane, I would have a clear escape route if it all failed. If I can limit everything to one year – the employment contracts, the leasing of the aircraft, the exchange exposure, and everything else that starting up a New York route involves – then I want to have a shot at it."

On the weekend as he mulled over the proposal, he cold-called People Express (the airline already running an Atlantic budget route) to see how they were doing. He cold-called Freddie Laker for advice on the idea. Branson's approach to finding a plane to lease was equally straight-forward: "On Monday morning I called up international directory inquiries and asked for the number of Boeing. They were bemused to hear an Englishman asking what kinds of deals were available on a jumbo."

Branson went on to take the opportunity, setting up Virgin Atlantic as a separate company. Virgin Atlantic took off and ten years later Branson went on to sell Virgin Music in order to grow his airline business further.

We are often so busy holding on to our precious outbound opportunities, the inbound opportunities pass us by, ending up in the hands of those who are more receptive. Advice, again, from Warren Buffet: "You do things when the opportunities come along. I've had periods in my life when I've had a bundle of ideas come along, and I've had long dry spells. If I get an idea next week, I'll do something. If not, I won't do a damn thing."

PHENOMENON #5
THE STRENGTH OF CERTAINTY

"It's as important to figure out what you're not going to do as it is to know what you are going to do."
– Michael Dell

Our success in life has more to do with what we say no to than what we say yes to. Many of us are saying yes to all the right things – but we're saying yes to all the wrong things as well.

Being clear on the game we play gives us the chance to say no to everything else. It allows us to stop pursuing multiple streams of income and focus on one big river. Oprah does not come back from a day meeting celebrities and get online for a spot of options trading. Bill Gates does not come back from a day inventing at Microsoft and try his hand at network marketing.

There is a reason why there are so few sportspeople who have reached world-class level at more than one sport. Our greatest asset is our time. When we try to split our time between two games, we cannot master either to the same degree as someone just focused on one.

Most importantly, it is only when others know what you stand for that you will attract the reputation and resources to support you on your path.

> *"If you don't stand for something, you'll fall for anything."*
> - Les Brown

PHENOMENON #6
THE POWER OF PERSEVERANCE

> *"You can never quit.*
> *Winners never quit and quitters never win."*
> - Ted Turner

Once you are on the right path, the most essential quality to possess is neither intelligence nor talent, but perseverance. One thing you'll notice about every one of the stories in this book is that each Wealth Creator is still playing the game.

At one of my seminars, I met an enthusiastic graduate from one of the many entrepreneurship MBA programs currently on offer. As if by way of introduction, he asked "What's your exit strategy?"

"What?" I replied.

"What's your exit strategy? What's your plan?"

I asked him if he could name any famous billionaire who had made all his wealth by setting a plan with an exit strategy, executing the plan, and then exiting. He couldn't. I'm not saying exit strategies are not useful. The first thing you're told when you get on a plane is where the exits are. But exit strategies are for the passengers, not for the pilots. The last thing you want to hear when you get on a plane is that the pilot will be bailing out at 30,000 feet. The last thing you want to hear if you're investing in Berkshire Hathaway is that Warren will be bailing out once the stock price hits $95,000.

It's not a coincidence that all the World's wealthiest entrepreneurs continue to work long after they need to. They don't see it as work, so there's nothing to retire from. If retiring means giving up work to do what you enjoy, Warren Buffet retired the moment he started investing. Pilots don't quit: they're too busy having fun flying.

Steve Case, co-founder of AOL, explains a critical key to his success like this: "If you really believe what you're doing is right, and you believe it's important, and you truly feel that you are a pioneer who is making a difference, you may make some mistakes, but your energy and commitment will help you overcome them. That perseverance is important because there are times when the so-called smart thing may be to throw up your hands and quit because it's hard, or you've hit a brick wall. But you have to think 'Well, we're just going to keep at it.' That's critical."

Why does Bill Gates keep going to work every day? "I have the most fun job in the world, and love coming to work each day because there are always new challenges, new opportunities, and new things to learn. If you enjoy your job this much, you will never burn out."

Where does Richard Branson keep finding the energy to keep playing the game? If it is no longer fun, he moves on: "I never went into business to make money - but I found out that, if I have fun, the money will come. If something stops being fun, I ask 'why?' If I can't fix it, I stop doing it."

Perseverance comes from passion and purpose. When you play your natural game, you won't quit. You'll be too busy having fun playing. Sustained attraction occurs when those with the resources to support you *know* that you won't quit. If they suspect that you will, their resources will flow elsewhere and your river will run dry.

PHENOMENON #7

THE MAGIC OF MOMENTUM

"When you're that successful, things have a momentum, and at a certain point you can't really tell whether you have created the momentum or it's creating you."
- Annie Lennox

Every winning sports team knows the power of momentum. When the momentum swings from one team to the other, the scores soon change. Momentum is group flow.

When we are living with momentum, small obstacles disappear. Decisions are made with certainty. No one wants to miss the boat, and attraction appears all around us. In his book "The 21 Irrefutable Laws of Leadership", John Maxwell got it right when he wrote "Momentum is really a leader's best friend. Sometimes it's the only difference between winning and losing." When I asked Maxwell what distinguishes a manager from a leader, he replied: "A manager solves problems. A leader creates momentum. When you have momentum, the problems soon solve themselves."

The wealth of every great entrepreneur comes quickly when their personal flow resonates with the flow of the market. Momentum comes from sustained flow in the same way that a bonfire grows from a sustained flame. When we experience sustained flow, the momentum that we create between ourselves, our team, our partners, our customers and the market, takes on a life of its own and sweeps us along. Wealth doesn't only come faster; it comes far easier.

CHAPTER THREE

THE WEALTH EQUATION

"Try not to become a man of success,
but rather try to become a man of value."
- Albert Einstein

RULES OF THE RIVER

If every great Wealth Creator has carved a river, how did they all get started? What are the rules they follow? Wealth creation is based on an equation of value and leverage. One determines the gradient of the river and increases the speed of flow; the other determines the width of the river and increases the volume of flow. Both value and leverage have opposite polarities. Understanding the equation, and focusing on your polarity, is an essential step to running your river.

SCULPTING THE RIVER

When I was 27 years old, I had the chance to work with the team that had taken Dell Computers international. In 1987, a 22 year old Michael Dell opened a Dell office in England. Andrew Harris headed the international operation and brought in a good friend, Martin Slagter, to run the UK and European operations.

By 1992, Dell's sales had grown to $2 billion, from $60 million six years earlier. However, 1992 proved a critical year for the company. A series of crises led to the company posting its first quarterly loss. Dell brought in new management and both Harris and Slagter left the company in 1993. They left with stock options that they cashed in making them both multi-millionaires; they used their cash to start an exciting new venture in the UK and US, Hand Technologies.

Hand Tech was at the cutting edge when I joined it in 1995. They were leveraging on something new – the Internet – to sell computers with the aid of a network of agents, who tended to be the 'techies' that people in each community would already be going to for advice on what PC to buy. Through Harris and Slagter's industry contacts, they had deals with Microsoft, Compaq, HP and Apple to sell their PC's online long before these giants were doing so themselves.

I became the General Manager for the UK and we quickly grew to employ over 1,000 reps in the first year. The team was intent on learning from the management mistakes that they had seen Dell make. We assembled a seasoned board of advisors, invested in cutting-edge systems, implemented tight financial controls. But somehow there seemed to be something missing…

While we were leveraging like crazy – on our vendors, our reps, the Internet – and appeared to be clocking some impressive growth, we did not have the kind of attraction that Dell had. After the first twelve months it seemed we still had to work just as hard to sell the next PC or recruit the next rep, even though we were over ten times bigger – and we were still a long way from making any money.

Slagter and I began to focus at our core value proposition: why weren't customers beating a path to our door? Our vendor margins and rep commissions didn't let us sell at Dell's prices. The service we promised from our reps we couldn't control. The reliability from our vendors – despite them being brand names - we couldn't guarantee. Meanwhile Harris, based in Austin, kept focused on greater leverage, saying, "The profits will come when we reach critical mass. The critical mass will come once we've built our brand."

From 1995 to 1997, with money from two successful rounds of funding fueling our growth, we grew to over 10,000 reps selling from the Hand Technologies website. But the cost of acquiring each new rep and each new sale seemed to be going up, not down. Meanwhile, Dell – even with its ongoing management and production problems - had grown from $2.9m in sales in 1993 to an astounding $12.3b in 1997, and it had been profitable in every quarter.

Whilst we could dismiss a phenomenon whereby lottery winners were losing their fortunes and put it down to carelessness, here was a far more baffling situation. From all accounts, Dell was continuing to have management and production issues, while we seemed to have a well-functioning team. Yet Dell continued to grow and attract new business at a phenomenal rate, and we had to fight for every penny.

Why is it that we all know of some businesses that seem to be run so well – with great management, nice systems, happy customers – and yet they still lose money? Why is it that we also know of businesses that seem to have one issue after another, yet more customers and more money keep flowing through the door at a dizzying rate?

In early 1997 we held a strategic meeting in Austin (which is also home to Dell's headquarters). Slagter returned from a visit to the local drycleaners visibly distressed. He had met a Dell staff member who he had hired years earlier who had told him what his current stock options in Dell were worth. Slagter did his sums on the trip back to the office, saying "If I had sat on a beach with my Dell stock options instead of starting Hand Tech, I'd be twenty times richer today."

To rub salt in the wound, Dell had finally 'discovered' the Internet months earlier, allowing customers to configure and buy their custom-made PC online. Sales quickly grew to $1 million a day, eclipsing the results we were achieving. While we were still struggling to fill our muddy pond with buckets of water, Dell had come by and with one simple gesture carved $1m-a-day of extra width into his wild, raging river.

I left the company in 1997 and traveled to Asia to start my next venture and Hand went the way of so many dotcoms, succumbing to the Wealth Paradox and closing shop in 2000, out of cash and out of luck. Meanwhile, Michael Dell has gone on to weather all manner of set-backs – many far larger than the ones we faced – and ended up fourth on the 2005 Forbes 400 with a net worth of $18 billion and a company which is now the world's largest PC manufacturer.

What set the two approaches apart? While we were busy focusing on the hundreds of tasks in our business, Michael Dell kept focused on one – perfecting his direct model. The value of his low price, fast delivery, and reliable service model attracted an ever-increasing flow of customers and cash that gave him the resources to get things right in all other areas of his business – in good times and bad.

Our plan, team, systems and financing counted for nothing if none of us were focused on playing the game of creating value, and leveraging. During those painful years, while Dell was busy playing his game, we never even found the pitch.

Every successful Wealth Creator has kept focus on playing their game: focusing on creating value, and then leveraging. This is what creates the money flow. This is the Wealth Equation.

THE WEALTH EQUATION

Wealth creation is not about making money. It is about creating flow. The Wealth Equation explains the plumbing:

WEALTH = VALUE x LEVERAGE

Money flow follows the same principles as water flow in a river. The two variables of the river that will determine the water flow at any particular section are the height and the width (or more accurately the area of its cross section - width x depth). Similarly, the two comparable variables that make up wealth and that will determine your money flow are value and leverage. Here's why:

VALUE

Water will always flow from high ground to low ground and always in that direction. The height differential will determine the speed of water flow at any one time. If you double the height of the river, you double the speed of water flow.

Similarly, money will always flow where there is a value differential, and always from high value to low value. Imagine I decide to sell my watch for $1,000. That means I don't value it as much as $1,000. You decide to buy it for $1,000. That means you value it more than the money. As a result, your money flows from you to me. You get my watch and I get your money. If a buyer and seller chose a watch of double the value, then $2,000 would have flowed. Double the value and you double the money flow.

LEVERAGE

Value on its own does not make the river. A river also needs width. In the 1980's, Bill Gates did not have the most valuable software, but he was better at leveraging it. While Steve Jobs at Apple was coming up with innovation after innovation in his software (Apple introduced the mouse and graphic user interface before Microsoft switched from MS-DOS to windows), Gates was encouraging the growth of the entire PC market to distribute his software.

While Jobs insisted that Apple software could only be used on Apple computers, Gates positioned Microsoft as a software company serving all PC's with a common operating system and software platform. As a result, the entire PC industry grew by leveraging on his products, and he could focus all his efforts on developing his software, while Jobs was diluting his efforts by trying to develop and own the software, the hardware and the distribution channel simultaneously.

Where value gives the river a gradient, leverage gives the river width. Where value determines the speed of money flow, leverage determines the volume of flow at that speed. In the 1980's while Jobs was trying to create an Angel Falls, Gates had carved a Mississippi.

By 1985, Jobs had lost his place at Apple - ejected from the company he started by his own board members. Apple's market share plummeted in the following years from over 50% to 5%. Gates, in 1986, took Microsoft public giving him an instant $236m fortune. (Jobs made a comeback when he changed his leverage strategy, building a billion dollar fortune in the following thirty years.)

THE POLARITIES OF VALUE

While value creation is a prerequisite to money flow, there are two opposite polarities to value creation: innovation and timing. These are related to the two opposite thinking dynamics: intuitive thinking and sensory thinking. Every successful Wealth Creator taps into their natural dynamic. If you do not follow your natural dynamic, wealth creation will feel like hard work. (And if it feels like hard work, you are already doing the wrong thing.)

INNOVATION

All value is created from the way we think. Some of us are born with 'high-frequency' thinking, which is called 'intuitive' thinking. Intuitive thinkers love coming up with new ideas and putting them into action. Bill Gates, Michael Dell and Walt Disney have all mentioned their natural creativity when they were younger.

We all have some element of intuitive thinking, but some of us have it more than others. Those who are constantly tapping into this 'high-frequency' thinking are often described as having their 'head in the clouds'. They can see the big picture, but often miss the detail. They are not as focused on what is there, but on what could be. They create value through one of the two opposites of value creation: innovation.

Intuitive thinking creates value through innovation

Innovation means creating something new of value – something bigger, faster, cheaper, smaller, smarter, better. Wealth Creators such as Steve Jobs, Ray Kroc, Richard Branson and Oprah Winfrey create their value through innovation. Their innovation has been focused on creating new products, new systems, new businesses or a unique brand. In every case, for each of the Wealth Creators above, the time invested in this one activity has been their number one priority from the beginning; in every case, each one of these individuals has delegated other aspects of their business so that they can focus as much time as possible on their natural way of creating value, and leveraging it.

TIMING

On the other hand, while Bill Gates has amassed a $51 billion fortune innovating at the cutting edge, Warren Buffett has grown a $40 billion fortune without creating anything high tech at all.

The opposite of 'high-frequency, intuitive thinking' is 'low-frequency, sensory thinking'. While intuitive thinkers create value by having their head in the clouds, sensory thinkers create value by having their ear to the ground. Sensory thinkers do not need to create anything new because they have an innate sense of timing. Why create anything if you know when to buy low and sell high? Warren Buffett, George Soros and Rupert Murdoch are all individuals who are known for seeking out patterns and opportunities that others miss.

Some of us have a more natural tendency towards sensory thinking than intuitive thinking. Sensory thinkers are alert to their surroundings and pick up signals that intuitive thinkers miss. Whereas intuitive thinkers always feel the need to push forward, sensory thinkers know that sometimes the best thing to do is to do nothing. They create value through the other opposite of value creation: timing.

Sensory thinking creates value through timing

Timing means creating value by acting at the right time. Wealth Creators such as Benjamin Graham, Peter Lynch and Donald Trump have created value through their investments, trading and deal making rather than by creating anything new.

Some people believe that creativity and timing can be taught. There is no doubt that you can work at improving both, but if it is not your natural frequency to begin with, in the heat of the moment you will fall back on your old habits. I have met many people who have used their natural creativity and optimism to build successful businesses only to then trade these earnings – unsuccessfully – on the stock market. That same creativity and optimism had led to awful timing, and they lost much (if not all) of the money they had reinvested.

Some even acquired sophisticated systems to support their trades. Ultimately, successful trading does not come from a system, but from good timing, which is not so easily bought. When asked about his trading style, George Soros, the world's most consistently successful trader with a net worth of over $7b said, "My peculiarity is that I don't have a particular style of investing or, more exactly, that I try to change my style to fit the conditions. I think my analytical abilities are rather deficient. I am not a professional security analyst. I would rather call myself an insecurity analyst."

As we will see, some of the Wealth Creators above - such as George Soros and Warren Buffett – are so clear on their own focus that they have stuck to their focus even in the face of public criticism. Others – such as Steve Jobs and Martha Stewart – have deviated from their core focus and paid the price (until they got back on track).

THE OPPOSITES OF LEVERAGE

Some people think that leverage alone can create wealth: "Leverage other people's money, time, expertise or knowledge, and wealth can be yours!" This could not be further from the truth.

Leverage has the power to massively accelerate the money you make *and* the money you lose. Leverage itself simply ensures a multiple output for every input – positive *or* negative.

If you have hired a team and then failed to find the value in their time, you will have ended up worse off than when you started. If you have raised money through financing and then failed to extract the value in that money then you will have ended up in trouble. *There is only one thing that you can leverage to create wealth, and that is value.*

Ensuring you find value *before* you leverage and then being careful to leverage *that value* is essential. How successful Wealth Creators do this is explained in the following chapters.

In the same way that there are two opposites of value there are also two opposites of leverage: multiply and magnify, which are related to the two opposite action dynamics: introvert and extrovert.

Here's how they work:

MULTIPLY

People who have a more introvert action dynamic naturally internalize and analyze their course of action, in comparison to people who have a more extrovert action dynamic and work through consultation with others. Introverts are process-oriented and leverage by multiplying.

Introverts leverage by multiplying

The way to multiply is to ask the question, "How can this happen without me?" Multiplying is about making things as simple as possible and then making lots of them. Wealth Creators such as Henry Ford, Warren Buffett, John D Rockefeller and Ray Kroc have leveraged through multiplying, whether through their systems, their investments or their franchises.

Introverts will always keep things simple while extroverts tend to make things appear more complicated. In his 1989 letter to shareholders, Warren Buffet said: "After 25 years of buying and supervising a great variety of businesses, Charlie and I have not learned how to solve difficult business problems. What we have learned is how to avoid them."

MAGNIFY

People who have a more extrovert action dynamic on the other hand are more likely to be found socializing than studying a spreadsheet. In fact, many extroverts have gotten themselves in trouble when, having created a successful business out front, they have tried to get in the back office to systematize it.

Extroverts are not process-oriented. They are people-oriented, and they leverage in a manner that is the complete opposite of multiplying. They leverage by magnifying.

Extroverts leverage by magnifying

Rather than asking "How can this happen *without* me?" the way to magnify is to ask the question "How can this *only* happen *with* me?" Magnifying is about making things as complex or unique as possible so that you become indispensable. Wealth Creators such as Martha Stewart, Oprah Winfrey, Jack Welch and Donald Trump leverage by magnifying, whether through their unique brand, leadership or deal making niche.

Introverts multiply: leveraging effectively where they are most comfortable – in the background. Extroverts magnify: leveraging effectively where they are most comfortable – out in front.

HOW TO FIND A BILLIONAIRE

The front page of a 2005 issue of Business Week entitled "Googling for Gold" declared that the Internet company, Google, has created five billionaires and over one thousand millionaires. This reinforces a fundamental truth: *If you want to find a billionaire, just look for a large group of millionaires, and the billionaire will be the one in the middle.*

Every great river is surrounded by tributaries. When a new source of value or a new form of leverage is found, it soon becomes clear that the wealthy do not become wealthy by making others poor. They become wealthy by making others wealthy.

This is possible because one person's value becomes another person's leverage.

Those playing the game understand this intuitively. For example, the people with the best products will look for the people with the best systems, and vice versa. Bill Gates sells more software by leveraging on Michael Dell's PC's and Michael Dell sells more PC's by leveraging on Bill Gates' software. JK Rowlings sells more Harry Potter books by leveraging on Jeff Bezos' Amazon.com and Jeff Bezo gets more customers by leveraging on JK Rowlings' books.

In fact, the value in Amazon.com's system allows *all* publishers to leverage more effectively. The value of Microsoft's software is that it allows *all* PC manufacturers to leverage more effectively. For each of us, *our greatest value is someone else's greatest leverage.* In the following chapter, we investigate the eight wealth profiles, and how each plays a different game based on the way they naturally create value and leverage.

CHAPTER FOUR

THE EIGHT WEALTH PROFILES

"The men who have succeeded are men who have chosen one line and stuck to it."
- Andrew Carnegie

PARALLEL UNIVERSES

Many explanations have been given for why some of us acquire great wealth while some of us do not. Many have taken certain explanations as persuasive enough evidence to give up trying. We say: "Well, he was born into the money"; "She has talent and charisma that I just don't have"; "He's obviously a great leader and I'm not."

Our greatest excuse for not taking action today is that we believe we don't have what it takes to make it tomorrow.

Let's imagine a parallel universe where some of today's most successful Wealth Creators ended up taking different approaches when they got started. What would have happened if Bill Gates had opted for a career as a footballer? Would Oprah Winfrey have made millions as a commodities trader?

Could Martha Stewart have made it as a stock market trader? (Actually, we'll come back to that one later!) Could Warren Buffett have made it big on MTV? Warren Buffett says that in the 1950's he invested $100 in a Dale Carnegie public speaking course "not to prevent my knees from knocking when public speaking but to do public speaking while my knees are knocking."

If any of these Wealth Creators had not followed their path of least resistance to wealth, we would not have heard of them today. Each of us has a path based on our natural habits and talents – the ones we were born with. When we follow our path – and *only* when we follow our path – do we give ourselves the opportunity to achieve our true potential. Your path will be one of the eight on the following square.

THE WEALTH PROFILE SQUARE

The wealth profile square gives us the relationship between the eight wealth profiles. If you are highest in intuitive thinking, you will float up to one of the high-frequency profiles: Mechanic, Creator or Star. If you are strongest in sensory thinking, you will gravitate to one of the low-frequency profiles: Accumulator, Trader or Dealmaker.

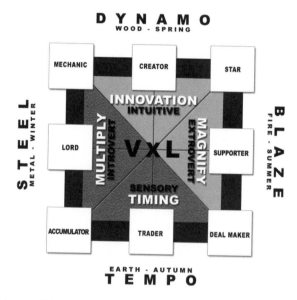

Introverts gravitate to the left: Mechanic, Lord or Accumulator, and extroverts gravitate to the right: Star, Supporter or Dealmaker. Each Wealth Creator has an absolute focus on creating wealth in the way that suits their natural strengths. Can we play more than one game? Of course, but it is only by keeping to one game that we begin to excel. The longer we play, the more distinctions we see, the greater our flow and the more we attract. Here's how the profiles differ:

THE CREATOR
"Creating a better product"

Creators can't resist creating. They keep creating long after they have run out of resources, money, and other people's patience. In fact, they have their greatest creative breakthroughs after most others would have given up.

Before Walt Disney's first animated movie was finished, his distributor went bankrupt. Before his second movie was finished, he ran out of money himself. To produce the now famous "Steamboat Willie" featuring Mickey Mouse in 1927, strapped for cash, he wrote to his brother Roy: "Slap a big mortgage on everything we got and let's go after this thing in the right manner."

Many creators do not make the best managers as they run faster than their teams, and are often on to the next venture before they have made money from the last one. The world is also full of frustrated Creators who have started a business and are now stuck running it. They did a great job creating it, but now do a mediocre job trying to manage others (often blaming their team for not "keeping up"). They move at speed, but can leave a big wake behind them.

Many Creators fail because of their over-optimism as to what their business and their team can achieve. This optimism has led many to take on far too much, leaving them little time to do what they do best.

Successful Creators have delegated everything except the creative process itself – and they focus on creating new products, or new companies, while others take care of the day-to-day business.

The successful Creators we will look at, who share a common strategy to achieve their successes, include Thomas Edison, Walt Disney, Bill Gates, Steve Jobs, and Richard Branson.

THE STAR
"Creating a unique brand"

The Creators set the stage, and the Stars steal the show. Stars get their most valuable feedback in the limelight, and find their flow while on their feet. As a result, they are able to evolve their attraction on the fly, and it is their personal magnetism that is their greatest value.

As innovators, Stars have an inner confidence that drives them to step up and take the lead. However, others sometimes see this as overconfidence. Reflecting on his outlook, Arnold Schwarzenegger comments, "I knew I was a winner back in the late sixties. I knew I was destined for great things. People will say that kind of thinking is totally immodest. I agree. Modesty is not a word that applies to me in any way - I hope it never will."

A Star profile should not be confused with sports stars or rock stars, who tend to get to their position largely on talent. There are Star profiles in industries ranging from property and media to hospitality who have ended up far wealthier than the most talented entertainers by following the Star profile strategy. There are also many extremely talented entertainers who have ended up flat broke.

Stars are naturals at creating a unique identity for themselves. It is their personal brand that attracts others. By magnifying their brand, they quickly magnify their attraction. Failed Stars do not realize this and have been attempting to build their wealth by improving their products, their systems or their teams – none of which come as naturally. Stars also get frustrated that others cannot do what they can do, and so make poor managers without the right deputies.

Successful Stars are happy to leverage on the products and platform of others in order to perform their magic. They lead from the front with their name shining in lights, while others count the receipts.

The successful Stars we will look at, who share the same winning and losing formulas in their path to success, include Oprah Winfrey, Martha Stewart, Arnold Schwarzenegger, Paul Newman and India's number one superstar, Amitabh Bachchan.

THE SUPPORTER
"Leading the team"

While Stars are busy shining, Supporters are busy lighting up others. Supporters are the strongest leaders, as they can translate value into action through people. As Jack Welch says, "Information moves so fast today, and everyone has more information than the CEO does. So the only role of the CEO is to be out there energizing people and turning this information into action."

The high-frequency innovators (such as the Creators and Stars) run at such speeds that their teams often lose confidence in their own ability to execute. Deal Makers, Traders and Accumulators can intimidate just as easily when they get into their zone. Supporters are masters at energizing teams by giving them the confidence they need to succeed. Quoting Welch again, "Giving people self-confidence is by far the most important thing that I can do. Because then they will act." Supporters supply the glue without which great plans would crumble.

Many Supporters struggle to find the right business to start, despite their fabulous network. This is because they are asking themselves what business they should start, when they should be asking themselves which value creator they should support. Rather than asking "What?" they should ask "Who?"

Successful supporters continue to play the game with the same value creator, building a culture of effective execution. Steve Ballmer has led Microsoft, giving Bill Gates the space to create, and his shares in Bill's company now give him a net worth of over $13 billion.

Some of the most successful supporters can also be found in their own businesses – such as in public relations, headhunting and consulting where others will pay big bucks for access to the people they know. Where others would take months to find the right person, it often takes Supporters just one phone call.

Notable Supporters that we will look at include Jack Welch, Michael Eisner, Steve Case, and Meg Whitman.

THE DEAL MAKER
"Bringing people together"

Like Stars and Supporters, Deal Makers leverage by magnifying out in front. While Stars are high in the sky, however, Deal Makers have their ear to the ground. Creating value through timing, not innovation, a Deal Maker lives in the present. As Donald Trump said, "I try to learn from the past, but I plan for the future by focusing exclusively on the present. That's where the fun is."

Successful Deal Makers tend to catch the imagination of the business world, with their sweeping gestures that make millions in a moment. Of all the profiles, the Deal Makers rely most on the relationships around them. While a Star's value grows as they become less accessible, a Deal Maker's value grows as they become more accessible. They are constantly on the phone and on the move. They create their wealth by spotting connections in the market. Once the deal is done, the new value created enriches everyone involved.

While intuitive thinkers shape their surroundings to suit them, sensory thinkers will shape themselves to their surroundings, letting others do the talking. They will recognize that often the best thing to do is to do nothing. Trump's advice in deal making: "If you walk into a negotiation and you know nothing about the other party, let *them* talk. Listen to their tone; observe their body language. The best negotiators are chameleons. Their attitude, demeanor, approach, and posture in a negotiation will depend on the person on the other side of the table."

Struggling Deal Makers are often stuck trying to start a business or caught up in detail, as the idea of wheeling and dealing, wining and dining, just sounds like too much fun! Others lose out by making connections without taking their share, or lose focus by failing to establish a niche to operate within. Whether it is David Geffen in Hollywood, Donald Trump in New York real estate, or Rupert Murdoch in media, every successful Deal Maker has picked a niche from which to attract the best deals in their market.

The Deal Makers we will cover include Donald Trump, David Geffen, Masayoshi Son, Henry Kravis, and Rupert Murdoch.

THE TRADER
"Buying low, selling high"

Traders are masters of timing but, unlike Deal Makers who make their money by bringing assets and resources together, Traders will buy and sell the assets and make their money from the spread. Extrovert traders will do this where they can influence the price through hard bargaining. Introvert traders prefer to trade through analysis rather than face-to-face bidding, and include many of today's successful market traders.

As a result of the popularity of online and retail trading, many people try their luck as market traders. Unfortunately, most are not, which results in them losing more often than they gain. True Traders have been trading all their life. They love finding the margins in market value and so it comes naturally, whether getting a bargain at the flea market or making a billion on the currency markets.

While Creators need to immerse themselves to create their wealth, Traders need to detach themselves. If markets were symphonies, the Creators are the composers while the Traders are the conductors. They naturally detach enabling them to remain grounded while others might be losing their heads. Value comes from waiting for and surfing the right wave while others get caught in the current. When asked if he went with the herd or against it, George Soros replied: "I am very cautious about going against the herd; I am liable to be trampled on. The trend is your friend most of the way; trend followers only get hurt at inflection points, where the trend changes. Most of the time I am a trend follower, but all the time I am aware that I am a member of a herd and I am on the lookout for inflection points."

Many failed traders have never taken control of the trade. As reliable and hard-working employees, they may see either the buy side or the sell side of a transaction within the company they work for, but often never the two together. Only when they are in control of both sides will traders become aware of the natural talent that they have.

The Trader stories in this book include George Soros, Peter Lynch, John Templeton and Jim Rogers.

.

THE ACCUMULATOR
"Collecting appreciating assets"

While Traders create wealth by accelerating money flow, Accumulators create wealth by decelerating it. Rather than making money by buying and selling off waves, they make money by buying and holding on rising tides. Accumulators always prepare and the most successful ones can be found doing their homework. As Warren Buffett said in an annual report, "Noah did not start building the Ark when it was raining."

Steady and dependable, if the profiles were compared to a football team, the Stars would be the strikers while the Accumulators would be the keepers. While Stars are quick to spend, Accumulators are quick to save. Accumulators often fail as a result of keeping too much to themselves, rather than building the advocates who will network on their behalf. They rarely act on impulse, and fail if they have not set the criteria to take action. Often accused of procrastinating, they simply need more data to make an informed decision.

When Buffett appeared on the TV program, Money World, he was asked what investment advice he would give a money manager starting out. "I'd tell him to do exactly what I did 40-odd years ago, which is to learn about every company in the United States that has publicly traded securities." Moderator Adam Smith said, "But there are 27,000 public companies." Buffett replied, "Well, start with the A's."

Once Accumulators connect to the right team, they can quickly be lifted while keeping the team grounded. They ensure that everything is in order and that what needs to get done gets done on time. Successful Accumulators are happy to remain down-to-earth, holding the kite strings while others fly high.

The successful accumulators we will cover include Warren Buffett, his mentor Benjamin Graham, Sandy Weill, Hong Kong's richest man, Li Ka Shing, and Microsoft co-founder, Paul Allen.

THE LORD
"Controlling cash generating assets"

Lords love the detail, and are renowned for their thrift. One of the world's most successful Lords, John D Rockefeller said when reflecting on his life, "How well I remember the words of my mother, willful waste makes woeful want!"

Lords can squeeze out the cash flow from assets without needing to own the assets. Rockefeller became a billionaire in the oil industry without needing to own a single oil well. Mittal has become a billionaire in the steel industry without needing to own a single mine. Whether commodity lords or land lords, they have the patience and diligence to collect and crank up every cent of cash flow they find.

While extrovert Supporters value people over numbers, introvert Lords value numbers over people, and don't have time for politics or niceties. They would rather deal with simple legwork than fancy footwork. When Rockefeller began buying up other refiners in the 1800's he did not wine and dine them, but instead said simply, "If you refuse to sell, it will end in your being crushed." And as he knew his numbers, he was right.

Lords love certainty and hate risk. They also prefer to keep to themselves, and those who have not yet found their wealth have often failed to see their analytical skills, risk aversion and need for control as their greatest strengths. When momentum grows, many Lords also cannot resist their tendency to micro-manage, which cash flow responds well to but which people do not.

Successful Lords are unrelenting once they find their niche, with the ability to consistently generate cash flow without the need for either innovation or timing, weathering market conditions and acquiring the competition until they are dominating entire industries.

The Lords we look at include Andrew Carnegie, John D Rockefeller, Jean Paul Getty, England's richest man, Lakshmi Mittal, and Google co-founder Sergey Brin.

THE MECHANIC
"Creating a better system"

If Creators need to have their head in the clouds, then Mechanics need to have their finger in the pie. While Creators are great at starting things, Mechanics are great at finishing things. They are perfectionists, which is why they cannot resist finding ways to do things better. One of Henry Ford's maxims was: "Everything can always be done better than it is being done."

While Stars twinkle, Mechanics tinker. They get hands-on with their systems and prefer to study how to improve things with their hands dirty. As a result, they have little interest in impressing with or indulging in their appearance. Bernard Marcus, chairman and Co-founder of Home Depot, recalled going out to lunch with Sam Walton – founder of Wal-Mart who became the richest man in the world in the 1980's. "I hopped into Sam's red pickup truck. No air-conditioning. Seats stained by coffee. And by the time I got to the restaurant, my shirt was soaked through and through. And that was Sam Walton – no airs, no pomposity."

Many Mechanics have yet to get going because they are still trying to figure out what business to start. Ray Kroc was 52 before he realized he didn't need to start his own business, he could take an existing business – McDonald's – and make it better.

Many Mechanics have companies with better systems than their competitors, but they have not leveraged these systems with stronger products produced by others, or their business is limited by their autocratic management style and high staff turnover.

Successful mechanics remain hands-on, fine-tuning their systems long after they have delegated many other areas of their business. This is where they see the greatest results, and where they gain the most satisfaction.

The successful mechanics whose stories we relate include Henry Ford, Ray Kroc, Sam Walton, IKEA founder Ingvar Kamprad, and Michael Dell.

THE WEALTH PROFILE SQUARE

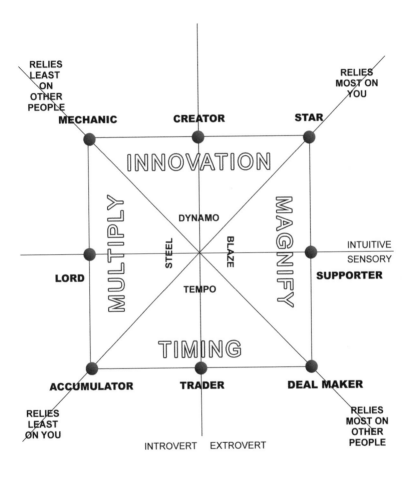

INTROVERT	EXTROVERT	INTUITIVE	SENSORY
More likely to act on own initiative	More likely to act through others	Thought process from own ideas	Thought process reaction to events

THE SIX STEPS TO WEALTH

The eight profiles each follow a common six-step strategy, establishing their value, leveraging that value, and creating a river of wealth. As we cover each profile in the following chapters, we see them repeating the same six steps, applying them in a way unique to their profile. Compare these steps to your own history:

1. BUILD YOUR WEALTH FOUNDATION

The first step, before carving the river, is to build the mountain. Your wealth foundation is your location, understanding, connections and knowledge of the game you are playing. Every one of us, no matter what our level of education, intelligence, talent or inheritance, can build our network and knowledge to begin attracting great opportunities daily.

2. MAXIMISE YOUR MOMENT OF WEALTH CREATION

Each profile has a different high-value activity that creates the greatest value or leverage. For example, the Creators who build the teams to allow them to spend their days innovating end up carving their rivers fast. The Deal Makers who build the teams to allow them to spend their days out at lunch and on the phone sniffing out the next big deal carve their own rivers equally fast. For many of us, we are investing less than 10% of our time on our moment of wealth creation. When we increase this to more than 50%, our attraction and flow multiplies dramatically.

3. CREATE VALUE

As the first part of the wealth formula, you need to be very specific on the value differential that you are creating. If a Star begins to focus on how to improve the system – instead of leaving a Mechanic to do that as she builds her brand, or if a Trader begins to focus on marketing his next fund – instead of leaving a Deal Maker to do that as he continues to focus at the market trends, the gradient of the river falls, and we take ourselves out of our flow.

4. ENSURE OWNERSHIP OF YOUR VALUE

Every Wealth Profile has a different value they create, and different ways to own it. The balance of ownership is essential. Too restrictive an ownership, and no one will want to leverage your value. Too loose an ownership, and you will lose the value to others. The world is full of entrepreneurs who impatiently began leveraging their value before they had ownership over it, and today their raging river is owned by someone else.

5. LEVERAGE YOUR VALUE

The value of other Wealth Profiles is your leverage, and your value is their leverage. Value creates the gradient of your river and dictates the speed of money flow. Leverage creates the width of your river and dictates the volume of money flow at that speed. Understanding the mechanisms that exist to leverage will transform the effective value that you can create.

6. SECURE YOUR CASH FLOW

The biggest downfall of many entrepreneurs, once they have carved out a river, is that they wait far too long to turn on the tap. For many unsuccessful entrepreneurs, everything that comes out of the river gets recycled back in, until the river dries out and the entrepreneur is left with nothing. The entrepreneurs covered in this book have secured their cash flow so that in good times and bad, their river continues to flow. Every Profile has a different way to extract cash from their river *on an ongoing basis*.

THE FIVE FREQUENCIES

Our primary profile is the game we play when we are in our flow. Each of us has a primary profile based on the balance of our frequencies. We were all born with a different mix of five 'frequencies', first identified in the Chinese 'Book of Changes': The I Ching. Through a 5,000 year path explored in Chapter 14, these frequencies have become the basis of modern psychometric tests, as well as the basis of Chinese disciplines such as Chinese Medicine, Martial Arts and Feng Shui.

We will come back to the peak frequency, water, later in the book. The other four base frequencies form the four sides of the Wealth Dynamics square. Each of these four frequencies is a state of change, like the four seasons. When you take the Wealth Dynamics profiling test, you identify how much of each frequency you hold. The balance determines which of the eight games you play most naturally: the one that creates the greatest resonance and harmony with your natural frequencies. The more time we invest in harmony with our strongest frequency, the sooner we get into our flow. Here are the four base frequencies:

	Frequency	Season	Element	Flow
1	Dynamo	Spring	Wood	Innovating
2	Blaze	Summer	Fire	Energizing
3	Tempo	Autumn	Earth	Connecting
4	Steel	Winter	Metal	Analyzing

The five frequencies form a cycle that begins and ends at water. Every project, business, industry, country goes through these frequencies as they cycle from creation to completion to creation again. You are currently going through this natural cycle with each relationship you have and each journey you embark on.

Our effectiveness changes as we resonate with our environment, and also as we resonate with our time. Even in the right environment, as time changes we can lose our flow – our winning formula can become a losing formula. Great entrepreneurs recognize this, and so will move industries and even countries to stay in the flow.

THE WEALTH FREQUENCIES

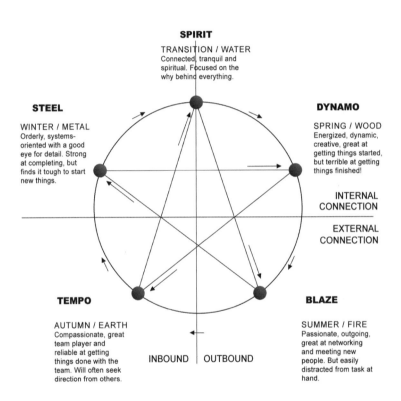

SPIRIT

TRANSITION / WATER
Connected, tranquil and spiritual. Focused on the why behind everything.

STEEL

WINTER / METAL
Orderly, systems-oriented with a good eye for detail. Strong at completing, but finds it tough to start new things.

DYNAMO

SPRING / WOOD
Energized, dynamic, creative, great at getting things started, but terrible at getting things finished!

INTERNAL CONNECTION

EXTERNAL CONNECTION

TEMPO

AUTUMN / EARTH
Compassionate, great team player and reliable at getting things done with the team. Will often seek direction from others.

BLAZE

SUMMER / FIRE
Passionate, outgoing, great at networking and meeting new people. But easily distracted from task at hand.

INBOUND | OUTBOUND

THE VALUE OF TIME

"It has been my observation that most people get ahead during the time that others waste."
- Henry Ford

Each of the next eight chapters focuses on a different wealth profile, with the stories of forty well-known Wealth Creators. As you read these stories, you might ask yourself what has been stopping you from taking the same bold actions that many of these individuals have taken. It usually comes down to one of three reasons: not enough money, not enough knowledge or not enough support.

These all come down to the same thing: *The illusion of limited resource*. As we see Wealth Creators build the network and connections around their game we see that their network shows limited resource for what it is – an illusion. With the right networks, they are not limited by money as they know the financiers with the money. They are not limited by knowledge because they seek out the mentors with the knowledge. They are not limited by support as they have connections to the people and teams ready to support.

Without exception, none of them started with money, knowledge or support. But they did start with their time. The same 24 hours a day that you and I wake up with. While we realize that the notion of limited resource is an illusion as we grow our wealth, there is one resource that really is limited, and that is our time.

The one thing that each of these Wealth Creators puts at a premium is the value of their time. That is why they never waste it doing the wrong thing. When Edison was asked if he ever lost patience when inventing, he said, "The thing I lose patience with the most is the clock. Its hands move too fast."

As you read through the next eight chapters, featuring the stories of entrepreneurs who found their flow, keep in mind that the wealthy got wealthy not by investing their money, but by investing their time. The sooner we value our time, the sooner we begin to invest it wisely.

PART TWO

Finding Your Flow

CHAPTER FIVE

THE CREATOR

"When you can't get a job,
you start your own business."
- Walt Disney

GETTING THINGS GOING

On the Wealth Dynamics square, Creators sit up at the top, bang in the middle of introvert and extrovert. Sure enough, Creators come in two forms: the introverted creators are the inventors, inventive and able to multi-task on many new ideas at the same time. Introverted creators such as Thomas Edison, Walt Disney and Bill Gates will focus totally on the creative process and let others run their business.

The extroverted Creator is a pioneer: innovative but focused, creating not just products, but business strategies as well. Extroverted Creators such as Richard Branson have multiple businesses but with others running each business. Both are visionaries and motivate others by their drive and innovation. All add the most value when they are free to create. The more they stay in their creative space, the better their creations become.

HEAD IN THE CLOUDS

Creators are best when their heads are in the clouds. At altitude, they can see the big picture, and will rely on their intuition more than any market research to guide them. Their over-optimism is their greatest strength when it comes to their vision and their greatest weakness when it comes to what they believe others can achieve. As a result, many Creators succeed in their creation, only to fail in their execution.

Creators are naturally intuitive, so tend to get involved in their own creativity, which can cause friction with others. They are big picture thinkers, which can often mean missing the details. Their drive gives them the momentum to spark their creativity, but this drive can also exhaust or disorientate others. As a result of this double-edged sword, Creators are often described by others as the best communicators and the worst communicators at the same time.

Creators are excellent at getting things started, but often terrible at completing. With a passion to always be occupied with the next big thing, many Creators also over-stretch themselves. They come up with a great idea that will bring them success, only to drop it before it has been properly executed to go onto something 'more exciting'. As a result, there are plenty of Creators with half-finished projects and the next big thing just around the corner.

Many Creators also happen to believe they are the best at what they can do – mainly because their brain often forms solutions or reaches conclusions that appear faster than others around them. The fact that these solutions may not be the most thorough is a mere technicality. In any event, this habit leaves many Creators getting involved in areas where they add little value, and when they get the ball they often run so fast they shoot over the horizon leaving the team behind.

Those Creators who have turned their back on their creativity have often done so as a result of others criticizing their lack of attention to detail, or their inability to complete the task at hand. Unsuccessful Creators are those who either have seen their creativity as a distraction in the serious business of earning a living, or who have become a victim of their success – living the consequence of some creative idea they had in the past, whether it is a company they set up or a career path they have entrenched themselves in.

The Creators that have made it have set up a structure to allow them to stay in their creative groove every day, with great teams and partners to execute. They know what value they deliver, and are crystal clear in owning that value through their equity, patents and trademarks. They are also generous in the way they share the pie, aware that it is only through the efforts of others that their creations can be fully leveraged.

THOMAS EDISON
"The Wizard of Menlo Park"

The electric world we live in today is the result of Thomas Edison's unwavering insistence on being able to dedicate his waking hours to his passion – inventing. A consummate Creator and one of the most prolific inventors in history (he held 1,093 US patents and 1,300 foreign patents in his lifetime), his most significant innovation was *creating an industrial process for creating* – pioneering the first industrial research lab at Menlo Park.

Edison worked as a telegraph operator in his early years, patenting his first invention, an electronic vote recorder, in 1868 at the age of 21. Two years later, Marshall Lefferts, a former president of the American Telegraph Company, saw promise in Edison and decided to finance him. Rather than pump the money into marketing his existing creations (a temptation many lesser Creators might have), Edison used the money to set up a space in New York and hired an English mathematician, Charles Batchelor, and a Swiss machinist, John Krueis, to increase his capacity to invent.

Within eight years, Edison and his team had 45 inventions patented, including the stock printer and quadruplex telegraph. Aware that true creativity occurs when others have long given up, he would often lock the lab doors and tell his staff they couldn't leave until they had cracked the project they were working on.

By the age of 29, Edison, having become wealthy off the royalties of his inventions, moved to Menlo Park. He continued to pump back the money he made to invent even more, saying: "My main purpose in life is to make enough money to create ever more inventions." It was here that Edison perfected a common trait amongst successful Creators – the ability to cash in on concepts even before they had become reality (what became known in Bill Gates' era as 'vaporware'). For example, the following year he filed the patent for the phonograph – before he had actually invented a working prototype, and in 1877 he persuaded a consortium to provide him financing through a rights and remuneration agreement for a marketable lighting system – before he had invented the light bulb.

The promises of great Creators will come to fruition with enough work. That year, Edison delivered the phonograph, and the year after, the light bulb. In each case, he delivered these inventions through his team at Menlo Park, and almost always as commercial modifications of other inventions that were taking place at the time.

So when he applied for a patent on the light bulb, the US patent office ruled that Edison's patent was based on the work of another inventor, and was invalid. The legal case dragged on for six years until a judge ruled that Edison's use of a filament in his bulb was a legitimate improvement that could be patented. Even so, Joseph Swan had beaten Edison to a similar patent in Britain, and so Edison joined together with Swan to form a joint company "Ediswan", to market the light bulb in Britain.

In 1889, the same year that he invented an early motion picture camera, Edison formed Edison General Electric to market his inventions. Three years later, he merged with Thomson-Houston to create General Electric. Having no interest in running the company himself, he continued to focus on simply inventing. In the following years, with his team, he created over a thousand new inventions, including the DC Generator, the electrical metering system, alkaline storage batteries, cement manufacturing equipment and the first synchronized movies with sound.

Did Edison's decision to invent more – instead of managing what he had already invented – affect the future of his business? General Electric went on to become one of the first twelve companies that made up the Dow Jones Industrial Average in 1896. Today, it is the only one of the twelve to survive – in fact, General Electric is today the world's second largest company, with $152 billion in 2004 revenues and assets of over $750 billion.

Over one hundred years after Edison started the company, in 2005, Fortune Magazine ranked GE first overall in their "Global Most Admired Companies" list.

Other major companies today, including RCA and AT&T, were launched by GE in its first twenty years, and Jack Welch, GE's CEO and Chairman in the 1980's and 1990's is featured in a later chapter.

WALT DISNEY
"The Mouse that Roared"

A person with a Creator profile quickly becomes aware their greatest value is in their creations – and that ownership of their creation is paramount. Walt Disney learnt it the hard way at the age of 22 when he found that he had signed away the rights to his prized animated creation, "Oswald the Lucky Rabbit", in a distribution deal with Universal Studios.

When in 1930, at the age of 29, Disney signed a $7,000-per-picture distribution deal with Columbia Pictures for the character he came up with after losing Oswald (a mouse called Mickey), he agreed to split the money but insisted on keeping copyright on the mouse. In 1948 he said, "Mickey Mouse to me is the symbol of independence. Born of necessity, the little fellow literally freed us of immediate worry."

Once a Creator profile has a bankable creation, wealth is created in leveraging that one product. While presenting himself as an animator, once Mickey was born, Disney began to leverage in many different ways. In the same year of 1930 he published 'The Mickey Mouse Book' and sold close to 100,000 copies. He signed an agreement with King Features to develop a Mickey Mouse comic strip. He hired an agent, Kay Kamen, who licensed the National Dairy Products Company to make Mickey Mouse ice cream cones – which sold 10 million cones in the first month.

Within a year, Disney was netting $300,000 in endorsement deals alone for Mickey Mouse, a phenomenal amount in 1931 – especially for a character that cost nothing but Disney's imagination to create.

For all Creators, being constantly creative is not just a natural habit, but also the route to increased momentum. Throughout the 1930's, Disney began to create a host of Disney characters with a team of talented animators. In 1937, the team created the world's first animated film, "Snow White and the Seven Dwarfs" with an unprecedented budget of $1m. The film went on to make $8.5m in its first release. (It has been re-released eight times since, distributed in forty-six countries, and grossed a further $100m.)

Disney remained a step ahead in his innovation and, with an animation team in place, focused his creative efforts and $100,000 of his profits on a 51-acre studio in Burbank, California. Disney called it "the house that Snow White built", and it began to churn out expensive animations. However, whilst to the outside world Disney appeared a success, he continued to spend everything he made, and by 1940 the studio had accumulated $4.5m in debt. A public listing temporarily eased the cash crunch but by 1953 – after Walt Disney had been in Hollywood for 30 years - the company was still scraping along with minimal cash.

As with all great Creators, success came when the company pursued a new avenue to leverage the creations. In 1954, Disney signed a long-term contract with ABC to start a Disneyland TV channel. In the first season, 30 million viewers tuned in and in turn boosted sales of Disney products, finally turning Disney's cash flow around. By the mid 1950's, Mickey Mouse ears sold at a rate of 25,000 per day.

Despite the publicly listed Disney studios making a decent profit, Walt Disney wasn't done yet. After trying, unsuccessfully, to convince the Disney board to finance a theme park based on the Disney characters, Walt Disney sunk his life savings in a separate company, Walt Disney, Inc. to launch Disneyland in Anaheim, California.

Launched in 1955, Disneyland sentimentally harked back to the two creations that gave Disney his success: Mickey Mouse and the Snow White castle. As with many of Disney's other ventures the park ran over budget, costing $17m to build against the original budget of $5m. As with many of Disney's other ventures the market response exceeded the expectations of the experts and 170,000 people visited in the first week. Today, 75 years after Mickey was born, the Walt Disney Company is worth $50 billion.

BILL GATES
"The Richest Man in the World"

Whilst billionaires create millionaires, the richest man in the world can claim to have created multiple billionaires. Paul Allen and Steve Ballmer, who went to school and college with Gates, are both billionaires (in Allen's case he remains one of the richest men in America despite leaving Microsoft in 1978).

Like all successful Creators, Gates focuses on his area of greatest passion and contribution: innovation, and leaves the day-to-day management of his company to others. For the last six years he has been the 'Chief Software Architect' at Microsoft, focusing on what he is best at and loves most: creating the future.

From the beginning, Gates followed in the footsteps of Edison and Disney by positioning himself in a growth industry he was passionate about – in this case software – and then building an innovation machine that continued to turn out one new innovation after another. Gates recognized that as a Creator, the greatest value in his new products was the value that others could easily leverage.

As an example, it was five years after Microsoft started that Gates saw the potential of selling operating systems to PC manufacturers after the MS-DOS deal with IBM in 1980. When MS-DOS was launched, Microsoft was a small $7 million business with 40 staff. By comparison, Apple Computer, the personal computing pioneer, was already a listed company with the Apple III launched. By 1982, Apple's revenues were over $1 billion.

Apple, however, continued to bundle their software and hardware exclusively – attempting to control both the innovation and the distribution sides of their business. When Apple came up with LISA – the first PC with a graphic user interface and mouse in 1983, Microsoft came up with Microsoft Windows 1.0 – which was then sold wholesale to the many PC manufacturers in the market. The two differing strategies led to Apple's OS market share falling to less than 3% and Microsoft's share rising to over 93% in the next 20 years – despite Apple having created an arguably superior solution.

This focus, at commercializing the inventions of his team and others, and then leveraging through an entire hardware industry geared to distribute his products, has led to Microsoft today having close to $40 billion in sales.

Why has Gates been so successful when there have been so many other smart and talented entrepreneurs who have entered the software market in the last twenty years? Gates' unrelenting focus on extracting commercial value and leveraging that value in spite of the many distractions around him is unmatched.

Over the last fifteen years, Gates has had his fair share of distractions: from competitors to changes in the industry, the advent of the Internet, and the efforts of regulating bodies to break Microsoft apart. Starting in 1990, when the US Federal Trade Commission launched a probe into possible anti-competitive practices, Microsoft has been sued – often successfully – by companies and state governments in the US and Europe. In June 2000, US District Judge, Thomas Penfield Jackson, ordered Microsoft to be split into two companies. In June 2001 – one full year later – an appeal court reversed the ruling.

Creators often complain that they can't get into their creative 'zone' because of the distractions around them. With the ongoing threat of his company being broken up, and his paper worth having fallen by some $30 billion since the heights of the dotcom boom, Gates has had more distractions than most – but has remained fixed on his daily task of innovation.

This ongoing focus is not only a result of choosing to have the discipline to only do what he loves. It also comes from the process that Gates has put in place to extract cash from his ongoing wealth creation. While poor Creators lock all their cash in their creations, Gates sells a portion of his Microsoft shares every quarter (20 million of them – that's over *$500 million cash in his pocket every quarter*).This cash flow ensures that whatever the future of Microsoft, his own personal wealth is secure.

With his personal cash flow secure, doing what he loves, Gates is in his flow. His net worth – the $51 billion on paper - is already being pledged in large parts to the Bill & Melinda Gates Foundation. This will be his legacy, which he will be working on full-time from 2008. This process of effective wealth creation and contribution will continue to unfold through the stories in the coming pages.

STEVE JOBS
"A Billion Dollars not Once, not Twice, but Three Times"

When Steve Jobs launched Apple with Steve Wozniak in 1976, they decided to name the company after the fruit that according to legend spurred Isaac Newton's theories on gravity. Since that moment, Jobs' entrepreneurial career has had a tumultuous battle against gravity – and from the latest score, gravity is losing.

From the beginning of Apple, Jobs demonstrated the tenacity and resourcefulness that defines every great Creator. Realizing they did not have the expertise or financing to build the business, Jobs brought on a local VC, Mike Markkula, who bought shares in the company and subsequently became CEO. He brought in Regis McKenna, the best public relations man in Silicon Valley, to market the Apple II, and over the next five years he continued to seek out the best minds and mentors he could find for his company. Markkula was responsible for the early financing of the company, and for taking Apple public in 1980.

Starting with the premise that the best ideas are already out there, Jobs also negotiated with Xerox to grant Apple engineers access to the Xerox PARC facilities in return for selling them one million dollars in pre-IPO Apple stock. It was from this visit that Jobs collected the ideas behind the fundamentals of today's PC – the graphic user interface, mouse and pointer.

On the day that Apple went public, riding the PC wave, Steve Jobs became worth $217 million. Each wealth profile has an Achilles heel, however, and Jobs' heel came to trip him over. Ambitious Creators can trip up by running against the grain of the team – especially if the team is riding a struggling business model. As IBM led the PC manufacturers into a Microsoft-enabled war against Apple, Jobs continued to insist that the Apple bundle of software and hardware remain as one package – preventing Apple from leveraging as either a software company or a hardware company with the rest of the industry. As a result, within two years of entering the market, the revenue of IBM's PC division had already overtaken Apple's.

Thinking (as Creators often do) that he knew best, with Apple now a billion dollar company, Jobs continued to drive his product development team purely from intuition. Apple's head of marketing, Mike Murray, commented, "Steve did his market research by looking into the mirror every morning." Sales stalled, Jobs' management style was seen by his board as a liability and, in 1985, he was thrown out of the company he had started nine years earlier.

That might have been the end of another entrepreneur story, was it not for Jobs' perseverance. Having left Apple, he launched NeXT, to provide PCs to the education market. Apple sued Jobs for launching in competition, prompting him to say, "It's hard to think that a $2 billion company with 4,300 plus people couldn't compete with six people in blue jeans."

Jobs sold all but one of his Apple shares, and Apple continued to languish, falling from 20% market share to under 5% by 1996. Jobs, in the meantime, struggled with NeXT, burning through $250 million of investors' money as he tried to market his new computers.

In the same year that Jobs founded NeXT, George Lucas was looking to sell a small computer animation group he owned. Disney rejected an offer to buy 50% for $15 million, and a deal to sell to Ross Perot and Phillips for $30 million fell through. Jobs ended up negotiating Lucas to under $10 million for the business, thinking he could market the high-end animation computers that the group had designed.

Jobs kept 92%, with the other 8% going to the two founders, Alvyn Ray Smith and Ed Catmull. Renamed 'Pixar', the company began marketing the Pixar Image Computer to the medical market – with little success. By 1989, with Pixar losing over $1 million each month, and NeXT faring little better, Jobs found himself left with less than 20% of the $150 million he had received when he sold his Apple stock. At the rate he was going, within two years he would be back to zero.

Taking drastic measures, Jobs sold the hardware side of Pixar for several million, taking a massive loss. Most people at this point would have thrown in the towel, but Jobs persevered, keeping the core team and looking for a way to make money from their animation talent. The perseverance seemed to pay off. An animated short movie they had produced, "Tin Toy", received an Oscar, and in 1993, Disney approved a full feature joint venture with Pixar called "Toy Story". The victory was short lived, however, with Disney shutting production of Toy Story down later in the year after losing confidence in the script. The following year, 1994, became Jobs' worst year ever.

1994 was the year that Disney lost four executives in a helicopter crash, including Chief Operating Officer Frank Wells. In the aftermath, animation head, Jeffrey Katzenberg, fell out with Michael Eisner and left to launch SKG DreamWorks with Steven Spielberg and David Geffen. Meanwhile, Jobs was left attempting to get Toy Story back on track while also having to close the NeXT manufacturing facility and sales operation. Most of the NeXT team left. The investors, having put in another $100 million, saw that money disappear too. From the deal that Katzenberg had originally negotiated, with Toy Story now back on Disney's agenda, it would need to earn at least $100 million for Pixar to make any money from it at all; more than any other Disney film had made at the time. Even so, Jobs decided to bet that not only would Toy Story be a success, it would enable him to publicly list Pixar and raise further funds.

In November 1995, Toy Story opened to enormous acclaim, becoming the highest grossing release of the year, generating over $450 million in cinema and video rental sales, and leading to a lucrative seven-film deal with Disney. One week later, Pixar had its IPO. The advisers argued for a $12 to $14 price range. The stock opened at $22, and ended the day on $39. Less than twelve months after his worst year financially, Steve Jobs was a billionaire.

Then, in 1996, Gil Emilio (the new CEO of Apple) went hunting for a new operating system and finally found it… in NeXT. Approaching Jobs for his system, Jobs was only interested in selling the entire company. Apple bought it for $377.5 million in cash and $1.5 million in Apple shares. In one fell swoop, Jobs could pay off all his investors and was involved with Apple again – after over ten years.

In 1997 Apple sales were $7 billion and losses were over $1 billion. Jobs took to the challenge of revitalizing Apple, first as consultant and then as "interim-CEO". By 1998, Jobs launched the iMac, which was followed – entirely by chance – with the iPod and then iTunes. Ironically, Jobs' need to rely on a leverage structure he could not own when he entered the entertainment world made it a natural step to approach the music giants when he launched iTunes. The partnerships he has now created have given him incredible leverage for his undoubted creative leadership – multiplying the effect of his creations into the billions.

Jobs is now transforming Apple into a cutting-edge multimedia company. 2005 sales were up to a record $14 billion, and Jobs net worth has risen to over $4 billion.

In January 2006, Disney (having rejected the chance to buy 50% of Pixar for $15 million ten years earlier) bought a transformed Pixar from Jobs for $7.4 billion in stock, making Jobs Disney's largest individual shareholder and a billionaire for the third time.

RICHARD BRANSON
"The Maverick Multi-billionaire"

How can we ensure we stay in the game? Today Richard Branson has over 200 companies, and his Virgin Group generates over $8 billion in revenue. As a creator of companies rather than inventions, Branson has been a master at leveraging himself out of sticky situations through his creativity.

Eight years after launching, in 1992 Virgin Atlantic needed to raise $10 million for seat-back video terminals to compete in the market. But with the global recession taking grip, all attempts to raise the money had been unsuccessful.

As a last resort, Branson called Phil Conduit, CEO of Boeing, and said he wanted to buy ten new Boeing 747-400s, but would like Boeing to throw in seat-back videos in economy as a condition of purchase. Branson then repeated the process with Airbus. Both companies welcomed the new orders and readily agreed. Afterwards, Branson commented, "We discovered that it was easier to get $4 billion credit to buy eighteen new aircraft than it was to get $10 million credit for the seat-back video sets."

Virgin was launched in 1968, first as a student magazine, and then as a mail order business. Soon after the mail order business launched there was a six-month postal strike. Within days of the strike starting, Branson opened the first Virgin record shop. The record shop then led to a record label, Virgin Records, launched in 1972. Virgin Records signed Mike Oldfield's Tubular Bells, the Sex Pistols, Culture Club, Phil Collins and other hit bands. But in 1979, just as Virgin was blossoming, interest rates soared and a recession hit. Branson persevered, growing Virgin on tight cash flow with his stores making a loss. He owed the bank close to £3 million (US$4.5 million) when he decided to launch Virgin Atlantic.

In 1984, the day after Virgin's leased jumbo arrived in the UK, it hit a flock of birds, destroying one of the engines. As it did not yet have CAA approval, the engine was not insured. As a replacement engine would cost £600,000, Branson called up Coutts (Virgin's bank) and pleaded for an extension of their £3 million overdraft to cover the engine. Several days later, after the inaugural flight and CAA's approval, Branson returned to London to find Chris Rashbrook, the manager of their account at his door. Rashbrook told Branson that Coutts would bounce all Virgin checks that took it over its limit.

Branson mobilized his various subsidiaries for cash, keeping them in their limit. After such a close call, later in 1984 Branson decided to bring in professional managers, Don Cruikshank and Trevor Abbott. Abbott became Branson's money man, continuing to find the financing that Branson's growth demanded. First, Abbott contacted a wide range of banks and extended Virgin's overdraft facility to £30 million. Then, to raise more money, in 1986 the Virgin Group listed. At this point, the company had 4,000 employees, and £189 million in revenue. The float raised £30 million, part of which Branson then used to finance Virgin Atlantic.

The following year, Abbott arranged a further £100 million loan with the Bank of Nova Scotia to buy shares in Thorn EMI, which Branson wanted to take over. Abbott and Branson began buying shares of Thorn EMI on the open market, and had spent £30 million by October 1987 – when the stock market crashed.

Virgin shares almost halved in value from 160p to 90p; Thorn EMI shares crashed from 730p to 580, and the £30 million became worth £18 million. The bank asked for an immediate cash payment of £5 million. Faced with a significant loss on his hands, Branson gave up the idea of buying Thorn EMI. In fact, by 1988, with the stock market becoming a poor source of financing and the constraints of running a public company around his neck, Branson chose to buy back Virgin PLC, setting the price at 140p (a premium of 70p) so no one who bought when it listed would lose. Abbott organized lines of credit for a £300 million overdraft, and Virgin became a private company again.

Twenty years after Virgin was launched, Branson had his freedom, and a company with over £300m (US$450 million) in debt.

All Creators know that there is cash locked up in their creations, and the greatest cash flow comes when this value is unlocked. Branson recalls, "We realized that we would have to sell shares in both Virgin Atlantic and Virgin Music in order to reduce our mountain of debt."

Branson sold 50% of ten of his mega stores to WH Smith for £12 million, which immediately paid down borrowings in Virgin Atlantic. He sold 10% of the airline to a Japanese travel group for £36 million. 25% of Virgin Music was sold to a Japanese media company, Fujisankei for £100 million. Showing how little relationship company value has against stock market value, through the Fujisankei deal Branson not only paid down some of his debt, but demonstrated that Virgin Music was worth £400 million, compared to the £180 million stock market valuation of the entire Virgin Group just one year earlier.

Despite the additional cash, Virgin kept trading in debt as Branson continued to grow the music and airline businesses. By 1991, Virgin's overdraft with Lloyds Bank had grown to over £50 million. Even so, Branson would not let the cash flow pressures stop him from acting at critical moments. The Rolling Stones became available for signing in 1991, and Abbott got a £6 million loan from Citibank to pay the signing fee, with repayment the following April: "We were living so much from hand-to-mouth that we didn't care about next April."

By the following year, the Lloyds overdraft had grown to £55 million. Virgin Atlantic needed a further £30 million, and a recession was taking hold. Finally, with cash flow pressures reaching a critical point and Virgin Music having built considerable value, Branson decided to sell Virgin Music in its entirety to Thorn EMI – for £560 million. In 1993, twenty-five years after starting Virgin, Branson was finally debt-free, with $500 million in the bank. Reflecting on the past twenty-five years he said, "We were lucky; each time something went wrong, we were the smallest jump ahead of the banks."

As time has gone by, Branson's ability to make money has grown dramatically. It took him twenty years to make Virgin Music into a billion dollar business. He turned both Virgin Blue and Virgin Mobile into billion dollar businesses in a fraction of that time. In 2000, Branson launched Virgin Blue in Australia with US$10 million in financing. He listed the company four years after launching it at a value of $2.3 billion. In 1999 Branson launched Virgin Mobile, and in 2006, UK cable company NTL paid $1.7 billion for it – while still keeping the use of the Virgin brand. Branson, who owned 71.2% of Virgin Mobile, made himself over $1 billion from the sale – and continues to receive $15 million a year for licensing the brand.

Edison, Gates and Jobs created "invention factories", with a stream of new inventions that they then extracted value from as their companies' grew in attraction. In a similar fashion, Branson has created an "enterprise factory", with a stream of new companies that he then extracts value from as the Virgin brand grows in attraction. Today, Virgin continues to attract thousands of new proposals each year.

With a constant inflow of new opportunities, where is Branson focusing? In September 2006, Richard Branson made a $3 billion pledge to fight climate change. All profits from Virgin Atlantic and Virgin Trains over the next ten years will fund investments in renewable energy technology through a new investment fund, Virgin Fuels.

CREATORS IN A NUTSHELL

Dominant Wealth Frequency: Dynamo

Action Dynamic: Introvert/Extrovert

Thinking Dynamics: Intuitive

Wealth Creation Key: Building a better product

Secondary Profiles: Mechanic, Star

Strengths: Visionary; creative; optimistic; stimulating; able to inspire others; can multitask; quick to generate revenue; great at getting things started

Weaknesses: Poor sense of timing; over-optimism with what others can achieve; easily distracted; quick at spending what they make; terrible at getting things finished

Successes: Best when free to create, with a team to execute and a team to hold onto the purse strings. Excels when kept focused on the creative process from inception to commercial completion – with a creative team that can help bring products and businesses to fruition.

Failures: Failure results from trying to control too much, run too fast, or expect too much of the team. Creators will often burn out their team, or move on to new ideas before their old ones are contributing cash flow. Once a team is in execution mode, a Creator will often be a liability in management, as he will automatically look for creative solutions to issues, when it is more likely to be a people or process issue that needs to be addressed.

Many Creators have never got started because, thinking they can do it all themselves, they have never invested the time to find the right mentors and supporters. Others have been shot down – often as early as in primary school – for being too rebellious or individualistic, and have repressed their creative passions in run-of-the-mill jobs where they can keep a low profile.

THE CREATOR STRATEGY

1. BUILDiNG YOUR WEALTH FOUNDATION

Creators can be extremely productive when using their creativity but may invest little time in this area. As a Creator, your biggest priority must be to build a team around yourself to support and execute the right ideas and plans.

Great Creators have a ready source of financiers and supporters they can call on to finance and support their new ventures. They also have the right distribution and deal-making partners who are ready to take their new products and market them, and they have their own brainstorming teams that will often come up with far better ideas than the Creator can on his own.

2. MOMENT OF WEALTH CREATION

Creators need to maximize their time invested dreaming up and creating new ideas, products and strategies. Yes, that's right, doing the things that are most fun. Key to this is choosing a market that you are passionate about – and that you can see yourself remaining in, attracting the butterflies, even when it's no longer about the money.

3. VALUE CREATION

The value creation in innovation is in maximizing the value differential in your business or products' unique selling points. Commercial value is quite different from uniqueness. Commercial value is what allows others to leverage a Creator's products profitably. This is the value you give, not the value you get. This alone will multiply returns. Great Creators identify and build product niches that they can dominate, which means narrowing their niche - you can't boil the ocean. Everything else is secondary: operations, systems – someone else can do it, and will do it better.

4. VALUE OWNERSHIP

Before leveraging, you need to own the product rights of whatever you and your team have created. That means trade marking, copyrighting or patenting. You need to ensure that you have ownership of the originality of what you create, or any cash flow you generate will be very temporary.

5. LEVERAGE

Extrovert Creators are much more likely to start their own business to support their product innovations. Leverage will come from multiplying reach and productivity through distribution networks and mass production, and magnifying the brand and goodwill through marketing and partnerships. Introvert Creators need to leverage even more by securing licensing agreements with distributors: hence the need to link with dealmakers.

6. SECURE CASH FLOW

The world is full of Creators who have not followed this strategy and so have missed their wealth and are spinning in the eddy currents, out of the flow. Many even find a way to leverage, but then miss the final key point: getting paid their worth. Cash flow will come from patent royalties, license fees, or often direct from your business: company profits or equity sales. You need to secure where the money is coming from, and how and when it will be paid, before rushing ahead and conquering the world.

CREATORS TO LEARN FROM

Thomas Edison (General Electric), Walt Disney (Walt Disney Company), Bill Gates (Microsoft), Steve Jobs (Apple/Pixar), Richard Branson (Virgin), Larry Ellison (Oracle), Thaksin Shinawatra (Thailand's richest man), JK Rowling (Harry Potter Books), Mark Burnett (Mark Burnett Productions), George Lucas, Steven Spielberg (SGK DreamWorks), Jeffrey Katzenberg (SGK DreamWorks), Anita Roddick (Body Shop), Narajana Murthy (Infosys, India)

CHAPTER SIX

THE STAR

"Fame is a bitch, man."
- Brad Pitt

NOT JUST A PRETTY FACE

On the Wealth Dynamics square, Stars sit up at the top right, creative and extrovert – which means they take their cues from the reaction of those around them. The more they stand out, the more at home they feel, and the more they attract.

Like Creators, Stars are best off when left to innovate. But rather than innovate products or systems, which they do not have the patience or inclination for, they innovate and magnify their brand. This often means making themselves less accessible to make themselves more valuable. Stars such as Oprah Winfrey and Martha Stewart have built entire empires around their names – with others managing the shop while they star in the show. In their cases, they have not only leveraged on the media to magnify their brand – they have created their own media to ensure their star keeps shining.

SHINING BRIGHTLY

Stars, naturally, are the easiest of the profiles to spot. After all, the value is in the person. Obvious Stars can be found in the sports, music, film and entertainment industries. However, the highest profile CEOs, salespeople and trainers also achieved their wealth by following their natural path as a Star.

Naturally extroverted, Stars will be happy around others and will be quite comfortable being the centre of attention. In fact, their creativity comes far faster when in conversation than when sitting alone. As a result, Stars are best when they can take the products and concepts of others, and add their own unique spin for effective promotion.

Stars are not the most diplomatic of profiles, often skirting controversy for the fun of it, causing disharmony and alienation at times. As Stars grow in stature, the demand on their time grows. To continue to shine brightly, however, they need to continue to deliver, which can lead to exhaustion and dissatisfaction if they have not learnt how to leverage effectively.

With the stress that comes with increased success, it is natural for a Star's ego to often get the better of them. This can lead to them forgetting the winning formula that brought them their wealth, and it becomes all too easy to burn out or self-destruct. When Stars shine, they also find it easy to make money, and even easier to spend. In fact, many Stars have crafted into an art form their ability to spend their money before they make it.

In leadership, while Mechanics are best leading from behind and providing systems to support, Stars are best leading from the front, and setting an example to follow. They are often the best sales people and promoters, but come unstuck when they then try and build teams to "multiply" their success. The successful Stars in insurance, real estate and other sales industries stay firmly in the sales process, with a support cast feeding the pipeline, magnifying their brand – and magnifying their earnings.

Those Stars who have ignored their path have often done so because of the knock-backs they have received in the limelight, and the responsibility that goes with it. Fallen Stars have often been trained to not draw attention to themselves, much as they secretly enjoy it. And others simply lack confidence and knowledge, so tread a careful path incognito, blissfully unaware of the simple steps they could be taking to claim their wealth.

High profile stars, such as Arnold Schwarzenegger, Paul Newman and Amitabh Bachchan have amassed fortunes in different industries on content created by others and leveraged through others, but modified and packaged around their own particular identity. Stars like Oprah Winfrey and Martha Stewart have lifted themselves from day-to-day execution to do what they love – stay in the limelight and light up the world.

OPRAH WINFREY
"The Queen of the Talk Shows."

Oprah Winfrey is worth more than every Hollywood celebrity she has had on her talk show. Are their multi-million dollar blockbuster movies not enough to propel them ahead of a talk show host? Oprah Winfrey, according to Forbes in 2006, is worth $1.4 billion. Oprah's wealth comes from playing the game exceptionally well, establishing ownership over her empire, and leveraging that brand over multiple media – something few Hollywood stars have managed to do.

As with all Wealth Creators, a Star's first step is to follow their passion. As with a good pair of shoes, passion doesn't come from analysis, but by trying it all on and finding what fits. Oprah tried news reporting on radio at 19, news reporting on TV at the age of 22, then co-hosting a chat show on radio, before hosting a TV morning talk show in 1984, when she was 30. The show, AM Chicago, became the number one talk show in America, and after ten years Oprah had found a passion that she has kept to ever since.

A year after playing Sofia in Steven Spielberg's "The Color Purple" in 1985, Oprah got her own nationwide chat show, "The Oprah Winfrey Show". She pioneered a format that dealt with every day life and the issues we face, which drew a growing daytime audience over the next nine years. However, in 1994 with many copycats following Oprah's show format and sensationalizing relationship issues and every day hardships, Oprah revamped her brand, re-positioning to "Change Your Life" TV. This proved to be a critical decision, enabling Oprah to carve a niche that has resonated with an ever-growing audience through the following decade.

A further critical moment came in 1998, when she bought the rights to her show from the ABC. Ownership of your own brand is paramount for a Star profile. With ownership, you are able to leverage and magnify your brand across multiple media. Oprah set up Harpo Productions ("Harpo" being her name spelt backwards) and invested $20 million on her own production facility in Chicago – making her only the third woman in history to own a major studio, after Mary Pickford and Lucille Ball.

With a production vehicle in place, she began to build her leverage. The following year, she launched the Oxygen cable TV network, a 24-hour channel dedicated to women. In 2000 she launched "O", a magazine that now reaches 2.4 million readers monthly. In each case, she brought in management teams while she continued to host her show. By 2006, her show had 49 million US viewers each week, and was being broadcast in a further 122 countries.

All great wealth creators see opportunity while others are looking the other way. As a great example, in 1996 Oprah found herself in the middle of an unwelcome legal case in which her brand power had landed her. A group of Texan cattlemen sued Oprah in a "food disparagement" suit after Oprah commented on a study on Mad Cow disease on her show, saying it "just stopped me cold from eating another burger."

The cattlemen said they had lost $11 million when the cattle market plunged after the show. The case dragged on and Oprah had to relocate her TV show to the local theatre in Amarillo, Texas, where the case was being heard, for almost a year. During this time, she hired a company called Courtroom Sciences to help her analyze and read the jury. Rather than worrying about the trial, Oprah saw promise in one of Courtroom Sciences' co-founders, Philip McGraw, and brought him in to her show, as Dr Phil.

Oprah went on to win the trial, leaving Amarillo saying, "Free speech not only lives, it rocks", before adding, "I'm still off hamburgers". As a result of her comments on mad cows, a chain of events has now led to Harpo Productions owning the number one and number two talk shows on US national TV: The Oprah Winfrey Show, and Dr Phil.

Oprah's charity work is legendary, and has grown with her fortune. As she says, "What material success does is provide you with the ability to concentrate on other things that really matter. And that is being able to make a difference, not only in your own life, but in other people's lives." To date her Oprah's Angel Network has raised over $50 million. As her brand continues to grow, she continues to keep grounded, writing in her magazine: "Though I am grateful for the blessings of wealth, it hasn't changed who I am. My feet are still on the ground. I'm just wearing better shoes."

MARTHA STEWART
"The Homemaking Queen"

Martha Stewart's Star path has been remarkably similar to Oprah's – leveraging her brand through existing media companies, and then taking ownership of her brand by setting up her own media company, with the many accompanying spin-offs. In Martha's case, however, she has taken her path to the extremes. As a result, we have seen her off the racing line – and into the gravel trap.

While Oprah initially built her brand through the radio and TV networks, Martha built her brand through her books, Kmart and Time Warner.

From a small catering business in Westport, Martha's first step up in brand building came when her husband, who was the CEO of a book publishing company, helped her to get her first book "Entertaining" published in 1981. A string of books followed, establishing her identity as America's lifestyle and homemaking star.

Every Star needs a dealmaker to grow their brand. In 1987, Barbara Loren-Snyder, from America's second largest discount retail chain Kmart, called Martha out of the blue and said, "I can make you a multi-millionaire and a star and it won't cost you a penny." Kmart was looking for a star to bring some glamour to their kitchen department. Martha agreed to a five-year contract at $200,000 per year.

While Stars are quick to make money, they are generally even faster to spend it. As soon as the contract was signed, Martha bought her dream house, a $535,000 farmhouse she wanted to renovate. Although Martha was quick to spend, it didn't mean the money had to be hers. She came up with a plan to fully fund the purchase, convincing Barbara and Kmart to loan her the money to buy the house. In return she would use Kmart supplies in the renovation, video the process and turn it into a Kmart promotional campaign.

This chance idea – that simply came from Martha's idea of leveraging her brand to get her dream house – turned out to be the launch pad for Martha's TV career. With 37 Kmart vendors on board, Martha became the face of their various advertisements in a national $20 million campaign. This then led to print advertisements, TV show appearances and a new book in 1989, "Martha Stewart's New Old House" which, with all of Kmart's dollars funding the hype, became an instant bestseller.

By 1991, Time Warner was ready to sign a ten-year contract to publish "Martha Stewart Living". Her magazine gave her another massive leverage point, with the production, distribution and marketing undertaken and financed by Time Warner. Circulation of her magazine grew to 725,000 by 1993. In that year she secured a similar arrangement with Time Warner for her own half-hour TV series, "Martha Stewart Living Television".

At this point, Martha took another big step up – again by bringing the right person into her team. Sharon Patrick, a former partner of management consultants McKinsey & Co, came in to organize Martha's business activities. Sharon went about renegotiating her deals with Kmart and Time Warner, and then set up Martha Stewart Living Omnimedia, which bought the rights to Martha's activities from Time Warner in 1997. Martha again leveraged on other people's finances to raise the money for this – with the $85 million price coming from a mix of shares, a loan, and a payment reportedly made by Kmart to Stewart which covered the cash portion of the deal.

Having leveraged off the promotional muscle of Kmart and Time Warner to build her brand, and then having leveraged on their finances to buy back the rights to her brand, Martha and Sharon took Martha Stewart Omnimedia public in 1999. The IPO made Martha a billionaire. By 2001, Martha reached the Forbes Richest List and was elected onto the prestigious board of the New York Stock Exchange.

But then, less than a week after her election to the NYSE, in December 2001, she made a share trade unrelated to her company, and her billion dollar winning formula suddenly became a losing formula. She sold 3,928 shares in ImClone one day before the Food and Drug Administration declined approval on ImClone's cancer drug, sending the stock into freefall. In June 2002, ImClone's founder, Samuel Waksal, was arrested and charged with insider trading. Eighteen months of negative press and speculation later, Martha resigned as chairman and CEO of her company.

Every Star's winning formula is their force of personality. Martha had used this successfully to build a billion dollar business. Force of personality, however, becomes a losing formula when you switch from the Star game to the Trading game. While federal prosecutors initially charged her with securities fraud, she was never found guilty of this charge. In March she was convicted for lying to regulators during their investigation – her natural instinct to protect her image at the critical moment, a strategy that served her so well as a Star, resulted in a jail sentence in the regulated trading market.

Martha spent five months in prison, from 2004 to early 2005. During this time, she rebuilt her brand with the announcement of new partnerships and TV shows, and shares of Martha Stewart Living Omnimedia jumped 70%. Today, she has recovered her wealth and is back in her flow.

ARNOLD SCHWARZENEGGER
"The Governator"

Wealth Dynamics uses many analogies with sports and likens the process toward financial fitness to that of working toward physical fitness. Schwarzenegger has often compared success in life with success in the gym, and as a seven-time Mr. Olympia, he is qualified to do so.

Schwarzenegger has reached the top of three entirely different, highly competitive vocations, by applying the same level of determination against the odds in each case, and by recreating his brand (and team) each time to have maximum attraction and effect.

His Hollywood success, and election as Governor of California, both occurred in circumstances where the odds were stacked against him. With the opposition and challenges he faced, many people in his position would have quit early in the process. In fact, most would probably never even have started.

Comparing this process to the gym, he comments, "The last three or four reps is what makes the muscle grow. This area of pain divides the champion from someone else who is not a champion. That's what most people lack: having the guts to go on and just say they'll go through the pain no matter what happens. Strength does not come from winning. Your struggles develop your strengths. When you go through hardships and decide not to surrender, that is strength."

While serving in the Austrian Army as a tank driver in 1965, Schwarzenegger, who had the dream of winning the Mr. Universe title, snuck off base to compete in his first bodybuilding competition. When his base found out, they put him in detention for a week. However his commanding officers realized he had come back with the Mr. Europe Junior trophy, and on release from detention transferred him from tank driving to full-time competitive bodybuilding.

By 19, he had won the titles of Best Built Man in Europe and Mr. Europe, as well as the International Power lifting Championship. At 20 he became the youngest competitor ever to win the Mr. Universe title. With ambitions of furthering his bodybuilding career, and finding his fortune, Schwarzenegger moved to the United States the following year. Despite having little money, and little fluency in English, he continued to compete, with Joe Weider as a mentor. Weider was the founder of the Mr. Olympia competition and had built a publishing business around his passion for bodybuilding, with titles such as Men's Fitness and Muscle & Fitness. Schwarzenegger competed for a decade in Weider's Mr. Olympia, winning a record seven times, between 1970 and 1980.

Determined to break into Hollywood, he starred in his first film "Hercules in New York" in 1970. His accent was so strong, he was dubbed, and, following advice to drop his complicated name, he appeared under the name "Arnold Strong". Over the next ten years, he continued to audition for parts, deciding to revert to his birth name saying, "If it's hard to remember, it'll be difficult to forget."

After two "Conan" films in the early 1980's, Schwarzenegger's break came, as breaks do for so many Star profiles, when he teamed up with an inspired Creator, James Cameron. Cameron's film, "The Terminator" starring Schwarzenegger, together with its two sequels, became a $390 million franchise. Fourteen years after beginning his quest, Schwarzenegger found the superstar status he was looking for.

Over the next seven years, before announcing he would be running for Governor of California, he continued his run at the box office, while carefully converting his success in both bodybuilding and Hollywood into sustainable cash flow.

Oak Productions (which he had set up in 1977 after his nickname "The Austrian Oak") received all his film fees, licensing fees and merchandising fees. Pumping Iron America (named after the bodybuilding film he featured in and which he bought the entire rights to as soon as he could afford it) received sales from his weightlifting videos, merchandise and clothing. Fitness Publications received fees from his books and magazine contributions.

Schwarzenegger was also careful to funnel the cash flow that his brand had attracted into real estate and stocks, so while his businesses gave him a net worth of between $100 million and $200 million, his portfolio increased this to a reported $800 million by the time he ran for Governor, making him the World's third wealthiest celebrity after Oprah Winfrey and England's Paul McCartney.

A Star's winning formula is their force of personality, and their ability to connect with their audience while staying in the limelight. While Oprah achieved this through her sincerity, Arnold achieved it through his sense of humor.

When he announced his entry into politics during the California recall election in 2003, he said on the Jay Leno show, "It's the most difficult [decision] I've made in my entire life, except the one I made in 1978 when I decided to get a bikini wax".

For a Star to shine, a critical factor for success is their team selection. Schwarzenegger was off to a good start, having married John F Kennedy's niece, Maria Shriver, back in 1986. Exposure to America's most famous political family had given him an invaluable introduction to politics. As he began to campaign against a background of criticism of his credibility, he brought in Warren Buffett, America's most successful investor, and former Secretary of State, George Schultz as advisors on his economic recovery council.

His choice of a team to build his credibility had a large part to play in his success in winning the governorship. For the first year – despite ongoing media attention devoted to his history of alleged inappropriate behavior – his popularity ratings remained steady at 65%, the highest for a California governor in 45 years.

While Schwarzenegger's final track record in politics has yet to be written, his success in building attraction around himself through his determination and force of personality have been proven time and again. Keeping himself grounded, with the right teams and the right wealth creation strategies, has allowed him to continue to shine.

A fellow Star profile, George Bush, compared himself to Arnold at a White House dinner after his election success: "We both married well. We both have trouble with the English language. We both have big biceps… Well, two out of three isn't bad."

AMITABH BACHCHAN
"Superstar of the Millennium"

Amitabh Bachchan is the undisputed king of India's Bollywood. Having appeared in more than 70 films, today he remains the highest paid actor in India's entertainment industry. His journey has been anything but smooth, however, and his story shows how easy it is for our winning formula to become a losing formula.

With an ambition for Bollywood, Bachchan gave up his job as a freight broker to get into film early on. It took 13 films, however, before he got his first hit, Zanzeer, in 1973 at the age of 31. His popularity grew through the 1970's and 1980's. By 1983 his star status turned into a national obsession. After being punched on the set of his film "Coolie", he fell against a table and ended up in hospital with near-fatal wounds. The national papers kept a running commentary on his progress, which also dominated the television news.

With his star shining brightly, Bachchan then took two turns in his career that each demonstrated just how quickly winning formulas can become losing formulas.

After the assassination of Indira Gandhi in 1984, Bachchan was convinced by Rajiv Gandhi to enter politics. His brand quickly got him elected into government. Passing your brand into the hands of others, however, is a surefire route to disaster. Rajiv Gandhi was elected as Prime Minister, but soon after taking office, his government was hit by the Bofors Scandal. The government was accused of receiving kickbacks from Bofors AB for a bid to supply India's 155mm field howitzers, and Bachchan found himself in the middle of the drama. Resigning his seat, Bachchan vowed never to get involved in politics again.

In 1995, Bachchan took another ill-fated diversion by starting ABCL (The Amitabh Bachchan Corporation Ltd). Stars are successful in business when their companies' are leveraging their brand and being run by others. Stars become extremely unsuccessful in business when they attempt to run the businesses themselves using their force of personality. Bachchan intended to create a production company to get involved in all aspects of the Indian film and media industry.

ABCL began producing and distributing films, and was the principle sponsor of the 1996 Miss Universe contest in Bangalore. Rather than building his own brand, Bachchan spent his days managing his company, and spending freely on films which then flopped at the box-office. Over two short years, ABCL racked up Rs900 million in debt before Bachchan closed it down - leaving his reputation in Bollywood at an all-time low.

Determined to pay back the debts, Bachchan promised his creditors he would compensate them by acting as "brand ambassador" for their businesses, appearing in their campaigns and promotions, and that he would repay them from the fees he earned when he returned to acting.

In 2000, Bachchan was chosen as host of India's TV quiz "Who Wants to Be a Millionaire?" which became a huge hit. He then starred in a series of hit films, becoming a far bigger star in his sixties than he was in his thirties and forties. The size of his following in India was highlighted when the BBC held an online poll for the "Superstar of the Millennium". Votes from India flooded in, giving Bachchan the position ahead of all the celebrities in America and Europe.

When Bachchan switched from a Star profile strategy to a Creator profile strategy, he unraveled all the wealth he had created in his first fifty years within two years, leaving him arguably in more debt than any of his fans. When he switched back to a Star profile strategy, Bachchan not only reversed his fortunes, but reignited his passion.

Now in his mid-sixties, Bachan continues to operate as Indian "Brand Ambassador" to a dozen major companies, charging around US$500,000 to each. He starred in thirteen films during 2005, and has become the highest paid actor in Bollywood.

PAUL NEWMAN
"Shameless Exploitation in Pursuit of the Common Good"

You will not see Paul Newman on the list of Hollywood's top earners, yet he has given away more money than most Hollywood superstars have ever made. In fact, the way that Newman's life has revolved around his passion and purpose is a living example for every Star.

Newman, born in 1925, has spent most of his life in the theatre and film. He had to wait until his 40's before starring in his most successful films, Butch Cassidy and the Sundance Kid with Robert Redford when he was 44, and The Sting when he was 48. He was nominated nine times for an Academy Award, but had to wait until he was over 60 before winning one, in 1986 for The Color of Money.

Despite his late success, Newman leveraged the brand he was building in Hollywood to pursue a passion and a greater purpose. His passion, motor racing, he discovered in 1968, when he trained for "Winning", a film revolving around motor sports. To begin with, he raced with the Bob Sharp Racing team, lending his brand to the team by appearing in some of their commercials. Fifteen years later, he combined his brand with the expertise of professional race manager, Carl Haas, to launch Newman Haas Racing.

This allowed him to pursue his passion at the top of the sport. The team won its first CART title with Mario Andretti the following year, and went on to attract other top drivers including Michael Andretti, Nigel Mansell, Paul Tracy, Christian Fittipaldi and Cristiano da Matta. Newman Haas Racing is the most successful team currently active in the Champ Car World Series. It has won five championships, the most recent with Sebastien Bourdais in 2005. Newman, who has just turned eighty, has stayed actively involved in the team throughout.

Newman's purpose, he discovered by accident. In 1982, he teamed up with his friend AE Hotchner on a bet, to see if they could sell the homemade salad dressing that the Newmans gave out as holiday gifts. Run by a small team, from the beginning the company let the public know that all profits would go to charity. "Newman's Own" leveraged on Newman's brand and gradually expanded into pasta sauce, popcorn, salsa and other things.

Aware that it was his brand that was getting the salad dressing noticed, Newman gave the company the motto: "Shameless exploitation in pursuit of the common good". In the first year, Newman's Own donated close to $1 million to charity. By 2006, the company had reached an astounding $200 million in donations to charities.

Newman's explanation of this phenomenon is worth hearing: "A lot of the time we thought we were in first gear when we were really in reverse, but it didn't seem to make any difference. We anticipated sales of $1,200 a year and a loss, despite our gambling winnings, of $6,000. But in these twenty years we have earned over $200 million, which we've given to countless charities. How to account for this massive success? Pure luck? Transcendental meditation? Machiavellian manipulation? Aerodynamics? High colonics? We haven't the slightest idea."

Newman was not new to philanthropy. When his only son, Scott, died of a drug and alcohol overdose in 1978, Newman started the Scott Newman Foundation to spread awareness of drug and alcohol abuse. Of the many charities that Newman's Own began to support, one of the main ones was Newman's "Hole in the Wall Gang Camp", which was a summer camp for seriously ill children, named after the gang in his film Butch Cassidy and the Sundance Kid.

However, the success of Newman's Own led to a chance meeting that has since catapulted Newman's involvement in philanthropy to an entirely new level. In 1990, Newman's Own won the Lawrence A. Wien prize for Corporate Social Responsibility. At the prize-giving ceremony, Newman met Peter Malkin, Wien's son-in-law, who told him how Lawrence Wien had led a personal crusade to improve corporate philanthropy by buying stock in 300 large corporations, and then attending their shareholder meetings and writing to their chairmen to pressure them to practice greater philanthropy.

Inspired by Wien's efforts, Newman joined up with Malkin to launch the Committee to Encourage Corporate Philanthropy (CECP) in 1999. Newman committed $125,000 a year over the next four years to fund the Committee, and it soon took off with further grants from major corporations and entrepreneurs.

In the five years since launch, the CECP has encouraged corporate giving, which has doubled from 1998 levels. In 2005, the CECP was chaired by Citigroup's CEO, Sandy Weill, and the membership list is a who's who of America's top CEOs and Chairmen, representing companies that gave over $7 billion to charities in 2005.

STARS IN A NUTSHELL

Dominant Wealth Frequency: Dynamo/Blaze

Action Dynamic: Extrovert

Thinking Dynamics: Intuitive

Wealth Creation Key: Creating a unique identity

Secondary Profiles: Creator, Supporter

Strengths: Vibrant; energizing; image-driven; quick to deliver; quick to connect; can take an idea and run with it; can think on their feet; can improvise quickly in tricky situations; holds the stage

Weaknesses: Can be overbearing; controversial; operates by force of personality; cannot let go easily; values image over execution; doesn't listen to others easily; quick to spend; quick to cut.

Successes: Best when free to express and develop their own identity and brand, with a team to support them and a team to negotiate the deals. Stars excel when they focus on performing or being in front of their market and clients, while the business the Star attracts is managed professionally by others.

Failures: Failure results from a Star driving their ideas through as a result of their force of personality. While they are great at driving their ideas through, they do not always have the best ideas. Stars who leverage ideas achieve greater success. Stars often stretch themselves too thinly, because they think they are the only ones who can 'do the job properly', and so often fail to build the right team or turn off the teams they build, resulting in low staff loyalty.

A Star's combination of quick decision making and over-confidence can lead to reckless decisions which sound convincing at the time but lead to failure later. Many Stars never get started as they fail to see that the value of their brand comes from being less accessible, rather than more accessible. They will show up one-to-one rather than magnifying themselves to show up one-to-many, through the various leverage channels that already exist. Stars often also fail by missing that their value lies in themselves and not their products – and so they limit themselves by promoting products created by themselves, rather than partnering and promoting far better products created by others.

THE STAR STRATEGY

1. BUILDING YOUR WEALTH FOUNDATION

Stars draw the admiration and curiosity of others, but may fail to package this properly. As a Star, your first step must be to define the area where you contribute most to others – your niche and your market. Then you need to commit yourself to this path.

Great Stars have entrenched themselves in their niche, so anyone with a new product or promotion is likely to be attracted to that Star to support them. They have their own dealmakers to manage the deals, business teams to manage their businesses and investments, and support teams to manage themselves! The key is to see your brand grow year on year despite the fact that the products or businesses you are creating the most wealth with may chop and change.

2. MOMENT OF WEALTH CREATION

Stars need to focus as much time and effort as possible on defining and refining their identity and then delivering against it. That's right – vanity rules! The biggest downfall of many a Star is their failure to create a unique identity around themselves that people can relate to, so they just become another face in the crowd. All other activities should take second place until you have become fairly certain that when people talk about you, based on your branding strategy, you have a pretty good idea what they are saying.

3. VALUE CREATION

As a Star, your value creation activities will be in the efforts you apply to building your exposure, crystallizing your brand, and fine tuning your talents to fit your brand. Who has the best products and leverage systems in your market? Link with them to build their wealth while they build yours.

4. VALUE OWNERSHIP

Most everyday Stars deliver their value liberally with no ownership or leverage. Regardless of whether you are a doctor, salesman or network marketer, you need to create ownership of your identity, which means owning all intellectual property rights relating to your material, your brand and your image, and managing how others use this, whether on a paid or promotional basis.

5. LEVERAGE

The most important area you need to leverage is your time. That means being ruthless about what is low value time that you should be delegating to others. The team you create should allow you to free up your time to accelerate the process of magnifying your brand. You must also create leverage through your packaging, duplication of content delivery and duplication of promotional material and vehicles.

6. SECURE CASH FLOW

Unlocking the cash flow when you are the product is a fine art. The most successful Stars will negotiate their returns up front, and link them directly to their pulling power, whether it be sales commissions, signing fees, service fees, license fees or endorsement fees.

STARS TO LEARN FROM

Oprah Winfrey (Harpo), Martha Stewart (MS Living Omnimedia), Arnold Schwarzenegger (California Governor), Amitabh Bachchan (Indian Celebrity), Paul Newman (Newman's Own), Bono (U2), Bill Clinton (US President), George Bush (US President)

CHAPTER SEVEN

THE SUPPORTER

"Getting the right people in the right jobs
is a lot more important than developing a strategy."
- Jack Welch

THE CONSUMMATE LEADER

Supporters are outgoing, loyal, reliable and fantastic networkers. With a blaze frequency, their value is in the heat of the moment – the relationships they create and the wealth of energy, enthusiasm and time they can offer. On their own, they will find themselves outwitted by the innovations and timing of others. But when given the opportunity to build their own team, the team can outpace, outsmart and outperform the most quick-witted competitor.

Supporters such as Jack Welch and Meg Whitman have built their reputation around their ability to mobilize teams to perform. In an innovative environment they thrive, with new products adding fuel to the flames: the more wood, the more fire. The sharper the products, the smarter their marketing and leadership. Innovation, though, is left to others as Supporters are too busy leading from the front to have their head in the clouds.

IT WASN'T ME, IT WAS THE TEAM

While dynamo frequencies, such as Mechanics, Creators and Stars, are busy creating value and have no shame in taking credit for it, Supporters see motivation as one of their key roles, and will always be the first to praise the team. This people-focus makes Supporters absolutely essential in any ambitious undertaking. Successful Supporters can be found working with every successful Wealth Creator. However, many Supporters have found success without aligning solely with one Wealth Creator. As a result, there are many CEOs of well-known, listed companies who are Supporters.

Supporters are both intuitive and sensory, which means that they often can act as the antenna for a more removed Wealth Creator. With strong interpersonal skills, a Supporter is more comfortable out meeting people than creating sustainable systems, and so it is easy for value to be lost as quickly as it is being created. Also, in the excitement of new opportunities and relationships, distractions and diversions are aplenty.

Most failed Supporters mistook their profile as an employee doomed to a life of salaried income, or they tried to start a business or investment with limited success. Others might have liked the idea of finding a dynamic moneymaker to team up with, but preferred variety and 'trying new things' over focusing on turning one spark into a flame.

Despite being one step away from the Star profile, the two are as different as thunder and lightning. Supporter profiles engender plenty of loyalty wherever they go, one of the Star profile's greatest challenges. This is because while Stars generate hands-off admiration, Supporters attract hands-on motivation.

The Achilles heel of a Supporter is this lack of focus, which can lead them to slip strategy – and slip profiles. As in the case of Michael Eisner, who slipped from a successful Supporter profile into a Star profile while running Disney, and Steve Case, who slipped from a Supporter profile into a Deal Maker profile while running AOL, when you shift from your profile it causes friction not just with your flow, but with your entire team. When your staff, your shareholders, and the people who supported you get rubbed up the wrong way, they soon rub you back, and rub you out.

The Supporters who have succeeded have continued to magnify their leadership to scale with the market. Their reputation in the market, and the networks they have built, become their greatest value. They remain in high demand whatever business they choose to run.

JACK WELCH
"Manager of the Century"

Jack Welch spent his life working for the company that Thomas Edison founded, General Electric (GE). Joining in 1960 as an engineer on a $10,500 annual salary, Welch worked his way up to Vice President after twelve years, and up to Vice Chairman before his twentieth year.

In 1980, the year before 45-year old Welch took over as CEO and Chairman of GE, Fortune voted the company the best-managed company in America. Starting from the front, Welch set the target of making GE the world's most valuable company.

He recounts, "Peter Drucker asks a great question: 'If you weren't already in this business, would you enter it now?' That's a great question. And we began asking it about every business we were in. What we decided was that we would keep a business if it required a high amount of technology, a lot of money to run, and there were reasonable cycle times, that is, it didn't operate on short cycles. These factors were our strengths. We're the fastest elephant at the dance, but we are still an elephant."

Welch's dancing elephant went from a $14 billion company with revenues of $26.8 billion in 1980 to a $400 billion company with $130 billion revenue when he left in 2000, making it the world's second largest corporation after Citigroup.

His strategy was focused on his strength, which was his people management. Explaining his approach he said, "I spend 60% or more of my time on people stuff, and that's the way it should be. I couldn't produce a show on NBC; I couldn't build an engine; I couldn't do any of these things. So my involvement revolves around people."

Welch stumbled on a fundamental key to leadership soon after joining GE in 1961. Welch's boss, Burt Coplan, handed him a $1,000 raise a year after he joined, and Welch promptly quit. Hearing the news, Coplan's boss, Reuben Gutoff, invited Welch and his wife to dinner, to persuade him to stay. The dinner and subsequent call from Gutoff had an impact on Welch who recalls, "During his two-hour drive back home to Westport, Connecticut, he stopped at a pay phone next to the highway to continue selling. It was one a.m.; Carolyn and I were already in bed, and Reuben was still making his case." Welch eventually got an additional $2,000 and an increase in responsibility, and decided to stay.

"Gutoff's recognition – that he considered me different and special – made a powerful impression. Ever since that time, differentiation has been a basic part of how I manage. That standard raise I got over four decades ago has probably driven my behaviour to an extreme. But differentiation is all about being extreme, rewarding the best and weeding out the ineffective. Rigorous differentiation delivers real stars – and stars build great businesses."

His first public speech as CEO, in 1981 on the "New GE", explained his vision. At the New York presentation, Welch outlined the "soft" issues in his vision. Quoting Von Clausewitz's "On War", Welch cited the Prussian army, "Strategy was not a lengthy action plan. It was the evolution of a central idea through continually changing circumstances". His vision included: "Creating an atmosphere where every individual across the whole company is striving to be proud of every product and service; an atmosphere where people dare to try new things". The speech was a flop, prompting one analyst to say: "We don't know what the hell he's talking about."

Criticism increased over the next five years, as Welch cut over a quarter of GE's workforce - 37,000 in sold businesses and 81,000 in continuing businesses - leading to his nickname at the time, "Neutron Jack". During those years he was investing in facilities at the GE headquarters and Crotonville, his new management development centre, and building his vision of a workforce of star players.

Despite the criticism Welch did not sway his strategy. In his book "Jack: Straight from the Gut", Welch says, "I could understand why it was difficult for many GE employees to get it. But I was sure in my gut it was the right thing to do."

Differentiation, the strength of every Supporter profile, underscored his entire approach. In the 1980s, differentiation in a manufacturing organization seemed in itself a paradox. Saying, "In manufacturing, we try and stamp out variance. With people, variance is everything", Welch put in place structures to ensure differentiation. Each year, the review structure would identify and reward the 20% of 'A Players' and would identify and release the 10% of 'C Players' from the workforce. This became known as the 'Vitality Curve', with the 'A Players' differentiated from the 'B Players' by the GE 'four E's': high energy; able to energize others; the edge to make decisions; and the ability to execute. Welch said, "In my mind, the four E's are connected by one P – passion." It was passion that separated the A's from the B's, and it was the each manager's job to turn B's into A's.

Welch's focus was "People first; strategy and everything else next". The 'Crotonville Pit' became the venue for open exchanges between staff to bring forward their ideas. Managers had to make a yes-or-no decision on at least 75% of the ideas on the spot. The process prompted one appliance worker to say, "For 25 years you've paid for my hands when you could have had my brain as well – for nothing". The exchanges went global with GE's 'Work-Outs' bringing together entire teams to exchange and share their ideas.

In 1989, with the aim of "Focusing the brain power of 300,000-plus people into every person's head", Welch came up with the idea of GE as a 'Boundaryless' organization, which would "put the team ahead of individual ego". This process is a key distinction between the leadership style of a Supporter and that of a Creator. Welch explained, "For our entire history, we had rewarded the inventor or the person who came up with a good idea. Boundaryless would make heroes out of the people who recognized and developed a good idea, not just those who came up with one."

This concept went on to form the basis of a restructure of the way that GE's staff worked, breaking down divisions between staff and customer, between divisions and between countries. As with his other leadership concepts, Welch kept focused on the one big idea, repeating, measuring it, and making it real to the team. "Whenever I had an idea or message I wanted to drive into the organization, I could never say it enough. I repeated it over and over and over, at every meeting and every review, for years, until I could almost gag on the words." This concept of simplifying the vision and then magnifying that one vision is common in all successful Supporters.

In summarizing GE's success, Welch says, "We've only done three fundamental things in this company in the 20 years I've been in this job. We've changed the hardware; changed how we behave, and changed how we work."

"Within the hardware framework, the most important thing was deciding what businesses we wanted to be in, and we used the 'number one or number two; fix, sell, or close the thing' idea to guide the organization's thinking. How we behave – this drive for boundarylessness, open idea-sharing – came from several years of town meetings where everyone in the organization was urged to participate. Our latest initiative – Six Sigma – defines how we work: we want to have a quality mind-set in everything we do. Now, what those three things have in common is people."

Welch's relentless people focus is summed up in his phrase, "Accounting doesn't generate cash. Managing businesses does." In 1999, Fortune Magazine named him "Manager of the Century". Despite building over $380 billion in shareholder value through 100 consecutive quarters of increased earnings, Welch's record salary of $94 million and retirement-plan of $8 million a year attracted criticism. In summing up his time as CEO and Chairman at GE, Welch said, "You get paid a lot, but the real payoff is in the fun."

MICHAEL EISNER
"Giving the Micky"

Michael Eisner's story reads like a Disney fairytale, without the happy ending. As with all Supporter profiles, Eisner's strength in marketing was spotted early on. Barry Diller took him on at ABC as his assistant in 1966 where he went on to become head of daytime and children's programming. In 1976 Diller, now at Paramount, headhunted Eisner to where he became President at the age of 34. Paramount had a strong team, with Jeffrey Katzenberg, another of Diller's assistants, rising up to become President of Production.

In the 1980s, Eisner had his golden years. Between his marketing and Katzenberg's creativity, Paramount had a string of hit TV shows included Taxi, Mork & Mindy, and films including Saturday Night Fever, Elephant Man, Grease, Star Trek, Airplane, Raiders of the Lost Ark and Beverly Hills Cop. Profits increased from $30 million in 1977 to over $100 million by 1982.

Eisner's winning streak continued at Disney, which he joined in 1984 as CEO. Roy Disney, Walt Disney's nephew, brought on Eisner along with Frank Wells, former President of Warner Brothers, to revive the Walt Disney Company. Eisner, in turn, brought on Katzenberg as Disney's new Studio Head.

Over the next ten years, Katzenberg focused on creative output, releasing the highest grossing animated features that Disney had ever released: Who Framed Roger Rabbit, The Little Mermaid, Beauty and the Beast, Aladdin and The Lion King, which became the highest domestic grossing animated film of all time until 2003.

In the meantime, Eisner repackaged classic Disney animation films on home video – including Bambi, Cinderella, and Katzenberg's hits. As a Supporter, Eisner leveraged every creation as far as he could, saying, "If you try to pinpoint what it is that will allow us to continue to survive and grow, it is asking whether we have done that last mile on the Broadway show for The Lion King? Have we gone the last mile on the Animal Kingdom? Making sure we have, that's what it's all about."

With Eisner driving leadership and marketing, Katzenberg driving new content, and Frank Wells managing the finances, in the first four years of the new team, Disney's market value quadrupled, and by 1988, after exercising stock options awarded when he arrived, Eisner's income was $40 million, making him the highest paid executive in America. From 1985 to 1990 the company posted record profits 20 quarters in a row. By 1990, Walt Disney Company was posting revenues of over $5 billion and profits of close to $1 billion.

1994 was a tragic turning point for Eisner and for Disney. Eisner lost his two key team members following a helicopter crash which killed Frank Wells in Nevada's Ruby Mountains. As well as losing Wells, Eisner lost Katzenberg, after he refused to give him Wells' vacant role. The separation was a messy one, with a protracted legal battle over Katzenberg's severance payment.

Eisner took on the responsibility of all three roles, writing in 1995, "What I'm doing now looks crazy: no president, no CFO, no treasurer," and adding: "Soon I hope to have a first class CFO."

That CFO came in the form of Stephen Bollenback, Donald Trump's CFO who had restructured Trump out of near bankruptcy. Bollenback encouraged Eisner to get into deal making, saying "We can borrow cheaply and easily and we ought to take advantage of that". On his advice, Eisner bought Capital Cities / ABC in 1994 for close to $20 billion – at the time the second-largest merger in US history.

Eisner went on to recruit Hollywood's most accomplished deal maker, Michael Ovitz, as Disney's new president. In contrast to Wells' Accumulator profile, Ovitz's Deal Maker profile led to enormous friction within Eisner. Almost immediately, Eisner set about clipping Ovitz's flow, writing in a letter to Ovitz, "The deal is not the essence of Disney... operations are the thing. I feel about acquisitions exactly as I feel about everything else. We don't need them."

Major arguments followed. As Ovitz tried to bring in major signings for Hollywood Records, Eisner vetoed the signings saying, "We'll grow our own acts". Ovitz retorted, "You can't just 'grow' a major music act." Ovitz had created incredible attraction as founder of the Hollywood agency CAA, but his profile was ill suited to the operations role that Eisner wanted him to fill. Ovitz left Disney in one of the decade's most public and acrimonious corporate splits. He received $38 million in cash and $100 million in stock, for 14 months work.

Supporters put an extremely high value on trust, and Eisner saw the actions of Katzenberg and Ovitz – both reacting to being taken out of their flow – as breaches of trust. In an interview with Fortune Magazine, he described Ovitz as "Too devious, too untrustworthy, and only out for himself".

By the end of the decade, struggling to find the right 'trustworthy' team to match his 1980's dream team, Eisner focused on trying to build the Disney brand without dedicated resources to improving creativity, leading to conflict with Walt Disney's nephew and board member, Roy Disney, who said, "Branding is for cattle".

Eisner continued to rely on those he felt he could trust, and Disney continued to falter. His dispute with Roy Disney, who felt the creative magic of Disney had been lost, led to Disney resigning in 2003 to fight for Eisner's ousting from the outside.

Following Disney's resignation, 4,500 Disney animators – nearly everyone who had worked there – signed a letter of support to Roy Disney, saying, "In the new corporate template we become little more that factory workers or unskilled laborers at the studio… Mr. Eisner's rejection of Walt Disney's heritage has been a colossal failure. Yet this is a man who has been paid over $700 million in compensation since 1996, while the feature animation department has been decimated by pink slips."

In 2004, 43% of Disney shareholders voted against Eisner's reappointment at Disney, led by Roy Disney. By 2005, Eisner had resigned from Disney and waived his ongoing entitlements.

When Eisner arrived, Disney had revenue of $1.6 billion. By 2005, it was over $31 billion. Yet his legacy is being defined by the nature of his departure. While Jack Welch laid the platform for GE to operate creatively, Eisner failed to build a similar creative platform at Disney. In the 1990's, as he leveraged the existing creations within Disney, he was not being served by a flow of new creations. Ironically, his departure, opened the way for Disney to purchase Pixar, leading to a stream of new creations, and Creator Steve Jobs becoming Disney's biggest shareholder.

STEVE CASE
"The Deal of the Century"

Steve Case's story is an incredible story of how, when you turn on your flow, you can create a hundred billion dollars, and when you turn it off, you can lose it just as fast. In 1992, the age of 34, Case listed AOL after three years of operation. He acquired CompuServe in 1998 and Netscape in 1999, merged with Time Warner in 2000, and by 2003, he was gone.

Supporters often fall into a rolling wave by luck. Case's background was in marketing at Procter & Gamble and then PepsiCo (The Pizza Hut division). In 1983, Case joined Control Video, a small video-games service company. It was here that he met Mark Seriff (who worked on Arpanet, the forerunner of the Internet) and Jim Kinsey. While Seriff managed the technical side and Kinsey managed the finances, Case managed the marketing.

With the video company not going anywhere, the three of them launched Quantum Computers, to provide online services to Commodore computer users. Then, when Commodore imploded, the three renamed Quantum Computers American Online (AOL) in 1989. Case was 31 years old.

As Case grew AOL into America's leading online subscription service in the early 1990's, he was exhibiting a key sign of flow – anticipating the critical moments, moment after moment. Barry Schuler, an AOL executive commented, "There were a half-dozen seminal moments in the history of the company, and Steve always made the right decision". Another AOL executive, Jack Daggitt, added, "Steve kept making the right decisions: one time, two times – you chalk that up to luck – but when you keep doing it, it moves to the realm of skill."

By 1996, AOL had grown to 4.5 million subscribers, but Case's focus on getting new subscribers had led to a crisis at AOL. Case hired Bob Pittman, co-founder of MTV, to take over the day-to-day running of the company. Pittman came on board to find massive service issues and escalating customer acquisition costs. AOL's paid service was losing ground to the free access web. They had to come up with new revenue streams fast. Business Week wrote, "If those new sources of revenue don't materialize, AOL does not have many other tricks".

Many businesses have great concepts, but understanding how to monetize those concepts is fundamental, and new ways to monetize can come out of the blue. In January 1997, Daniel Borislow, who ran Tel-Save (a low cost long-distance call service) appeared at AOL with a $50 million check. Borislow wanted exclusive rights to sell his service to AOL members. Pittman put his top dealmaker, David Colburn, in negotiation with Borislow. AOL ended up with $100 million in upfront cash and a share of ongoing profits in return for the rights.

As a result, 100,000 new customers a month signed up to Tel-Save. By 1998, Tel-Save's stock market value had soared to $2 billion. AOL had found new value to leverage: exclusive marketing partnerships to reach their members. 1-800-Flowers bought the flower concession for $25 million. Amazon paid $19 million to be the exclusive bookseller on the external aol.com website. Barnes & Noble paid $40 million to be the exclusive bookseller inside.

Within a year of the Tel-Save deal, AOL's stock price climbed 231%. Suddenly, Case's relentless drive to build subscribers above all else appeared a stroke of genius.

In the dotcom frenzy of 1998 and 1999, vendors were willing to pay enormous amounts to have an exclusive deal with AOL as it multiplied their stock value at public listing. Having a deal with AOL became a right of passage for many dotcoms on their way to IPO.

David Colburn's deal making team became the driver of AOL's revenue, squeezing increasingly outrageous amounts from eager vendors and leading a colleague to say, "David will look you right in the eye and take your wallet out of your pocket." Another said, "These were win-win deals: we win and then we win again".

AOL began taking a share of their vendors' stock, multiplying their gains further when the company listed on the frothy stock market. Subscribers grew to 20 million on a fixed pricing structure and after the acquisition of CompuServe and Netscape. Between 1998, AOL's stock surged from $2 to $40. By 1999, Steve Case was worth $1.5 billion, and AOL was worth more than IBM, Disney or Time Warner. AOL revenue jumped to $4.8 billion from $1.4 billion the year before.

A deal making culture pervaded the company, and armed with AOL's high-flying stock as currency, Case went out looking for the deal of the century. He approached Disney, but following the Capital Cities / ABC merger, Eisner was averse to any further deals. Case then approached Jerry Levin at Time Warner. At the time, AOL had $5 billion in revenue and 15,000 employees. Time Warner had $27 billion in revenue and 70,000 employees. Yet the valuation of AOL would give it 65% in a new merged company against 35% for Time

Warner. As Levin considered a deal, AOL's stock price continued to escalate, reaching $95 by late 1999.

Over the following months, Case found himself in the minutiae of deal making, and out of his AOL leadership role. As the deal progressed, Levin and Case were both in their own world, while a sea change in the market was occurring. As the new millennium opened, Case and Levin gave their advisors a three-day weekend for due diligence before announcing the deal of the century: a merger between AOL and Time Warner. One of the bankers said, "If you do a deal over a weekend, you take shortcuts; it was sloppy." An AOL lawyer said, "It really was a joke... we were just going through the motions."

On the 10th January 2000, AOL announced it would buy Time Warner for $165 billion; Time Warner shareholders would get 45% of a new merged entity, AOL Time Warner. This was by far the biggest acquisition in corporate history. Yet it was a castle crafted on sand, where the craftsmen were oblivious of the knock-out wave about to reach the shore. As the Internet bubble burst, the enormity of the deal was nothing compared to the dramatic carnage that followed.

Within a year, the merger went from the biggest deal in history to the worst deal in history. In 2002, AOL Time Warner had to report a loss of $99 billion as a result of a write down in goodwill - the largest loss ever reported by a company. AOL Time Warner went from $280 billion market value in 2000 to $84 billion in 2004. By 2005, over $200 billion of shareholder value had been wiped out.

In his flow, Case built a fortune of $1.5 billion over 15 years. Out of his flow, Case lost $200 billion in shareholder value in just five years: more than the entire wealth of Bill Gates, Warren Buffett, George Soros, Jack Welch, Richard Branson, Oprah Winfrey, Donald Trump, Steve Jobs and Rupert Murdoch, plus all the founders of eBay, Amazon.com, Yahoo! and Google combined ... poof!

In December 2005, AOL's subscriber base had halved from its peak. Google bought 5% of AOL for $1 billion, valuing the online business at $20 billion. Steve Case resigned from the Time Warner board in October 2005, and today focuses with his wife on the Case Foundation, promoting social entrepreneurship.

MEG WHITMAN
"The Empress of eBay"

Since 1998, Meg Whitman has been the President and CEO of eBay and, unlike Case, she remained focused on leading and leveraging the business throughout the dotcom crash. As a result, she has built eBay into a community of 135 million users worldwide, leading her to say, "If we were a nation, we would be the ninth most populous nation in the world." By 2005, Whitman was worth $1.6 billion and Fortune Magazine ranked her the most powerful woman in business.

eBay was founded as 'AuctionWeb' in 1995 by Pierre Omidyar in California. The first item to be sold via the online auction house was Omidyar's broken laser pointer for $14.83. When Omidyar contacted the winning bidder and asked if they understood it was broken, the buyer replied, "I'm a buyer of broken laser pointers".

Omidyar hired Jeff Skoll as eBay's first President and full-time employee in 1996, and the company was renamed eBay in 1997. By 1998, the company had 30 employees and began interviewing for a new president. Meg Whitman's early career was in marketing, at Procter & Gamble, Bain and Company, and Walt Disney, where she rose to Senior Vice President by 1992. Whitman took an interview with eBay "in order not to make the headhunter mad". She took the job and went on to grow the company to 11,600 employees and $4.55 billion revenue over the following seven years.

Her leadership freed up Pierre Omidyar's time, and he went on to form the Omidyar Network to fund social enterprise with his $10 billion fortune. It also freed up Jeff Skoll's time (the second largest shareholder of eBay) and he has gone on to form the Skoll Foundation and the Skoll Centre for Social Entrepreneurship at Oxford University to promote social entrepreneurship around the world.

As with other Supporters, Whitman keeps her market instinct ahead of analysis. In an interview with USA Today in 2005, Whitman said, "This is a completely new business, so there's only so much analysis you can do. It's better to put something out there, see the reaction and fix it on the fly. You could spend six months getting it perfect in the lab or six days in the lab; we're better off spending six days, putting it out there, getting feedback and then evolving it."

Like Welch, Whitman has stayed focused on a small number of fundamental principles that can scale with the growth of the business. In each action and strategy, she reminds her team and the market: "What we do at eBay is we connect buyers and sellers better than anyone else in the world." When looking to innovate, she does so through the community, saying, "Our users are our best R&D lab".

Whitman's summary of the Internet is equally clear. In a 2006 interview with FT she pronounced that the five things people do on the net are "find, buy, pay, share, entertain". She has made a number of high profile acquisitions that, unlike AOL Time Warner, have added to the eBay river. Whitman bought Paypal for $1.5 billion in 2002 and Skype for $2.6 billion in 2005. Asked if she had plans to keep buying, she said, "We always look at acquisitions if they furthers our strategic objectives. But probably, for the moment - and I've said this before - we're pretty focused now on maximizing the three businesses that we have. And we've got three of, I think, the best brands on the Net. Let's just optimize those."

Through her focused leadership, Whitman has built greater wealth than anyone else in this chapter. How does she build trust within her team, and keep out of the contract disputes that tied up Eisner? "We don't have contracts at eBay. I've never had a contract. This was a bit of a surprise because at Disney, everyone had a contract. When I came to eBay, Pierre was incredibly clear: we're not having contracts for anyone. We're not having severance agreements, we're not having any of this." The eBay philosophy is that it is not contracts, but commitment that keeps the team driven.

Whitman has kept in her flow year after year, continually adding new value to eBay, and optimizing that value through the ups and downs of the market. By 2006, Whitman had built eBay into a $34 billion company. What keeps Whitman going in an executive role, when she has over a billion dollars in wealth herself? "I love this company. And it is endlessly interesting."

SUPPORTERS IN A NUTSHELL

Dominant Wealth Frequency: Blaze (Fire)

Action Dynamic: Extrovert

Thinking Dynamics: Intuitive/Sensory

Wealth Creation Key: Supporting Wealth Creation by leading the team

Secondary Profiles: Star, Deal Maker

Strengths: Relationship-focused; confidence-building; able to lead; able to follow; enjoy team building; enjoy networking; great cheerleader; very loyal to the right team; strong up front

Weaknesses: Little patience with spreadsheets; restless in the back office; easily defocused; loves to chat; can change direction often; often seeks too many opinions; wants constant variety

Successes: Best when able to take an idea and run with it. Will shine if given the opportunity to build a team and execute around a task, project or product. Supporters move at a more bearable pace than Stars, and so build stronger team loyalty. They excel when they can leave the creative development and bean-counting to others, and get on with the task of leading the team.

Failures: Supporters cannot be micro-managed, as they need the space to burn brightly. Conversely, Supporters will also get stuck if left with no base to work from. For fire to burn, it first needs wood. For Supporters to succeed they first need the idea to run with. Many Supporters never get started because they can't figure out what business to start. Supporters also fail when they start a business based on their network, such as a restaurant or retail store, only to be out-innovated by competitors. Supporters fail by painting themselves in a box – kindly taking tasks off their team to enable them to perform, only to be left doing the exact things they should not be doing.

THE SUPPORTER STRATEGY

1. BUILDING YOUR WEALTH FOUNDATION

Supporters already know many people and are undoubtedly a popular person around town. But to create your foundation for wealth as a Supporter takes a clear strategy to connect what you already have, together with your natural talents and time, to one or more Wealth Creators. That means packaging your network and your team.

Focus on building a reputation and network around your area of greatest passion. Connect with the Deal Makers and Stars who will connect you to even more of the right people to know.

2. MOMENT OF WEALTH CREATION

Supporters maximize the time that they invest in pinpointing and developing their areas of greatest contribution to the prospective or actual Wealth Creators they are going to support. That means spending time with them and being clear on how you can add the most value – not just by clarifying where your strengths are, but by helping them see where they are weakest and where they are entrenched in lower value activities.

3. VALUE CREATION

The value creation activities you need to focus on are building and nurturing the relationships with the Wealth Creator and with your network, including the team players working with you. Building trust and commitment are the two greatest areas of importance.

4. VALUE OWNERSHIP

For you, the value that you need to own is the relationships themselves - most importantly, the relationship with your team and the Wealth Creator. Without this ownership, no matter how good you are, wealth creation will be limited. But note – ownership is not simply a contract (although that is important) and it is not about constant proximity. It is about unwavering trust and reliability.

5. LEVERAGE

How do you leverage when the value is in the relationship? By magnifying your time, your knowledge and your resource base through a competent and loyal team.

6. SECURE CASH FLOW

Many Supporters go through the entire process and then fall down on the final one. They end up delivering fantastic value but have nothing to show for it but their salary. Steve Ballmer didn't become wealthy from his salary. He became wealthy from his shares in Bill's company. Similarly, you must secure a cash flow linked to the success of the Wealth Creator.

That means, make sure you have an equity share or profit share of his company – and make sure it is a large enough share and he is a good enough Wealth Creator that the end result will be a worthwhile one!

SUPPORTERS TO LEARN FROM

Jack Welch (GE), Michael Eisner (Disney), Steve Case (AOL Time Warner), Meg Whitman (eBay), Steve Ballmer (Microsoft), Louis Gerstner (IBM), Lee Iacocca (Chrysler), Tony Blair (UK Prime Minister)

CHAPTER EIGHT

THE DEAL MAKER

"I don't make deals for the money. I've got enough, much more than I'll ever need. I do it to do it."
- Donald Trump

THE ART OF THE DEAL

With a sensory dynamic, Deal Makers are reactive, acting on the right opportunities as they happen. On the lower, right corner of the Wealth Dynamics square, Deal Makers can be found aggregating the connections within an industry or region, such as Rupert Murdoch in media or Masayoshi Son in Japan. Deal Makers can also be found wherever there exist assets with significant value differentials, such as in property, corporate mergers and acquisitions, or the entertainment business with its multi-million dollar brand brokering.

While others may burn relationships to build bridges, Deal Makers will burn bridges to build relationships. After all, who needs a bridge when you *are* the bridge? Deal Makers are the great connectors, and the best ones understand how to monetize their network to develop (and control) their own Grand Central Station.

LET'S DO LUNCH

Deal Makers are in their flow when they spot the differential in the deal. While Traders will multiply the trades and control the spread, Deal Makers will control the deal and magnify the spread. As a result, a Deal Maker can make a billion dollars in just one deal. A Deal Maker's natural communication skills put them in this position, and for this skill to shine, they need to be in front of people. They will always add far more value negotiating over a salad than over a spreadsheet.

Deal Makers are natural communicators, influencers and negotiators. They have a great sense of timing. As a result, they can easily become intoxicated by their own success, looking for each deal to be bigger than the one before. This trend, however, is often the undoing of a good Deal Maker, who will go one deal to far and get burnt badly before they learn their limits.

Most failed Deal Makers are really deal-makers-in-waiting. They have never seen this as a credible way to create wealth and have never pursued this path. Or they have just never been aware that this was their main talent and would never find out unless they stumbled into it by chance. However, of all the profiles, when a Deal Maker finds his path, his wealth is one of the first to arrive!

It is also far too easy for Deal Makers to make connections naturally, but miss out on their wealth because they did not secure their cash flow. Without a niche, the right team, and the right momentum, it is often the Deal Maker who is the first to get cut out of the team. The sharp Deal Makers corner their market – in all four corners, so every game gets played on their turf.

Successful Deal Makers understand this, and strike a balance between the two sides of their market. Masayoshi Son became the richest man in Japan by bringing America's biggest Internet brands into Japan, benefiting the American companies, and benefiting the Japanese consumers. As each side of the equation grew, so the deals grew.

Other Wealth Profiles are often seduced by the ease with which Deal Makers make their deals, have been seduced by the combination of fire and earth to escalate value in a handshake, only to be burnt and buried in short order.

As Donald Trump said, deal making is an art, not a science. At the critical moment, what you say and how you say it can make all the difference: you can lose a million by what you say, and you can make a million by saying nothing at all.

DONALD TRUMP
"The Donald"

While Deal Makers tend to let their deals do the talking, Trump stands out thanks to Creator Mark Burnett, who has built Trump's brand (and his own wealth) through the hit TV show, 'The Apprentice'.

Trump's first big deal, in 1974 at the age of 28, is an example of how deal making is not about the resources you have, but the resources you can assemble. Trump found a vacant hotel on land owned by Penn Central Railroad, which owed New York City $15 million in back taxes that the city needed. Trump planned to buy the land for $12 million, persuade the city to accept part payment of the taxes owed in cash and part in profit share, then find a big hotel operator to run the hotel and convince a bank to loan $80 million to build it.

With little of his own money, but plenty of his time, over the next two years he worked on the deal. Eventually he succeeded in the purchase, with Bowery Savings Bank fronting the money, Hyatt opening the hotel as the Grand Hyatt, and Trump launching his real estate career.

Trump's father was a successful developer in Brooklyn, and in 1975 Business Week reported the Trump family's fortune at $100 million. Trump chose to move out of his father's shadow and focused on Manhattan property. Over the next fifteen years he built his reputation in New York, building Trump Tower, the Wollman ice-skating rink, and a series of casinos in Atlantic City.

As with every Deal Maker, he stayed hands on in his deal making, while delegating everything else, saying, "Every time I come over to a site, I make a lot of money. My father used to tell me that you can't make money sitting behind a desk."

By the late 1980's, banks were lining up with easy credit for Trump. Trump's attorney, George Ross said, "If he needed $60 million, the bank gave him $80 million, even if the project wasn't worth $80 million". Trump bought the Plaza Hotel four months after the 1986 stock market crash for $407.5 million, borrowing $425 million from a syndicate of banks to fund the deal. Trump gave a personal guarantee against the loan – something his father had always advised him against doing. Five months later, he bought the Eastern Air Shuttle service for $365 million, again with a personal guarantee, and renamed it the Trump Shuttle.

By 1989, Forbes Magazine said Trump was worth $1.7 billion, but behind the scenes he was fully leveraged with debt payments he would soon struggle to make. More significantly, Trump had begun to lose his focus, spending less time on deal making and more time promoting his brand. By 1990, the property market turned, leaving Trump in trouble.

Trump, however, didn't blame the markets. He blamed his own lack of focus, saying, "In the late eighties I lost focus. I'd fly off to Europe to attend fashion shows, and I wasn't looking at the clothing. Then, the real estate market crashed. I owed billions upon billions of dollars - $9.2 billion, to be exact."

As the new decade began, Trump was faced with the loss of three top executives in his casino business as a result of a tragic helicopter crash. The press was hounding him about relationship problems with his wife Ivana and mistress Marla Maples, and he was billions of dollars in debt. Trump had just launched the $1 billion Trump Taj Mahal Casino, and within months was not able to make a $41 million bond payment due on one of his other casinos. His bankers gave him a $56 million emergency loan and deferred $2.7 billion in debt in return for security over his three casinos. Trump was put on an allowance and charged with running the operations, taking him out of his flow.

With over $3 billion of outstanding business debt and $900 million in personal guarantees, Trump described how he was called in at 3am to attend a meeting at Citibank. He said, "That was the low point. There were thirty bankers sitting around a big table. I phoned one Japanese banker, then an Austrian banker, and then a third banker from a country I can no longer remember."

Trump's woes became public, and in 1990 Jersey Record columnist, Mike Kelly, wrote, "If we still had debtors' prisons, Trump would be in the dungeon" and adding, "Donald Trump is a Third World Nation."

Trump regained his focus, renegotiating his debts while aiming to keep control, if not ownership, of his assets. He continuously focused on making it to 1995 intact, saying later, "I knew that if I could survive until 1995 and hold on to most of my properties, which I did, the market would come back, and it did."

With the press against him, the banks watching him and his wife divorcing him, Trump worked down his debt. In 1995, he took his casinos public, raising $2 billion and making him debt free. By 1997, Trump was back to being a billionaire. Reflecting on his experience, Trump later said, "I was a schmuck, but I was a lucky schmuck".

Over the next eight years Trump built back his reputation in New York property, remaining focused on the deal. With no computer or email, Trump remained constantly on the phone. "My phones are so busy that I require two executive assistants, and they never stop. They alone handle, on average, more than 1,250 calls a week ... my whole life is just one big negotiation."

To understand people more effectively, Trump read up on psychology, saying, "For me, reading the work of Carl Jung was a step in the right direction. If someone had told me in business school that studying psychology would be important for financial success, I would not have believed it." Trump equates this ability to tune in to the people around him as the "technique for seeing into – versus reading into – the people around you".

In the new millennium, Trump was approached by Mark Burnett, who pioneered the reality TV genre with "Survivor", and in 2004, "The Apprentice" was launched, taking Trump back to a focus on his brand. Over the next two years, on the back of the success of "The Apprentice", Trump's name began appearing through books, key note talks, and talk show appearances. His fee for each show went from $500,000 to $3 million. Yet this was peanuts compared to the money he had been making through his property deals.

Was Trump, again, in danger of losing his focus and, again, swapping show for flow? In late 2004, Trump Hotels & Casino Resorts, which operated all of Trump's casinos, went into bankruptcy with $1.8 billion in debt. In 2005, the company was restructured and re-emerged as

Trump Entertainment Resorts. Trump held a 30% stake of the loss-making company, but resigned as CEO.

In 2005, Trump also faced a major set back with his biggest New York project. Trump Place became the name for the fifty-six acre site that made up Manhattan's West Side rail yards. Originally purchased by Trump in 1985 for $100 million, the area went through a series of planning disputes over the years before Trump was forced to sell it to Hong Kong investors as part of his debt restructuring in 1994.

Trump managed the project for a fee, and retained a profit share. It continued to bear the Trump name as construction finally started on residential units in 1997. Then as "The Apprentice" was reaching record ratings in 2005, the Hong Kong investors, headed by Henry Cheng, sold seventeen acres of the site to the Carlyle Group for $1.76 billion. Trump sued, claiming the sale was over a billion dollars less than it should have been. Trump lost the suit.

While Trump continues to make millions from leveraging his brand, he can continue to make (and lose) billions from his deals. We, in the meantime, continue to benefit from his experiences. Trump follows in the footsteps of billionaires like Carnegie and Getty by writing books on wealth. His book "How to Get Rich" gives a range of gems under headings such as: Keep your door open; Make sure both sides come out winning; Let your guard down but only on purpose; and, If you have them by the balls, their hearts and minds will follow.

DAVID GEFFEN
"When You're Hot, You're Hot"

David Geffen's story is the classic entrepreneur journey from mailroom to millions – literally. Determined to get a job at the William Morris Agency, the largest talent agency in the world, 21-year-old Geffen started with a job in the mailroom. On his first day in 1964, he arrived in suit and tie to sort the mail, and began to diligently study the company structure and communications through the mail he was sorting. Hearing that Nat Leftkowitz, the head of Morris' New York office, came to work on Saturdays, Geffen began to do the same, eventually introducing himself after an 'accidental' meeting at the elevators. Leftkowitz invited Geffen for a sandwich, and then took him under his wing, mentoring him, introducing him to his wife, and inviting him to dinner at their apartment. Geffen's mailroom colleagues were stunned at the speed with which Geffen had moved.

Within two years, Geffen was given a secretary and a corner office, and set about signing clients. While Stars naturally stand out, Deal Makers naturally fit in. Earning $300 a week, Geffen stretched his budget to buy $450 suits to ensure the top executives would see he already considered himself one of them. Building his network diligently, within a year he was being headhunted by rival agencies. The Ashley Famous Agency offered him $1,000 a week to sign up new talent, and Geffen took the offer.

Immediately after starting in his new role, he got on the phone. Rather than seeking out the best talent, he wanted to hire the top talent agents, to give him an ongoing flow of talent. He called Albert Grossman, the biggest manager of artists in the business. Grossman said he was happy with the agency he was working with, run by Todd Schiffman. Geffen immediately noted Schiffman's name and sought him out in Los Angeles. Geffen flew to meet Schiffman and persuaded him to join Ashley Famous, bringing his clients, including Grossman, with him.

Within a year, Geffen set up David Geffen Enterprises, signing up Crosby, Stills & Nash and securing them a recording deal with Atlantic Records. Geffen found a new mentor in Atlantic Records' Chairman, Ahmet Ertegun. When Geffen asked him how to make it in the music business, Ertegun replied, "Walk very slowly". Geffen asked him to explain, and he said, "You walk very slowly and maybe by chance you'll bump into a genius, and he'll make you rich."

Geffen started walking slowly, bumping into (and signing as clients) Jackson Browne, Van Morrison, the Eagles, Cher, Bob Dylan, Aerosmith, Guns n' Roses and Nirvana.

Geffen continued to move, to CMA, then to Warner, then to his own management company and record label, Asylum Records. With each move, he took his clients with him. In 1972, Warner bought 50% of Asylum Records for $7 million, despite earnings of only $150,000 for the label in the first year. Geffen received $2 million in cash and $5 million in Warner shares, along with an annual salary of $150,000. Geffen was 28 years old. That year, Newsweek wrote an article on Geffen entitled "Golden Boy" in which Geffen said, "I thought I'd be a success even back in the mailroom at William Morris. It was just inconceivable to me I couldn't win it all."

In 1980, Geffen negotiated a 50-50 partnership with Warner to launch Geffen Records, where Warner would cover all expenses, and Geffen would still enjoy half the profits and half the equity.

Geffen soon signed up Donna Summer, Elton John, and John Lennon. His first record, Double Fantasy, by John Lennon and Yoko Ono, launched in tragic circumstances. Shortly after the record's launch, Lennon signed an album for a 25-year-old, Mark Chapman. Chapman returned later the same day with a gun. Geffen's profile grew unexpectedly, as front-page stories of the murder featured photos of Geffen escorting Yoko Ono out of the hospital.

Over the next four years, Geffen Records increasingly suffered from struggling sales. By 1984, the company was yet to show a profit. Geffen saw this as an opportunity to renegotiate with Warner, and managed to reclaim Warner's 50% stake. Geffen got back into his flow, wheeling, dealing, signing up rising stars and striking it lucky with hit records from Whitesnake and Guns n' Roses.

In 1990, Geffen was ready to sell his company, speaking to Disney, Thorn EMI and Time Warner about a potential acquisition. As Geffen was doing his best to orchestrate a great deal, the President of MCA called unexpectedly, saying, "We're going to make you the biggest offer this company has ever made, and I'm going to send it to you by messenger right now." "It's 1990," Geffen replied, "Send me a fax."

MCA bought Geffen Records for $545 million in stock, giving Geffen a 12% stake in MCA and making him the largest shareholder. By luck, MCA was bought by Matsushita later in the year for $6.59 billion, giving Geffen $660 million in cash and making him the largest American beneficiary of a Japanese acquisition in history.

Geffen was just getting started. As Jeffrey Katzenberg was publicly ejected from Disney in 1994, he convinced Geffen to join him together with Steven Spielberg to form a new studio, DreamWorks SKG (after their three initials). While Spielberg and Katzenberg were the creative geniuses, it was Geffen's deal making that got the venture going. With $100 million equity from the three partners, Geffen persuaded Microsoft co-founder Paul Allen to invest $500 million, and convinced Chemical Bank to provide $1 billion in financing. Together with advances from home video and pay-TV partners, Geffen had soon leveraged their start-up financing to $5 billion. This gave the team the comfort that every single movie, record and TV show that they produced in the first five years could fail and they would still be standing.

DreamWorks SKG got off to a slow start, and the press began to report that the dream team may have lost their edge. But as the team built up momentum, the hits followed. Spielberg produced the blockbusters 'Saving Private Ryan', 'Gladiator' and 'A Beautiful Mind'. Katzenberg exceeded his Disney animation magic with 'Shrek', 'Shark Tale' and 'Madagascar'. In 2004, DreamWorks Animation was listed on the New York Stock Exchange worth $2.1 billion. In 2005, Paramount bought DreamWorks' live action studio for $1.6 billion.

Geffen continued to multiply his wealth through his investments, reaching $4.4 billion in 2006, taking him from mailroom clerk to the wealthiest person in Hollywood by far. Over the years, Geffen has built a reputation as a philanthropist in medical research and AIDS, and more recently he has pledged to give all the money he is making away. Asked by New Yorker magazine whether he felt he was a success, he said, "My life is a success – I am a happy man."

MASAYOSHI SON
"The Software Samurai"

Like Trump and Geffen, Masayoshi concentrated all his deals in one niche. Like a modern day Marco Polo, Masayoshi left his home country to collect his fortune and return with the spoils. His niche was the Internet, and his strategy made him the richest man in Japan. Son had grown up inspired by Japanese entrepreneur, Den Fujita, who had brought McDonald's to Japan. Determined to meet his role model, at 15 years old he hounded the McDonald's head office in Japan until he got a meeting with Fujita. At the meeting, Son asked Fujita for advice on what to focus on, and Fujita said, "Computers".

Masayoshi traveled to California in 1973, and began importing cheap video games from Japan to the US. Games like Space Invaders caught on, and within six months he had imported 300 machines and become the top games vendor in the area. While still studying at the University of California, he made his first million.

In 1980, he returned to Japan and started Softbank at the age of 23. Following in Fujita's footsteps, he focused on bringing American brands to Japan. Taking Fujita's advice, he focused on computers. He talked the banks into financing his business, and over the next ten years he grew the company into 15,000 dealer outlets with $350 million in revenue. Son kept his eyes on the market, and in 1994, as the Internet began to take off, he started to buy into US Internet companies that he could bring to Japan, including buy.com, E*Trade, Webvan and a 30% stake in Yahoo! for $100 million.

Son took advantage of the time lag between the Internet trend in the US and in Japan. Using Yahoo! Japan, he steered visitors to his other virtual properties. Meg Whitman remarked on how clever his strategy was saying, "He was so smart, because he was the first to understand the power of the Internet in Japan. And he made this Yahoo acquisition, and he saw what was happening in the United States, which was several years ahead of Japan. And he said, "I'll take one of those, one of those, one of those" and put it all together when there was virtually no competition on the Internet. So he seized first-mover advantage in the best business models."

Throughout the 1990's, Son connected himself with the key players in the US Internet and PC market. Wanting to be close to the action, he ended up owning the action - buying Comdex, the industry's main annual exhibition, in 1995 for $800 million. Son clearly saw the value of owning the market where the opportunities occurred, and Softbank went on to joint venture with Nasdaq to open Nasdaq Japan, the stock market exchange which hosted Japan's Internet IPOs.

By 2000, Son had spent over $3.8 billion on deals in over 300 companies in Internet, telecommunications and media. Then, in 2000 the market went into freefall. Softbank's value fell from $190 billion to $23 billion – a massive $167 billion fall. Written off by many as a major loser in the dotcom bust, Son was un-phased. He believed that his greatest assets were intangible brands that did not appear on his balance sheet. Still armed with over $1.3 billion in cash, Son continued to consolidate Softbank's role as the gatekeeper of Japan's cutting edge technology. His strategy led to a further string of acquisitions.

By 2006, Softbank had grown its market capitalization back to over $32 billion. Already owning Japan Telecom, in 2006 Son bought Vodafone Japan, and began rolling out a broadband wireless network with Motorola, combining Internet assets with mobile networks in anticipation of the coming wireless web. Worth $70 billion at the height of the dotcom boom, Son began 2006 with a $7 billion fortune, remaining the richest man in Japan.

HENRY KRAVIS
"The Buyout King"

Deal Makers have a tight inner-circle that control the deals in their niche. Henry Kravis epitomized the power of Deal Makers in the 1980's, making billion dollar deals by leveraging debt, a decade before dotcom venture capitalists started leveraging stock market equity. His $30 billion dollar leveraged buyout of RJR Nabisco inspired the book on 1980's deal making, "Barbarians at the Gate".

Kravis joined forces with his cousin, George Roberts, and Jerome Kohlberg to start Kohlberg Kravis Roberts (KKR) in 1976. Kohlberg, an analytical Lord profile, was working at Bear Stearns in the back office arranging complex finance structures when he pioneered one of the first leveraged buyouts in America in 1965. The concept was to buy majority control of a business using investors and bank debt, and give existing management a piece of the company. The management would then work to pay off the debt and interest, and the dealmakers would profit from a fee on the deal and a stake of the company.

Kohlberg had the concept, but had no interest in spending his time deal making. Henry Kravis and George Roberts on the other hand, were getting started in corporate finance and already had a network in New York. The three made a perfect team. Kohlberg's analysis identified the companies with the right profile. Kravis and Roberts would then pitch the idea of a buyout to the management.

KKR set up office in New York with $100,000 from Kohlberg and $10,000 each from the younger cousins. By having connections with the right investors and the right companies, KKR positioned itself effectively as the middleman with the expertise to put the right deal together. They made a fee as advisor to the company's management team and they made a fee from the investors − 1% to 1.5% of the cash invested and 20% of the profits the investors made.

KKR's first deal came through Roberts' connections: AJ Industries, which they bought for $26m, of which $24.3m was loan financing. By 1978, with three deals done, the team switched from raising funds on a deal-by-deal basis and instead started a limited partnership fund, with KKR as the general partner retaining full control over the deals.

As with all Deal Makers, the longer they played the game, the larger the deals got. KKR began to target the insurance companies and pension funds as a source of financing. In 1982, they raised $316 million in a second fund − ten times the size of the 1978 fund. By 1983 KKR were able to claim a 62.7% return on investments compared to a 9% return on the stock market. Both investors and potential acquisitions began to knock on their door. By now leveraged buyouts had become an industry in themselves, with 175 deals worth $16.6b taking place in 1983.

The following year, KKR did their first $1 billion deal, broadcasting company Wometco Enterprises, leading Roberts to say, "Lots of firms can do smaller deals, but over $1 billion, we don't have any competition". By 1988 the LBO market had ballooned to $77 billion, and the success of the early dealmakers had led to an oversupply of financing and an undersupply of deals. 1988 became a pivotal year: a feeding frenzy of corporate deals that culminated in KKR leading a record-breaking leveraged buyout of RJR Nabisco for $30 billion. KKR received $75 million in fees from that one deal.

By 1989, with the crash of the junk-bond market and an effective end to the increasingly cheap and easy financing of the 1980's, the leverage buyout market had seen 2,385 buyouts worth $245 billion. Starting from nothing, KKR's share of that was $63 billion.

Many of America's best-known companies have passed through Kravis' Deal Maker hands, including Texaco, Gillette, Safeway and Samsonite. Today, Henry Kravis is an active philanthropist and Vice Chairman of Rockefeller University with a $2.5 billion fortune.

RUPERT MURDOCH
"Outwit, Outplay, Outfox"

Murdoch built his global media empire from one newspaper in Adelaide, Australia, fifty- four years ago. Today, News Corporation, is a publicly listed company on the Australian, New York and London stock exchanges, and is one of the world's largest media companies with over $23 billion in revenue.

Murdoch inherited the Adelaide News when his father, Sir Keith Murdoch, died in 1952. Murdoch was 21 years old. From early on, he preferred to buy rather than start new businesses, saying, "In terms of starting new businesses, I've always been a skeptic."

While Mechanics, with their systems, limit choice (typified by Henry Ford's famous statement "You can have any color as long as it's black"), Deal Makers, with their networks, broaden choice. It is this passion for broadening of choice that has driven his strategy: "Communicating news and ideas, I guess, is my passion - and giving people alternatives so that they have two papers to read (and) alternative television channels."

Murdoch's relentless strategy, acquiring media titles and using their cash flow to acquire further titles, has taken him into new countries and new markets as opportunities emerged. From the age of 29, Murdoch went on a buying spree. Seeing the opportunity in England, he bought the News of the World and the Sun, followed by the Times in 1981. Using cash flow from his tabloid titles, he funded his satellite

TV network, Sky. Murdoch's heavy expansion in the 1980's came with a series of crises. First, he overcame a dispute with trade unions in Wapping, followed by an urgent restructuring of his debt as the 1990's recession hit. He dealt with both in his flow, taking advantage of the poor market to force a merger with his competitor, BSB, to form BSkyB and dominate the UK satellite TV market. His actions led Sunday Times editor, Andrew Neil, to call Murdoch "probably the most inventive, the bravest dealmaker the world has ever known".

Relying on cash flow and debt financing for his acquisitions, Murdoch repeated his formula in the United States, buying the New York Post in 1976, and Fox Studios and seven Metromedia TV stations in the 1980's. To overcome US ownership laws and complete the transaction, Murdoch became a US citizen in 1985.

From dominating the press, to dominating satellite TV, Murdoch continued to move wherever he spotted the greatest flow to leverage. When questioned by a reporter whether he still stood by his earlier words that newspaper classifieds were media's "rivers of gold", he replied: "Sometimes rivers dry up." Murdoch had already moved his focus to broadband and content in online networks, buying MySpace for $590 million in 2005, gaming company IGN for $650 million, and a share in DirecTV for $6 billion. For Murdoch, this was a natural progression: "The Internet is about giving lots of people lots of choices. Everything we've ever done is about giving people choices."

How does a dealmaker oversee a $20 billion empire with 750 companies in 50 countries without getting bogged down in detail? Deal Makers do not need excess paperwork. Murdoch explains, "We have weekly reports - flash reports - which state profits and losses for nearly every single division. Our finance people put that together. I've had that since the day I started, when it was in pen and ink, right down to the overtime - every detail. Just a sheet of paper."

Today News Corporation encompasses HarperCollins Publishers, BSkyB, News International, 20th Century Fox, Fox TV and Star TV. With a $6.7 billion fortune in 2005, Australia's richest man now lives in America and, at 75 years old, continues to play the game. In an interview with The Bulletin, when asked what he would like to see differently, he said, "I'd like to see the future a bit more clearly."

DEAL MAKERS IN A NUTSHELL

Dominant Wealth Frequency: Blaze/Tempo

Action Dynamic: Extrovert

Thinking Dynamics: Sensory

Wealth Creation Key: Connecting the right people at the right time

Secondary Profiles: Supporter, Trader

Strengths: Outgoing; entertaining; approachable; mischievous; always connecting people; quick to spot opportunity; operates out front; creates cash through conversation

Weaknesses: Needs structure to deliver; dependent on the value of their network; often too quick to please; can easily lose identity; often gets carried away; quick to blow off course

Successes: Best when free to network, working out and about. Deal Makers need constant variety to play the game. With a strong team to crunch the numbers and prepare the paperwork, they excel when their hands are free and their eyes open. Every successful Deal Maker has a niche which they dominate, and as a result all deals get attracted to them.

Failures: Many Deal Makers are busy networking naturally, with little ownership of the deal. They make the connections and then find themselves on the outside. By owning a niche and having forward momentum, contacts won't cross a powerful Deal Maker. It's tempting for Deal Makers to get the best deal for themselves rather than those around them, but only by building a track record of win-wins will connections keep coming back for more.

Deal Makers are often so busy helping others, they neglect their own team. Only by building a team of the best experts and connectors, can the Deal Maker focus all efforts on what they do best, with every hunch and every lunch taking them a step closer to the next big deal.

THE DEAL MAKER STRATEGY

1. BUILDING YOUR WEALTH FOUNDATION

Your wealth is in your relationships, and the higher level your relationships, the higher level the deals will be that you do. The time it takes to do a deal that makes you $100 is not so different from the one that makes you $1 million. Build your relationships but set the level you want to play at!

Focus on building your managers and players to support the deals you can do, and align yourself with the mentors, connectors and financiers who can provide you with the resources to make deals happen.

2. MOMENT OF WEALTH CREATION

You need to maximize the time invested picking deals, finding the right people and managing negotiations. As a Deal Maker, choose your niche and grow your network. Seek out value differentials to bring potential buyers and sellers together. You need to clear the decks to give you the time to do this job well, and with the right advisors around you, a fantastic deal could be just a month away.

3. VALUE CREATION

The value creation activity you must focus on is building a team to seek and attract the best deals. This team becomes an appreciating asset, growing in value with every new deal that you make, and you can fine tune the team as you go. Your internal value will be in developing your negotiating skills and tuning yourself in to whichever market you choose to focus on.

4. VALUE OWNERSHIP

Wealth comes from not just finding the deal, but controlling it. That means your ownership will come down to the relationships on either side of the deal, and the details of the deal – both legal and financial. You become the critical link without which the deal cannot take place, and that is where you capitalize on the value created.

5. LEVERAGE

You are magnifying your record, which means that you are building credibility as you go, and will need to be leveraging on someone else's credibility when you begin. Your leverage will also come over time as your team develops knowledge, your relationships build depth and your own knowledge increases. To begin with, leverage your time and other people's credibility.

6. SECURE CASH FLOW

Ensure you have determined your cash flow in advance to avoid confusion. Too many deals have gone through in which the Deal Maker remembered everyone except himself. Your cash flow must come from the deal itself, as that is where you are delivering value. So although you may want some equity stake for your efforts, your focus must be on the front end commission, back end commission and auxiliary fees you are charging to make the deal happen. To really reach your wealth fast, the money you make should be in relation to the wealth created – not to the time spent.

The value in a deal often grows not as a result of the product or business that is changing hands or merging, but simply as a result of the timing in the market or the demand for the deal. Your ability to pass a deal between multiple connections to end up with the right price and right players is an art which comes from practice. So find your mentors and learn from the masters.

DEAL MAKERS TO LEARN FROM

Donald Trump (The Trump Organization), David Geffen (SKG DreamWorks), Henry Kravis (Kohlberg Kravis Roberts), Masayoshi Son (Softbank), Rupert Murdoch (News Corp), Roman Ambramovich (Chelsea Football Club owner), Kerry Packer (CPH), Kirk Kerkorian (Tracinda Corporation), PC Chatterjee (Indian deal maker)

CHAPTER NINE

THE TRADER

"We were just feeling our way."
- George Soros

BUY LOW, SELL HIGH

Traders sit on the base of the Wealth Dynamics square. Like Creators, some Traders are introvert and some are extrovert. Introvert Traders operate best through data and research, and can make their money in front of a computer screen. Extrovert Traders will trade with people. They sense the lows and highs when with people; they can see them in your eyes.

Traders are sensory, reacting to events as they take place. For this reason they are more likely to have a day-by-day action strategy than a three-year plan. Market Traders like George Soros and Peter Lynch make it look easy, but it is in their canny sense of timing rather than a fixed system that they make their money.

EAR TO THE GROUND

While Creators have their head in the clouds, Traders have their ear to the ground. The earth energy of Traders keeps them grounded when markets take off, and their low altitude gives them a detailed view of the terrain. Having a ground-level view, they will notice patterns and inflections while others are preoccupied with the big picture. A Trader's strength operating at point blank range is also their weakness: they rarely plan ahead.

Traders are emotionally drawn to the trading process, which can become consuming. As a result of their reactive nature and reliance on other events or other people, Traders are not always proactive at grabbing hold of their future and ensuring their wealth. Traders work best when they tune in to their internal rhythm. Even so, many

Traders find themselves in their rhythm, but doing something that isn't firing them up: head down and stuck in the mud.

While Traders naturally nurture relationships, they are not the first to create new ones, lending their sensory nature to service above sales. Many may have tried some other vehicle in which they did not have to rely entirely on their own initiative, such as network marketing, real estate or insurance. However, until they take stock and follow their path, their true wealth will continue to elude them.

Traders struggle when given a blank sheet to fill, but will quickly find the patterns in a puzzle. They find their flow when they grow a connection with their market, and with their team. When they are taken out of this connection, it takes them time to tune back in and find their rhythm again. Coupled with their ability to multi-task, this is a double-edged sword; Traders often take on different activities that keep taking them out of their flow.

Great Traders make it look easy and every market – whether an up-market or a down-market – will have Traders who are making money, while others are losing money. While Deal Makers may do one big deal in the year, Traders will make many trades. It is in this consistent activity that they gain the edge. Their ability to detach, and observe their own activity relative to the market, leads them inevitably to home runs – and these home runs supplement an already impressive batting average.

Successful Traders seek out a changing market where they can take advantage of their incredible sense of timing. They are careful to own both the buy side and the sell side of the trade. After all, the value is not in either side, but in the spread. Ultimately, the world's best Traders have made their wealth not from one trade, but from an ongoing trading history which others are willing to invest in. This increased leverage allows them to literally move markets – shaping the very waves they are surfing on.

GEORGE SOROS
"The Man who Broke the Bank of England."

While Creators are constantly seeking certainty in their creations, Traders are constantly seeking uncertainty in their markets. Arguably the world's most famous trader, George Soros, said, "I look for the flaw in every investment thesis. When I find it, I am reassured. As long as I can see only the positive side I worry."

Anyone who invested $1,000 in Soros' Quantum Fund in 1969 would have seen it grow to $2 million thirty years later. This translates to a year-on-year compound return in excess of 30%.

The theories that powered Soros' trading strategy originated from the philosophy of Karl Popper: a 20th century evolution of the tenets within the Tao Te Ching. Soros studied under Popper at the London School of Economics before moving to the US. He coined the term "reflexivity", which theorizes that self-awareness influences reality: that the interpretation of markets causes exaggerated actions within their movements, resulting in booms and busts.

Hungarian born, Soros began his trading career at the age of 26, working as an arbitrage trader when he arrived in the US. For ten years he worked in trading and investments before persuading his company to set up a fund for him to run, called First Eagle, in 1967. Two years later, he set up a hedge fund, Double Eagle. With 17 years of trading experience under his belt and with the investor contacts he had built up, he set up the Quantum Fund with Jim Rogers in 1970. Soros was 40 years old. The Quantum Fund started with $12 million of investor's money, managed by Soros and Rogers, who earned 20% of profits which they reinvested in the fund.

Soros' approach was typical of a Trader, where it isn't work rate that defines success, but the opposite: "The amount of work you need to do is inversely related to your success. The less successful you are, the more you're going to have to work to correct the situation. If the portfolio is doing well, you'll have less work to do." He adds, "I do the absolute minimum that is necessary to reach a decision. When I have to, I work furiously because I am furious that I have to work."

Soros built the Quantum Fund by staying hands on and sensing the critical moments. Far from having a fixed system of trading, Soros includes philosophy and his own physiology in his approach: "When I was actively running the fund, I suffered from backache. I used the onset of acute pain as a signal that there was something wrong in my portfolio. The backache didn't tell me what was wrong – you know, lower back for short positions, left shoulder for currencies – but it did prompt me to look for something amiss when I might not have done so otherwise." Soros added, "That is not the most scientific way to run a portfolio."

Throughout the 1970's, Soros had already become an active philanthropist, supporting activists in South Africa during apartheid, and the growth of democracy in eastern Europe. Soros' Open Society Institute was named after Karl Popper's work "The Open Society and its Enemies", and his fund, the Quantum Fund, was named after the inherent uncertainties in Quantum mechanics. By 1980 the fund was worth $100 million, and Soros was worth $25 million.

In 1987, Soros wrote "The Alchemy of Finance". This was a "real-time experiment" in which Soros recorded his trading process. It was "not a scientific experiment, but an alchemical experiment, because I expected the fact that I was conducting an experiment to influence the results." As so often happens with a master of an art, the process of explaining success made him even more successful. Soros says: "The real-time experiment turned out to be a very good idea because it stimulated my thinking. Having to explain my reasons for making decisions forced me to become more coherent."

The Quantum Fund grew faster during Soros' "real-time experiment" than in the period leading up to it. Then, on Black Wednesday in September 1992, Soros became world famous when he 'shorted' over $10 billion worth of English pounds, making over US$1 billion in one day.

The selling pressure that Soros put on the pound in 1992 forced the Bank of England to borrow nearly $15 billion to buy back pounds in an attempt to prop up the currency. When that failed, England was forced to withdraw from the European Exchange Rate Mechanism and devalue the pound. After that, Soros was known as "the man who broke the Bank of England".

Every great Trader has leveraged their trading record by attracting a team of great traders and outside funds – through the time and money of others. In this way, Traders are freed up to direct the profits to their purpose. In the 1990's, the Quantum Fund continued under the management of an expert team of traders, while Soros continued to pursue his philanthropic activities. He continued to build his worldwide influence, becoming part of a group of international private investors with an estimated $100 billion in assets.

In 2000, the Quantum Fund's Chief Investment Strategist, Druckenmiller resigned following more than $5 billion in losses due to the dotcom crash. Soros had already made the move to focus entirely on his philanthropy, and following Druckenmiller's resignation, he said, "Quantum is far too big and its activities too closely watched by the market to be able to operate successfully in this environment. My own needs are for a more reliable stream of income to fund my charitable activities. To meet those needs, we shall convert the Quantum Fund into a lower risk/lower reward operation."

Despite the losses, the assets of the Quantum Fund still exceeded $14 billion, and despite having already given away $4 billion, Soros was worth $7.2 billion in 2006.

In 2006, Soros toured the world, advocating the concept of "Open Societies", in which he takes self-doubt and imperfect understanding to a global level. His cause is driven by his wealth, and in his own words, Soros' wealth has also been driven by his cause: "When I set up my first foundation in 1979, I had no public image. At that time I was a small fry in the market, managing a fund with $100 million in capital. Today we have more than $10 billion."

While Gates has harnessed his Creator profile to identify innovative ways to distribute his fortune, Soros has harnessed his Trader profile to advocate the expression of uncertainty and tolerance within the promotion of Open Societies. Ultimately, your profile does not only determine the way you make your money, but can also determine the most effective path for you to give it away.

PETER LYNCH
"The Twenty-Seven Bagger."

Like Soros, Lynch persisted in his flow until he had a trading team and a trading track record that could not be beaten. Like Soros, he also now dedicates himself entirely to philanthropy and has gone to lengths to share his success strategies. Lynch headed the Magellan Fund, America's largest investment fund, throughout the last two decades, so it would be easy to take his advice on stock-picking at face value, missing the broader principles that took Lynch into his flow.

While many new stock traders are eager to get started with their own money from day one, Lynch had over ten years of trading history, learning from others and trading with other people's money, before making great wealth himself. When he traded his own money, it was from reinvesting the commissions he earned from trading. Like Soros, by the time Lynch began risking his own money he was already a successful trader.

In fact, Lynch got into trading after working for eight years as a golf caddy, during which time he caddied for the president of one of America's major investment groups, Fidelity Investments. Hired as an intern at Fidelity in 1966, Lynch rose up the ranks of the investment company until he became head of the Magellan Fund in 1977, at the age of 33.

RISK can be seen as a an acronym for "Reaction to Incomplete or Summary Knowledge" – by the time Lynch was making million dollar investments with his own money, the risk on that money was less than the risk on a beginner's first $100 bet. Lynch had invested years of time playing the game, and building his knowledge.

While many new traders try to get into the game playing on their own, Lynch, like Soros, worked with a team. Lynch had a trader buying and a trader selling, and he would invest his entire time getting a feel for the market and the companies in it. Lynch said about his education, "Studying history and philosophy was a much better preparation for the stock market than, say, studying statistics. Investing in stocks is an art, not a science, and people who've been trained to rigidly quantify everything have a big disadvantage."

Lynch compared the logic of a prepared trader against the illogic of the market, saying, "Actually, Wall Street thinks just as the Greeks did. The early Greeks used to sit around for days and debate how many teeth a horse had. They thought they could figure it out by just sitting there, instead of checking the horses."

Lynch checked thousands of horses, visiting 40 to 50 companies each month, asking questions and looking at them in detail. While Soros was a speculator, Lynch was a percolator, spreading his bets over a wide playground: "I always thought if you looked at ten companies, you'd find one that's interesting, if you'd look at 20, you'd find two, or if you look at hundred you'll find ten. The person that turns over the most rocks wins the game. And that's always been my philosophy." Lynch built up investments for Magellan in over 1,000 companies, categorizing them into one of six types: Slow Growers; Stalwarts; Fast Growers; Cyclicals; Turnarounds; and Asset Plays. He had a different buy, hold and sell strategy for each type, and would recheck and re-categorize each company regularly.

Like successful players of every profile, Lynch's strategy was to ensure that he stayed ahead in down markets, knowing the up markets would take care of themselves. In his book "One up on Wall Street" he explains, "If you're in the market, you have to know there's going to be declines… every couple of years you're going to get a 10 percent correction. That's a euphemism for losing a lot of money rapidly. That's what a "correction" is called. And a bear market is 20-25-30 percent decline… If you're not ready for that, you shouldn't be in the stock market. I mean stomach is the key organ here. It's not the brain. Do you have the stomach for these kinds of declines?"

Lynch's trading decisions came from a wide variety of inputs – from the fundamentals of the companies he looked at, his knowledge of market history and psychology, his categorization system, his clearly defined decision-making criteria and passion in pursuit of the "Ten Bagger" – a company that would return him ten times his investment. His commonsense advice led to gems such as: "You won't improve results by pulling out the flowers and watering the weeds"; "A stock does not know that you own it"; "Go for a business that any idiot can run - because sooner or later, any idiot probably is going to run it"; and, "Sometimes it's always darkest before the dawn, but then again, other times it's always darkest before pitch black."

During Lynch's 13 year reign, the Magellan Fund became the largest investment fund in the US. Today it has more than $50 billion in assets. As with all the Wealth Creators in this book, Lynch generously shared the strategies to his success, writing three books on trading: 'One Up on Wall Street', 'Beating the Street', and 'Learn to Earn'.

By the time Lynch resigned from the Magellan Fund in 1990, after 13 years, the fund had recorded annualized returns of over 29%, and had investments in over 1,000 different companies. For all of Lynch's advice on pursuing the "Ten Bagger", anyone who had invested in the Magellan Fund when he arrived, would have seen their investment grow by 2,700% - a "Twenty-Seven Bagger".

JOHN TEMPLETON
"The Billionaire Contrarian"

As we reach a halfway point in our account of Wealth Creators, a pattern begins to emerge – we see that many of them have great ability not just to make money, but also to give it away. John Templeton is another example of a billionaire Wealth Creator who now works full time at giving his fortune away. Templeton spent his life as a trader, making a reputation for himself in 1939, at the age of 28, when he bought $100 of shares in every listed stock on the New York Stock Exchange. At the time, on the brink of World War II, the NYSE had 104 listed companies, of which 37 were in bankruptcy.

Templeton said, "I was sitting in my office at 30 Rockefeller Plaza in Manhattan when the news came out that Hitler had invaded Poland. It was obvious within a few days that it was going to lead to the Second World War. During war, everything that was in surplus, and therefore unprofitable, becomes scarce and profitable. Three years later I had a profit on 100 out of the 104."

Templeton was aware that his spread would be greatest in imperfect markets, so he began looking globally for markets that had not yet matured to invest in. Becoming the first truly global investor, Templeton focused on overseas companies and launched his own fund, Templeton Growth, in 1954. He was 33 years old. Over the next 40 years, the fund grew phenomenally through Templeton's hands-on trading of international equities and his contrarian strategies – buying as others were selling, at a macro level. $100,000 invested in 1954, with dividends reinvested, would have grown to $55 million in 1999.

Templeton moved from New York to the Bahamas in 1963, reflecting the global nature of his fund. In 1992, Franklin Resources bought his fund for $440 million, and today the investment company is worth over $24 billion. Flush with cash, in 1992 Templeton turned his focus to his philanthropic work. As trading was his passion, Templeton also kept active in the market, continuing with his contrarian philosophies. At the age of 88, Templeton made a hefty profit during the dotcom boom and crash. In a 2004 interview with SmartMoney he said, "I have put these philosophies into a simple statement: help people. When people are desperately trying to sell, help them and buy. When people are enthusiastically trying to buy, help them and sell."

If the Wealth Dynamics square was a hose pipe of attention, the wood profiles above would be a directed jet, the earth profiles below would be a sprinkler, the fire profiles on the right would warm the flow and the metal profiles on the left would cool the flow. Traders, with a wide peripheral view, are the most sensitive to the environment around them. As a result, it is no surprise that every Trader we cover is dedicating their lives to broadening open-mindedness and tolerance on a social scale.

While Soros has focused on open-mindedness in socio-political growth, Templeton, like Lynch, has focused on open-mindedness in spiritual growth. Templeton set up the John Templeton Foundation to fund and encourage research into the link between science and spirit. He also established the Templeton Prize in 1972, for progress toward research or discoveries about spiritual realities. The prize is the richest in the world, exceeding the Nobel Prize at over $1 million, and is presented by Prince Philip at Buckingham Palace each year. The prize is intended to promote "a clearer acceptance of the diversity of gifts within the major religions of the world". The first one was awarded to Mother Theresa in 1973. With a strong sense of the flow of time, through which he achieved his wealth, Templeton has focused this award on recognizing today's living legacies. At the launch of the award he said, "We are indebted to our forefathers who recorded in books their spiritual discoveries and revelations. Alive today are other persons to whom God is revealing further holy truths."

In his book, "Wisdom from World Religions", written in 2002 at the age of 91, Templeton brings together spiritual principles from all the world's major religions, from Taoism, Hinduism, Islam and Buddhism to Christianity, Judaism, Sikhism and Confucianism. In the book he explains the key to his wealth: "An attitude of gratitude creates blessings, Help yourself by helping others; You have the most powerful weapons on earth — love and prayer."

Recently, Templeton also talked of commerce being the most powerful force for good, saying, "For one thing, it enriches the poor more than any other system humanity ever has had." A prerequisite, of course, is the intent of commerce. He adds that if a business is not ethical, "it will fail, perhaps not right away, but eventually." Templeton was knighted in 1987 for his philanthropy.

JIM ROGERS
"The Indiana Jones of Finance"

How does a Trader link their profile with their passion? Jim Rogers has combined his Trader profile with his passion for travelling and for teaching. When he couldn't find a commodities fund to invest in, he created his own. When he couldn't find a global index to trade, he invented one, which today is the fastest growing index in the world.

Rogers stumbled on his path by accident. Offered a job on Wall Street, Rogers quickly discovered his passion for trading: "It was unbelievable," he said, "I didn't know a stock from a bond, but learning as much as possible about the world was already my passion, and I discovered that Wall Street would pay large sums of money just to figure out what was happening. I would have worked for free if I could have afforded it."

To avoid the draft, Rogers went to Oxford on a scholarship for two years, studying philosophy and economics. He spent his time reading The Economist and Financial Times, and daydreaming about becoming a "gnome of Zurich" – one of the mythical Swiss bankers who control the worldwide flow of capital.

In 1980, after six years of trading on Wall Street, Rogers met George Soros, and the two of them founded the Quantum Fund. At Quantum, Rogers was fully in his flow: "Every day I woke up racing to get on the bus to go to work. There was nothing that made me more excited and happier than the markets. That's all I wanted to do. I adored it. I was so consumed and mainly just in a constant panic to know everything I could know. It's like you're continually doing a four-dimensional puzzle, because no matter what you do, they change the pieces every day and you have to put the puzzle together again. How much more exciting could it be than to sit there and try to put this puzzle together every minute of every day, and figure it out before other people did? Omigosh, I can't tell you how much fun that was!"

The flow at Quantum led to a return of 4,200% over ten years while the S&P 500 rose by 47%. By the age of 37, Rogers had made $14 million by reinvesting his commissions into the fund. By 1980, with Soros looking to continue to grow the fund, Rogers decided to 'retire' from the fund and to leverage his time by combining his passion for travel with his passion for trading.

Rogers packed his motorcycle and set off with his girlfriend, Tabitha Estabrook, on a trip around the world. As they travelled he looked for ground-level investment opportunities, and documented the ones he found. When they rode through Botswana in 1991, Rogers saw a growing economy, and bought into all nine stocks traded in the local market. Since the market was turned into a formal stock exchange in 1994, it has grown by 800%. Rogers repeated the strategy in 1994, when he bought shares in almost every company on the Austrian stock market after learning of a change in trading rules. The market in Austria rose by over 400% in the following years. The book that resulted from the journey, "Investment Biker", made Rogers a cult hero in the trading community. The 65,095 mile trip also led to an entry in the Guinness Book of World Records.

No one retires from their profile, and Rogers continued to trade – with an unparalleled ground-level view of the world's economies. Rogers moved from equities to commodities. Realizing there was no suitable commodities fund or index he decided to set up his own. He launched the Rogers International Commodities Index in 1998, made up of 35 companies focused on commodities. Then, to leverage his own index, he launched a private futures fund to track the index, which soon attracted funds from investors.

In 1999, Rogers embarked on a second trip, this time in a custom-built Mercedes with Paige Parker, to chronicle the world at the turn of the century. The trip began in Iceland on the 1,000[th] anniversary of Lief Eriksson's landing in America. After two years, 116 countries and 152,000 miles, Rogers returned with another book, "Adventure Capitalist" and another Guinness World Record. During his years of travelling, which spanned the dotcom crash, his commodities index had continued to grow. By 2006, the fund had made a 263% return, making it the top-performing investment index in the world.

Rogers' third book, "Hot Commodities", was launched at a time when oil and metal prices were going through the roof, making him a sought-after guru. When told that whatever he touched turned to gold, with the value of lead growing at double the value of gold he advised, "You'd make far more money if you could turn your gold into lead."

Despite the demands on his time, Rogers' outlook on the US economy led him to move to Asia in July 2006. Saying, "The US owes the world $8 trillion dollars. It's a huge international debtor, and I'm not the only one who understands that." He added, "Long-term I expect the dollar to be seriously depressed." Rogers moved to Singapore, seeking a new base in Asia. Predicting a boom in Chinese stocks, Rogers began buying in tourism, agriculture and airlines. With China's economy hitting record growth, increasing 11.3% in the second quarter of 2006, Rogers is preparing a profitable future for both himself and his family: Rogers made sure his daughter had a Chinese nanny to teach her the language in New York, and now aims to live in a Chinese-speaking city. Asked whether his continued success is a result of luck, he replies with a Chinese saying, "Luck always follows the prepared mind."

TRADERS IN A NUTSHELL

Dominant Wealth Frequency: Tempo

Action Dynamic: Introvert / Extrovert

Thinking Dynamics: Sensory

Wealth Creation Key: Buying low and selling high

Secondary Profiles: Deal Maker, Accumulator

Strengths: Sensory; balanced; observant; insightful; grounded; creates loyalty easily; can multi-task; gets the right price; gets to the point; often sees things that others miss

Weaknesses: Can get bogged down in data; gets buried in activity; can miss the big picture; can lose confidence quickly; internalizes stress and doubt; once a position is set, hard to shift; can live in the moment at the expense of the future

Successes: Works best when in the thick of the action. Traders need to be hands on and actively engaged. When they are engaged, they remain grounded but if the anchor is up they are easily set adrift. When they are given the autonomy to make moment-by-moment decisions, without needing to leave the field of play, they excel.

Failures: Traders fail when their multi-tasking takes them into areas of creation, administration or presentation, which are out of their flow. Without the right team to support them, Traders will tend to take too much on and will sink under the weight of their workload.

Traders will be happy to take cues from others and then execute once the brainstorming is over. As a result, they are often overlooked in creative environments for the essential role they play in keeping the team grounded and the customers happy. Traders who fail to communicate their natural strengths end up frustrated without the connection and contentment they find in their flow.

THE TRADER STRATEGY

1. BUILDING YOUR WEALTH FOUNDATION

You need to fine tune your trading skills, which will only happen when you choose your market and build the network to support you and allow you to leverage your time and expertise.

Every market is a competitive one where the best Traders are easily found. Every market has networks of knowledge, strategies and systems. Connect to the one that resonates with you and get to work shadow trading with others to accelerate your learning (before you begin risking your own money against seasoned veterans).

2. MOMENT OF WEALTH CREATION

Maximize the time that you invest in analyzing opportunities, trends, and the differential values of the assets that you are trading. Also maximize the time that you are investing in timing trades and connecting with the people who you will be trading with (wherever that is relevant). In trading, it is easy to measure, so always keep score.

3. VALUE CREATION

The value you are creating comprises internal values, as all external values are locked into the trades, so are temporary by nature. The internal values that you are building are your access to information, your depth of market knowledge – overall, of individual buyers, sellers and products – and also your sense of timing, which will continue to sharpen with experience and knowledge.

4. VALUE OWNERSHIP

You must own the timing in both buying and selling the trades. Strange as it may sound, if you are a stock market trader this is already a given. But if you decide to begin an import business and start trading in motorcycles or wicker baskets, then suddenly you find you have a run on stock and a stop on orders, that loss of control in timing could mean the loss of your entire business. So don't leverage until you know you have this ownership secure!

5. LEVERAGE

You can begin by leveraging your time, as your wealth will ultimately flow from your internal value. All successful Traders find leverage first by multiplying (the number of trades they process), then by magnifying (increasing size of each trade and the resource base they have to trade with).

6. SECURE CASH FLOW

The Trader will always make their money from the spread. Where a Deal Maker relies more on his interpersonal skills, a Trader will rely more on the trading process – with the buyer or seller often being entirely unknown. And whilst a Deal Maker can do one deal with no upfront commitment and very high margin, a Trader is more likely to have the upfront commitment and a much lower margin.

That means that cash management becomes key. However, as you are making money from the spread, do not be limited by your buying power. Control the buying and selling, and then raise the capital and finance you need to do the deals that will make you the money.

When you are in your trading flow, you can move from market to market depending on your trading horizon and appetite for volatility. That means it may be a regulated trading exchange such as equities, currencies, commodities or derivatives, or it may be a market such as property, businesses, tradable assets or even trading within a particular country, market or online trading site.

TRADERS TO LEARN FROM

George Soros (Quantum Fund), Peter Lynch (Fidelity), John Templeton (Templeton Growth Fund), Jim Rogers (Rogers International Commodities), Charles Merrill (Merrill Lynch)

CHAPTER TEN

THE ACCUMULATOR

"Our favorite holding period is forever."
- Warren Buffett

IN FOR THE LONG HAUL

The Accumulator is the safest of the profiles, relying on a system of incremental growth to achieve wealth. There are many books on long term investing, as it appears to be a relatively straightforward process to follow. Many wealth seekers adopt the Accumulator strategy but either lose patience or get itchy feet and move on. The natural Accumulator becomes successful by patiently sticking with it.

Accumulators don't need a lot of people to make a lot of money. Buffett's investment company, Berkshire Hathaway, has 15 staff. On the left side of the Wealth Dynamics square, they can be happily hands-off, seeking out the next gem to add to their collection, while the others grow in value with little more than the occasional polish.

DOING YOUR HOMEWORK

As they expect to be hands-off, Accumulators will take longer to do their homework and to decide on what to accumulate. They will look for talent or assets that need little maintenance. After Buffett has invested in a company he won't interfere in the operations, saying, "At Berkshire we don't tell 400% hitters how to swing."

While many billionaires own properties, stocks and other assets, there is an important distinction between wealth creation and wealth retention. Billionaires in each of the eight wealth profiles attract through their *wealth creation* – which is the art of turning their time into money by following their flow. Once they have money, they will put it into *wealth retention* – which is the art of turning their money into more money.

In *wealth creation*, they focus and create one big river, investing all their time in what they love. In *wealth retention*, they diversify and create multiple streams. Bill Gates will buy shares in Berkshire Hathaway as part of his wealth retention, relying on Warren Buffett to leverage his money into more money, more effectively. Warren Buffett will give his money to the Gates Foundation, relying on Bill Gates to leverage his giving into more giving, more effectively.

Accumulators often struggle if they attempt to start up companies and create products, but make money naturally when leaving the start-up to others. As with all wealth profiles, few started with money. They started with their time and, once they had demonstrated their natural ability to pick appreciating assets, money got attracted to them.

Their analytical skills and sense of timing make Accumulators excellent project managers who will find the way to deliver what is needed on time. This ability to be extremely reliable has led many Accumulators up the ranks in areas that are not their passion. Many end up being faced with office politics, which they have little interest in and are ill equipped to handle.

Accumulators who wake up to their profile often find they have spent their entire life collecting, and they did it naturally. When this ability is redirected to collecting appreciating assets their wealth soon flows.

While Creators and Stars often make things complicated, Accumulators like to keep things simple. In his 1989 letter to shareholders, Warren Buffet said, "After 25 years of buying and supervising a great variety of businesses, Charlie and I have not learned how to solve difficult business problems. What we have learned is how to avoid them."

Accumulators are also the most risk averse profile. Accumulators don't like to speculate. Where Traders seek spread, Accumulators seek a margin of safety. Benjamin Graham, the first successful value investor and Warren Buffett's first mentor, made the distinction between investing and speculating saying there are two rules to investing. The first rule is 'don't lose'. The second rule is 'don't forget rule number one.'

BENJAMIN GRAHAM
"The Dean of Wall Street"

Benjamin Graham is recognized as the "Father of Value Investing", and is credited as the mentor of many modern investors, including Irving Kahn, William Ruane and Warren Buffett.

Starting as a bond salesman at a Wall Street brokerage house when he was 20, Graham generated little commissions, earning $28 a week. When the quality of his research reports was noticed, however, a position was created for him in the firm as "statistician" – a role that the industry today calls a security analyst.

In the 1920's, Graham began formulating his principles of value investing. By 1926 he had attracted $450,000 in funds when his big break came. Reading through an Interstate Commerce Commission annual report on railroads, he came across a small footnote on some pipeline assets owned by the Northern Pipeline Company, as a result of the breakup of Standard Oil in 1911. A train trip to Washington led him to the discovery of unvalued railroad bonds owned by the company, amounting to $95 per share against the share price of $65. Graham began buying up all the shares he could afford, and over the next two years persuaded the company to distribute the surplus capital to shareholders. With the support of the largest shareholder, the Rockefeller Foundation, the shares in Northern Pipeline rose to true value, and Graham's fund grew to $2.5 million by 1929.

In 1929, the stock market crash hit Graham as hard as the rest of America. On Black Tuesday, $14 billion was wiped off the market. Over the next three years the market continued to falter, and by 1932 Graham was left with less than 25% of the $2.5 million he had before the crash. Graham moved to a cheaper apartment and began to earn money from writing. He wrote a series of articles for Forbes magazine on his experience during the crash, and hired David Dodd, a colleague at Columbia, to help him write an investment book.

Graham also decided to leverage his students from the lectures he was giving at Columbia University for his research. The students were tasked to compare the "intrinsic values" of all 600 industrials listed on the New York Stock Exchange with their market prices, which led to the discovery that one in three companies had a market price that was below their net working capital.

Graham began buying up the best bargains. While still recovering from the crash, in 1934 at the age of 40, Graham published his first book, "Security Analysis". It soon became an investor's bible. His second book, "Intelligent Investor", was described by Warren Buffett as "the best book on investing ever written".

By 1948, Graham had turned his investment vehicle into a public company, Graham Newman Corporation. Graham became far more disciplined in his approach, and the results showed. In 1951, Newman sent his top student to research GEICO, a direct mail auto insurance company they were looking to invest in. The student visited the company on a Saturday and the janitor sent him to the only person in the office, Lorimar Davidson. The two chatted for five hours and the student was impressed enough to pledge three-quarters of his own net worth – at that time $9,000 – to buy shares in the company. On his recommendation, Graham bought 50% of GEICO, for around $720,000, using a quarter of his fund's assets.

In the following two years, the company's share price increased by 50%. The 21-year-old student, Warren Buffett, was rewarded with a $4,500 profit, which grew to significantly more over time. Today GEICO is part of Berkshire Hathaway, and valued at over $9 billion.

The GEICO investment was an example of Graham's distinction between speculating and investing. Investing was based on knowing the "intrinsic value" of a stock based on the health of the company, rather than stock market fluctuations. Graham's concept of "margin of safety" became the key measure for Accumulators, where the difference between the intrinsic value and the market value could be measured. The lower the market value was against the calculated intrinsic value, the more attractive the investment was to buy.

Graham's view was that wealth creation does not come from taking greater risks, but from taking *less* risk. He believed that with research, better bargains led to higher margins of safety, and it was in these investments that risk would be lowest while returns would be highest. Risk's correlation was not with reward, but with research.

Graham gave detailed, common-sense strategies for value investing, so why didn't everyone who read his books become wealthy? Graham pinpointed the need for the right "temperament" saying, "While enthusiasm may be necessary for great accomplishments elsewhere, in Wall Street it almost invariably leads to disaster." Having the temperament of an Accumulator – patient, analytical, reliable – was one step to following Graham's strategies effectively.

A second step was in effective leverage. Graham's disciples who went on to become billionaires were Accumulators who became wealthy by growing and leveraging funds made up of other people's money, eventually recycling the money they made from their river into their own flow. Those who attempted to use his strategies simply to invest their own limited supply of money would need to wait until old age before finding their fortune.

WARREN BUFFETT
"The Sage of Omaha"

Warren Buffett's story underlines the importance of finding the right mentor, and adding to their flowing river as you master the practice of value and leverage. Buffett started his learning early. At the age of 13, Buffett submitted his first income tax form, deducting his bicycle as an expense for his paper rounds. The following year, Buffett had accumulated enough money from paper rounds to buy 40 acres of farmland. He continued this accumulation trend, through booms and busts, building a $42 billion fortune, which he is now giving away.

Determined to have the right mentor early on, Buffett applied to Columbia Business School where Benjamin Graham was lecturing. He subsequently worked for Graham until Graham's retirement in 1956. In 1957, Buffett had learnt enough to launch his own fund. Needing capital, he approached the investors from his previous funds. He asked one of his partners, a doctor, to find ten other doctors who would invest $10,000 each into his partnership. Eleven doctors agreed to invest. He continued to leverage his contacts in this way, with investors recommending investors and by 1962 the Buffett Partnership, which began with $105,000, was worth $7.2 million.

Buffett invested $1 million of his $5 million fund in Dempster Mill Manufacturing, bringing in management to turn it around, and making a net gain of $2.3 million within two years. From then on, Buffett's direction evolved from Graham's investing strategy. He saw himself as a capital allocator, where his input could support the intrinsic value growth of a company. He began to repeat the formula of buying a controlling stake of undervalued businesses through his partnership, then adding value and seeing his investment grow.

Buffett had a big break in 1962, when American Express shares fell from $65 to $35 following a scandal. As the rest of the market was selling far below intrinsic value, Buffett bought the company's stock, investing $13 million - 40% of his assets. Within two years, the shares had tripled in price and the partners made a $20 million profit. Four years later, Buffet made a fateful purchase of a textile company, Berkshire Hathaway. He recalls, "We went into a terrible business because it was cheap. It's what I refer to as the "used cigar butt" approach to investing. You see this cigar butt down there, it's soggy and terrible, but there's one puff left, and it's free. That's what Berkshire was when we bought it – it was selling below working capital – but it was a terrible, terrible mistake."

Buffett bought Berkshire Hathaway and then tried to turn it around, but couldn't. So he turned this 'terrible, terrible mistake' into a listed vehicle to manage all his other investments. As a listed company he could now raise funds through the stock market. Through his experience with GEICO, he also understood the value of owning insurance companies, giving you an instant cash base from policies to invest with. In 1967, he bought two insurance companies for $8.6 million which came with a combined investment portfolio of $31.9 million. Over the next two years he grew the portfolio to $42 million – more than paying for the entire purchase price of the companies. Buffett continued with this strategy and by 2004, Berkshire Hathaway owned 38 insurance companies.

With ready access to cash to feed his flow, Buffett had built the leverage mechanisms he needed to sustain ongoing growth. He set a target to grow the intrinsic value of his investments by 15% per year, which he then proceeded to do. Reinvesting all gains, Berkshire Hathaway has grown through forty years with no dividend payments.

In 1969, Buffett dissolved his partnerships and injected his funds into Berkshire Hathaway. The following year, Berkshire made $45,000 from its textiles business, and $4.7 million from investments. Accumulators love under-priced markets – especially when they are flush with cash. The 1972 market sell-off came at just the right time, leading Buffett to say that at the time he felt "like an oversexed guy in a harem." He added, "You're dealing with a lot of silly people in the marketplace; it's like a great big casino and everyone else is boozing. If you can stick to Pepsi, you should be OK."

By 1979, Buffett's fortune had risen to $140 million, but he continued to live on a $50,000 salary. Accumulators are famed for their frugal life, and Buffett has continued to work from the same office and live the same lifestyle that he had before his wealth. The security and comfort that comes from familiarity extends to their relationships. In 1978 Charlie Munger joined Buffett as Vice President, and over the next 28 years they have built one of the most enduring partnerships in modern business history. Buffett married his wife, Susan Thompson, in 1952. They lived in the same Omaha home that they bought in 1958 for $31,500, until Susan passed away in 2004.

In the 1980s, access to money became far easier, as the leveraged buyout market and the junk bond market took off. Buffett, however, stayed out of this market, despite junk bonds becoming a $210 billion market and investors claiming returns of 60% and more. Buffett noted, "Mountains of junk bonds were sold by those who didn't care to those that didn't think and there was no shortage of either." During the 1987 stock market crash, Berkshire lost 25% of its value. Undaunted, the following year Buffett began buying stock in Coca-Cola, eventually buying seven percent of the company for over $1 billion. This turned out to be one of his most profitable investments.

In 1988, the leveraged buyout frenzy culminated with the buyout of RJR Nabisco for $30 billion by KKR. The deal making company earned a record-breaking $75 million for putting the deal together. Despite the size of the deal and heady returns, Buffett stayed on the sidelines until the junk bond crashed and then, in 1989 and 1990, he quietly bought $440 million in discounted RJR Nabisco bonds. In 1991 RJR Nabisco decided to retire most of the bonds at face value and Buffett made $150 million – double KKR's highly publicized fee.

Buffett repeated this practice of buying discounted bonds after the dotcom crash. During the dotcom boom, while facing open criticism for not achieving the same astronomical returns as Nasdaq, Buffett wrote, "We have embraced the 21st century by entering such cutting-edge industries as bricks, carpets, insulation and paint – try to control your excitement." After the crash in 2002 he bought discounted bonds including $158.4 million in those of Amazon.com.

By keeping to his strategies, Buffett has achieved a 22.2% compound growth rate over 40 years. Berkshire Hathaway has grown from $22 million to $143 billion in value. In June 2006 he announced that he would give 85% of his $42 billion fortune to the Gates Foundation. This was the largest act of charitable giving in history.

LI KA-SHING
"Superman"

Based in Hong Kong, Li Ka-Shing is the wealthiest person in Asia, the richest Chinese and the ninth richest man in the world. Like Buffett, Li has accumulated ownership of companies under a listed holding company. His holding company, Cheung Kong Holdings, owns businesses in real estate, construction, banking, telecoms, media, retail, hotels, power, steel, ports and shipping.

In 1940, when Li was 12, his family fled China as the Japanese invaded, making a home for themselves in Hong Kong. Determined to be successful, Li worked 16-hour days selling metal wares door to door, and found a tutor to teach him English. Preferring operations to sales, by 1949 he had gathered enough money from friends and contacts to open a manufacturing plant making plastic flowers. Nine years later, unable to renew his lease, Li bought his own site and found himself in the real estate market. In 1967 Cultural Revolution riots led to a drop in property prices and Li began buying bargain parcels of land. At the age of 39, Li found his flow.

Li built his investments as a typical Accumulator, saying in a recent interview, "I loathe the social scene; I don't like cultivating relationships, and I'm too emotional. These are all weaknesses in doing business. But I also have some strengths. First, I have a thirst for knowledge. Second, I work hard, which can compensate for some of the weaknesses. Most importantly, I know what's right from wrong. I long for a frugal life. In general, frugal people have more time. This attitude has not affected my business, but has actually helped me to achieve the best results and best returns for my shareholders."

Li's thrift on himself, and largesse towards charities, is legendary. In 2002, Bloomberg asked Li, "Do you still wear a $50 Citizen or Seiko watch? Is it always set eight minutes fast? … Do you still live in the same house you have lived in for 20 years?" Li replied, "Except for the fact that my watch clocks a full 20 minutes ahead, your facts are basically correct. My standard of living has remained at about the same level as when my business first began to take off in 1957, perhaps even more modest. I have always enjoyed a simple lifestyle. I have very modest needs in terms of material comfort. Spiritual peace and comfort, however, are very important to me. I only have a desire to do more meaningful deeds."

Li's ability to absorb knowledge and data led him to devise a structure of control for his activities leveraging on Hong Kong's growing stock market. Li had a goal of beating the colonial company, Jardine Matheson, which had grown from opium sales, tea and real estate into Hong Kong's largest conglomerate. To build their wealth, Accumulators need to control but don't need to own the assets. While Buffett leveraged by taking a controlling share in asset rich insurance companies, Li leveraged by issuing dual class equities and creating cross holdings that gave him control with minority ownership.

Within Cheung Kong, Li built a stable of listed companies, enabling him to raise funding from the public when he needed it, while also ring-fencing the liabilities and focus around each company. In 2006, Li had ten listed companies under the group. Each company had its own management team leading Li to comment, "Even should I myself or any senior management retire from office, it would not have any real effect." Like Buffett, giving management freedom to grow the business freed up Li's time to seek out synergies and the most effective allocation of capital. By 2006, his port operations controlled 12% of all container port capacity in the world. He had over 6,800 retail outlets in supermarkets, chemists and electrical stores. His water was the top selling brand in Hong Kong. One in twelve homes in Hong Kong had been developed by Li. The group's market capitalization was HK$766 billion (US$100 billion) - accounting for one in every eight dollars invested in the Hong Kong stock market. Li typifies the thinking process of an Accumulator: "If you think, then you will be prepared. If you are prepared, then you will have no worries."

While he will only spend HK$200 on the watch he wears, Li has already given HK$7.7 billion to charity. Li set up his charitable foundation, the Li Ka Shing Foundation, 26 years ago, in 1980, with the mission to nurture "a culture of giving" in society. He shared, "We focused mainly on education and medical care projects. It is my belief that knowledge can change one's fate. My father died of tuberculosis when we could not afford medical care. I know the feeling of helplessness and loneliness."

Li's slogan "Knowledge Changes Fate" covers his contributions from medical care to libraries and universities. Li says of his early years, "I bought secondhand books whenever I had spare money and I absorbed them before trading them in for more books. Even today I read before going to bed every night. Knowledge is not a guarantee of a life of riches but it does open the door to more opportunities. And recognizing more opportunities is really the best that you can expect."

In 2000, when receiving an Entrepreneur Award in Canada, Li said "Fifty years ago, I named my company Cheung Kong Holdings after the Yangtze River that flows through China, a great river that aggregates countless streams and tributaries. These days I think about where this "river" should flow. Throughout the years, a charitable foundation I set up has sponsored more than $C700 million to many causes, and in particular education and medical development. I will continue to do the same and more, not out of a sense of duty but because it is a maxim by which I choose to live my life."

Li now calls his foundation his "Third Child". He recalls, ""I was tossing and turning one night. The next day, when I was having dinner with my family, I told them that I have a third child. They fell silent. They were shocked and thought that I had finally lost it.

Actually it was an epiphany. If I had a third child, wouldn't I want to build a solid foundation for his future? By treating my private foundation as my third son, I could allocate more assets to it and enable it to benefit more people. I hope our 1.3 billion compatriots can understand this reasoning because our Chinese tradition is to pass on our wealth from one generation to the next. But if we can use our wealth to benefit society, then everyone will be happier."

In 2005, Li sold his $1.2 billion stake in CIBC, Canada's third largest bank, with all proceeds going to his Foundation. Having already been named by The Times and Ernst & Young as the Entrepreneur of the Millennium, in 2006, Li became the first recipient of the Malcolm S Forbes Lifetime Achievement Award, for "a lifetime of achievement as a hero of entrepreneurial capitalism."

SANDY WEILL
"The King of Capital"

What if it were possible to retire in your 50's, only to return and apply a lifetime of experience into your flow. Might it be possible to achieve more in the next twenty years than in the previous fifty? That's exactly what Sandy Weill did. Within fifteen years of coming out of retirement, he had built the largest company in the world.

Sandy Weill got started in Wall Street as a broker for Bear Stearns in 1955, when he was 23 years old. Weill was far happier studying financial statements at his desk than making cold calls, and for weeks his only client was his mother. While Deal Makers magnify out of their niche, Accumulators multiply out of their numbers, and Weill began to get a reputation for the quality of his investment research reports. Teaming up with three partners, his firm, CBWL, began to attract clients looking for quality research. Weill set to work to ensure that CBWL had the most efficient back office operation in the industry, saying, "This pipeline will be the platform for our growth." Over the next 14 years, Weill accumulated trading partnerships in a series of mergers which, by 1979, had grown into a firm with capital of $250 million, making it America's second largest securities brokerage firm after Merrill Lynch. In 1981, Weill sold the company to American Express for $900 million in stock. He took on the role of president of

American Express in 1983, and became chairman and CEO of the company's insurance subsidiary, Fireman's Fund.

Weill did not gel with American Express' corporate culture. Monica Langley, in her biography of Weill, says, "American Express always had a five-year strategy in place. Sandy's long-term planning ran to where he was going to eat dinner that night." The company's chairman, James Robinson, sent Weill to a speech coach to polish up his presentation skills. In constant conflict with the company, in 1985, Weill retired from American Express at the age of 52.

Weill took time out, but then decided that his career was not over yet. Like Buffett, Weill understood the leverage potential of a well run insurance and finance empire and in 1986 he invested $7 million of his own money in Commercial Credit, a consumer finance company, taking over as CEO. Cutting costs and reorganizing, he went on to list the company. In 1987 he bought Gulf Insurance, and the following year he bought Primerica, an insurance and brokerage company, for $1.5 billion. Further acquisitions followed. When the junk bond market crashed and Drexel Burnham Lambert fired it's junk bond chief, Michael Milken, Weill bought up the Drexel branch offices at the cost of their fixtures and fittings: $4 million. From the purchase, Weill inherited 500 brokers who went on to deliver $100 million in revenues and $20 million in profits over the next year.

In 1992, he bought 27% of Travelers Insurance for $722 million. At the age of 60, Weill was just getting started. He reacquired his old brokerage, now called Shearson Lehman, from American Express for $1.2 billion. Leveraging on outside financing and smart transactions, by the end of the year he had bought the rest of Travelers Corp for $4 billion in stock and consolidated his holdings under Travelers Group. Investing all his time in seeking out the next acquisition and adding further efficiencies, in 1996 he bought Aetna Life & Casualty for $4 billion. In 1997 he bought Salomon Inc for $9 billion in stock, and this allowed him to merge the investment-banking firm, Salomon Brothers with Smith Barney, giving Weill the world's second largest securities firm, Salomon Smith Barney.

In 1998, already owning interests in insurance, broking and financial services, Weill set his sights on controlling the ultimate leverage vehicle – his own bank. He approached Citicorp CEO, John Reed, about the idea of building a financial services powerhouse. That year, Travelers Group joined with Citicorp in a $76 billion merger - at the time the biggest in history. The new company, Citigroup, had assets of around $700 billion and served 100 million customers in one hundred countries.

For the merger to be approved, Weill needed Government banking laws to change. Accumulators network by having great networkers do the networking for them. Weill recruited to his board ex-President Gerald Ford along with ex-Treasury Secretary, Robert Rubin. With a respected Democrat and an influential Republican on board, the law took less than two years to change. Meanwhile, Weill continued to build the business, turning Citigroup into a trillion dollar financial powerhouse and, according to the Forbes Global 2000, the largest company in the world.

After the turn of the millennium, as the company dealt with the fallout and scandals of Worldcom and Enron, Weill stepped back from the management, resigning as CEO in 2003 and resigning as Chairman in 2006. When he left at age 73, the group he built had 450,000 employees around the world and total assets of over $1.6 trillion.

PAUL ALLEN
"The Accidental Zillionaire"

What happens when you persist down the wrong path, but are simultaneously following your flow by accident? Laura Rich's biography of Paul Allen is called "The Accidental Zillionaire" because, while Allen left the software business he co-founded with Bill Gates in 1983, he continued to get richer and richer. She says, "One should earn money or good fortune, and since Allen hasn't worked at Microsoft in two decades, he seems, to many people, just 'lucky.'"

While Allen has lost billions trying to create "The Next Big Thing", he has made more billions through his accumulation. In 2006, 23 years after leaving Microsoft, he was ranked by Forbes magazine as the sixth richest person in the world, worth an estimated $22.7 billion. Less than 25% of this was in Microsoft stock.

It was Allen who persuaded Gates in to drop out of Harvard and start Microsoft with him in 1975. Allen was the detailed programmer who knew the latest developments in the industry, and Gates was the creative genius who found the ways to monetize Allen's hard work. In 1983, at the age of 29, Allen was diagnosed with Hodgkin's disease. The same year, his father died. After receiving treatment, spending time with his family and reflecting on his life, he decided to resign from Microsoft to travel the world.

When Microsoft went public in 1986, Allen's 28% share became worth $134 million. Allen was motivated to get back in business, but he told Gates he was going to branch out on his own. Determined to live a meaningful life, Allen set up the Paul G Allen Family Foundation. Dedicated to health and human services, Allen decided to build his fortune to give back. He launched Asymetrix to create the 'next big thing' but this became the first in a series of 'creative' ventures that failed to achieve Allen's ambitions. Allen's strategy for building new products was to ask his team to "bring me some good ideas", leaving them with little strategic direction or creative input.

In 1991, Allen invested in SkyPix, a new broadband satellite network, and started Starwave, to support SkyPix's channels. Again, Allen assembled a team and asked them to come up with "something groundbreaking". SkyPix went bankrupt in 1993 and Starwave was redirected into CD-ROM content. Meanwhile, Allen tried his luck again, setting up a third company, Interval Research, to be an incubator for new ideas. He filled the 'ideas lab' with expensive inventors, instructing them to "follow a good idea wherever it goes". By 1995, Asymetrix's debt had grown to $50 million. He had spent over $96 million on Starwave, and a similar amount on Interval.

Realizing that his creative endeavours were not coming to fruition, Allen capitalized on Starwave's accidental shift to Internet content in 1997 to persuade Disney to buy the company for $350 million. He then shut down Interval. Allen was out of the content creation business after ten years, breaking even on his investments.

If Allen failed in his creativity, how did he magic up a $22 billion fortune? While he was working on his ideas, Allen had set up Vulcan

Ventures to look after his philanthropy. His sister, Jody, looked after the fund until Allen found a young 26 year old manager, Savoy, to leverage the fund in growth opportunities. Allen and Savoy did their homework and started small. A $20 million investment in USSB, a broadcast company turned into $46 million. An $18 million investment in Certicom, an IT security company, turned into $36 million. Then, in 1992 Allen bought $500,000 of AOL shares during its IPO, and continued to buy shares until he had a 24.9% stake. By the IPO, AOL only had a 5% market share of the online market. Allen wanted a management say in the company but, when Steve Case refused, Allen sold his stake holding in 1994, making a $100 million profit.

The same year, he bought 80% of Ticketmaster for $300 million when he saw the potential of their online ticketing. This time, Allen did not interfere with the management, deciding that his time was better spent looking for ways to grow the value of the business from the outside. Three years later, Allen sold the company to Barry Diller, making a $40 million return. Allen's greater return was from the new network the investment gave him. Through Ticketmaster, Allen became exposed to the stars being promoted by the company. Allen met Hollywood Deal Maker, Geffen, who went on to offer him a 24% stake in the new studio SKG Dreamworks for $500 million. To date, Allen has seen the value of that investment double.

Even the dotcom bust didn't slow Allen's new-found appetite for savvy accumulation. Although he lost on his Internet investments, he had become focused on cable companies. He began following the fundamental Accumulator key of asset control above asset ownership and in 1998, he bought a $2.6 billion controlling stake in Marcus Cable and a $4.5 billion stake in Charter Communications. By the end of 1999 he had invested a total of $18 billion and controlled the fourth largest cable system in America, causing one executive to say, "It was like you woke up one day and Paul Allen owned half of cable."

In the new millennium, Vulcan Ventures expanded from cable pipelines to oil pipelines, buying a controlling stake in a series of energy companies. Today, Allen focuses on his cable investments, property investments, and his Foundation, which gives $30 million each year. Allen lost money following the *wrong* path and made money on the *right* path – and on balance he is $22.7 billion ahead.

ACCUMULATORS IN A NUTSHELL

Dominant Wealth Frequency: Tempo / Steel

Action Dynamic: Introvert

Thinking Dynamics: Sensory

Wealth Creation Key: Buying and building appreciating assets

Secondary Profiles: Trader, Lord

Strengths: Reliable; careful; considered; meticulous; delivers on time; rarely over promises; provides gravity to a team; looks for what can go wrong; strong at turning a plan into a process

Weaknesses: Often procrastinates; easily distracted by detail; often needs more data before proceeding; can be slow to build up momentum; often more pessimistic than optimistic; often ends up collecting clutter; quick to walk away from chaos

Successes: When left to work at their own pace, Accumulators become the proverbial tortoise that wins the race. Slow and steady, they pick up the pieces that others leave behind. Shunning the limelight, they deliver through their results. They are happy for others to make a song and dance as they will be the ones calling the tune.

Failures: For the strengths that an Accumulator has in seeking out appreciating assets, they never take the first rung in the value and leverage chain, opting instead for an easy entry path even though it may not be their strength at all.

Most failed Accumulators have never built the capital to get started, or understood the financing or refinancing strategies to release cash flow while retaining ownership. As a result they have done nothing at all. Other Accumulators have gotten involved in their own business, and have made the mistake of investing what money they have in assets that are depreciating, not appreciating. Either way, simple switches in strategy are often all it takes to turn the spiral around.

THE ACCUMULATOR STRATEGY

1. BUILDING YOUR WEALTH FOUNDATION

You are not naturally inclined to throw wild parties for the neighbourhood, so the idea of building a network may be far from your mind. But you need one to get to your wealth. If you don't have the money to invest, you need to know the people who do – and they need to know you. Find advocates who will network for you!

Money will always follow results, and when you follow your path, your results will shine through. Find financiers to finance and peers to lend you breadth of experience. Find a strong Supporter to network on your behalf, and a great Mechanic to put your systems together.

2. MOMENT OF WEALTH CREATION

You need to maximize the time you invest in developing your selection system for the appreciating assets that you are focusing on. Focus on one area that you have a high interest in, and seek out those that already are masters in that area. This might be an asset class, like businesses or properties, or it might be a region, like China or India. You also need to free up your time to build your sensitivity and awareness for the right buying opportunities, and to time these opportunities to get the right purchase price.

3. VALUE CREATION

The value creation activities to focus on are internal values: developing your market knowledge in terms of overall trends and where and when buying opportunities occur. Your ability to sense future trends, forecast and predict asset appreciation will also sharpen your purchasing skills. Your understanding of how to finance and refinance your assets without needing to sell them will be a key factor in effectively compounding your gains.

4. VALUE OWNERSHIP

The ownership that you need, surprisingly perhaps, is not of the physical assets you are accumulating. You simply need ownership of the purchasing decision process, and of the rights of the asset –

which means even though it may be part owned by the bank as a result of financing, or by a fund that you set up and that investors are receiving a return from, you hold full control on whether to hold or sell that asset at any moment in time.

5. LEVERAGE

With this ownership, your leverage will come from the system that you create to identify and select the right purchases, together with your leverage on your purchasing power, through the financing that you can raise. Your greatest leverage is your performance history, as ultimately investors like a safe pair of hands delivering reliable returns.

6. SECURE CASH FLOW

To hold on to your assets for the long term, the two ways to return liquidity back into your pocket is either by creating a fund or investment company that you pass the asset rights to, and from which you sell shares, or by refinancing your assets as they appreciate, allowing you to take out the appreciation in cash in return for added gearing. Either way, you end up with cash and with the rights to the assets still in your hands.

Once you have established the right niche and begun to nurture a growing garden, you will find the best assets and opportunities being attracted to you. Stay in your flow, at your pace, and your wealth will emerge more from a rising tide than a breaking wave.

ACCUMULATORS TO LEARN FROM

Benjamin Graham (Graham Newman Corporation), Warren Buffett (Berkshire Hathaway), Li Ka Shing (Cheung Kong Holdings), Sandy Weill (Citigroup), Paul Allen (Vulcan Ventures), Carlos Slim Helu (Telmex), John Maynard Keynes (Economist), JP Morgan (JP Morgan & Co)

CHAPTER ELEVEN

THE LORD

"Formula for success: Rise early, work hard, strike oil."
- Jean Paul Getty

THE LORD IS IN THE DETAIL

Successful Lords are not seen, and rarely heard – until they emerge in control of an entire industry. Lords such as Carnegie in the early 1990's, and Mittal in the early 2000's, emerged in control of the steel industry after quietly building their empires for years.

Lords can be found wherever there is a fixed asset that is generating cash, whether it is a rented property or a leased vehicle. They become the aggregator for the cash flow of an industry, whether it is diamonds, oil or steel. Lords have become billionaires by quietly controlling every aspect of the delivery chain, whether in oil, steel, property, consumer rentals or a website called Google.

KEEPING THE CHANGE

Lords are famous for cutting costs and finding efficiencies in their business. The same economic thinking extends to their personal lives. Lords live frugally, watching every penny. They also look at the entrepreneurs and stars of the world and in most cases believe they could never do what they do in the limelight, and would never want to either. Lords are at home with themselves and don't believe you need to draw attention to yourself to create wealth. If you do, it seems a heavy price to pay.

Lords don't have time for politics or niceties. They would rather deal with simple facts than complicated people. When Rockefeller began buying up other refiners in the 1800's he did not wine and dine them, but instead said simply, "If you refuse to sell, it will end in your being crushed." And as he knew his numbers, he was right.

Lords will be first to analyze a situation, and will not act unless they have some level of certainty about the results they can expect. This can often cause friction with others. If Lords puts themselves in a fast-paced, high-growth environment, they will often be seen by others as counter balancing the chaos that surrounds them. However, this role will often put them out of reach of their flow, as they are seen in a support role and could be replaced. And here lies the critical point.

Successful Lords not only know they can be replaced, they want to be replaced. With their assets working for them, they have the time freedom to do whatever they want. Lords who have not become successful are passing their wealth every day. They simply have not had the luck to stumble upon a Lord who can show them how. When a Lord-in-waiting realizes that few Lords use much of their money at all to create their cash flow, then motivation suddenly sets in.

Lords are often the most useful profile to have at a brainstorming session. Why? When a group of Creators are left together with their heads in the clouds, the best ideas can be left floating in the ether. A Lord will document the ideas, categorize them, prioritize them, and see to it that there is a process designed to pull them from the top drawer to the bottom line.

As Lords have a strong introvert dynamic, many have never found their flow as they have kept to themselves. When connected to the right team or mentor, they soon sparkle. Supporters warm to the summer energy of fire frequency. Lords cool to the winter energy of metal frequency. They find their flow in certainty rather than variety, and are best when delving into the detail.

In any industry's winter season, products become commodities where companies compete on price. This is where Lords shine, weathering the peaks and troughs of their industry pricing by the unassailable position they have built by being in their flow. Andrew Carnegie, Jean Paul Getty, John D Rockefeller and, more recently, Lakshmi Mittal and Sergey Brin, dominated their markets by the yield-per-dollar they could generate from their scale and efficiencies.

ANDREW CARNEGIE
"Man of Steel"

Lords thrive on finding efficiencies in cash generating assets. Andrew Carnegie extracted margins by capitalizing on economies of scale in the age of steel. His cash management and margins were the cushion that enabled him to weather the American Civil War, 19th century banking collapse and crises in the early industrialization of America. Modern American cities, built on steel, are his legacy.

Carnegie's family moved to America from Scotland when he was 12 years old, and Carnegie began working at a local cotton mill in Slabtown, Pittsburgh. Graduating to a messenger boy at the Pittsburgh Telegraph Office, Carnegie came across James Anderson, who was setting up free libraries for "working boys". Having had no formal education, when Carnegie entered his first 'library' of 400 books, he said, "The windows were opened in the walls of my dungeon through which the light of knowledge streamed in." Carnegie credits Anderson for his success, saying, "To him I owe a taste for literature which I would not exchange for all the millions that were ever amassed by man."

Carnegie was soon noticed by Thomas Scott, a superintendent of the Pennsylvania Railroad at the time. Scott made Carnegie his secretary for $50 a month, and began to mentor him. He rose up the ranks and then, in 1862, Carnegie got his lucky break. Scott and Carnegie, seeing the success that an engineer, Linville, had had in constructing iron bridges, proposed to him to form a company together with Piper and Schiffler, who owned the bridges on the Pennsylvania line. Each of the five took a 20% share of the company for $1,250. Carnegie borrowed the money from the bank for his own share. At the age of 27, he was in business – entirely through the resources of others.

Having the right team is critical for every profile, and Carnegie relates, "We had the best talent of that day – Linville the engineer, Piper a hustling, active mechanic, and Schiffler sure and steady."

The following year, with an extensive network and know-how in the rail industry, Carnegie put his Lord profile to work, moving from iron bridges to manufacturing rails in 1864 and locomotives in 1866.

This began a trend of vertical integration that is typical of successful Lords. By controlling each step of the supply chain within an industry, cash remained in the control of the Lords and margins could be built through economies of scale.

It was a small step from iron rails and bridges to iron manufacturing, and Union Iron Mills was formed in 1867 in partnership with three others. This was when Carnegie's Lord profile sparkled. He found that financial controls in the industry were lax, saying, "It was a lump business, and until stock was taken and the books balanced at the end of the year, the manufacturers were in total ignorance of results. I felt as if we were moles burrowing in the dark, and this to me was intolerable." Carnegie set to work on an accounting system that ran throughout the process until "we began to know not only what every department was doing, but what each one of the many men working at the furnaces was doing...our strict system of accounting enabled us to detect the great waste possible in heating large masses of iron."

By 1870, Carnegie had found his flow by extracting from his one iron smelting furnace. "The Lucy furnace became the most profitable branch of our business, because we had almost the entire monopoly of scientific management. Having discovered the secret, it was not long before we decided to erect an additional furnace."

As the Civil War ended, high import tariffs and new technology from England, made steel manufacture in America viable. To underwrite the risk of starting a steelworks, Carnegie sent his men to get forward orders from railway companies for steel rails, giving him enough bookings to cover his risk and start the steelworks before the competition knew what he was up to. Carnegie began buying into iron ore mines to feed his furnaces, and coke companies to heat them. As he grew, he bought the management with the company. Henry Frick, the owner of the Frick Coke Company which he bought in 1882, eventually took charge of all of Carnegie's manufacturing.

Carnegie's steel empire continued to grow. Output swelled from 600,000 tons in 1888 to 2 million tons in 1897. Profits grew from $2 million to $40 million. It was not, however, through the peaks in the markets that Carnegie made his reputation, but in the troughs. While speculators and businessmen were caught wrong-footed by the early financial crises in the American economic system, Carnegie's caution at speculation and debt had led to him always remain credit-worthy. Carnegie said, "I have adhered to the rule never to purchase what I did not pay for, and never to sell what I did not own," adding, "The losses men encounter during a business life which seriously embarrass them are rarely in their own business, but in enterprises of which the investor is not master." As a result of his safe hands, he was able to attract financing far easier than his competitors.

After writing his book "The Gospel of Wealth" in 1900, Carnegie stepped away from his business. J.P. Morgan bought Carnegie Steel for $500 million and renamed it US Steel in 1901. It was the largest buyout in history at that time, and the company was the first to exceed $1 billion in valuation. That year, US Steel produced 67% of the steel in America. US Steel remained the largest steel producer in America for the next one hundred years.

For the last twenty years of his life, Carnegie turned his attention to philanthropy and the creation of free libraries. The impact that James Anderson and the "working boy" libraries had on him stayed with Carnegie throughout his life. His entire fortune went to the creation of over 2,800 libraries in America and Europe.

JOHN D ROCKEFELLER
"The First Billionaire"

Rockefeller's story is a great example of how a detail-oriented entrepreneur could become the richest man in the world, leveraging the majority of America's richest natural resource of the early 1900's – oil – without the need to own a single oil field, or a single drop of oil.

Like many Lord profiles, Rockefeller had a closer relationship with numbers than people. His biographer, David Freeman Hawke, wrote, "John D Rockefeller seemed to have no inner life unconnected with numbers." At 16 he began work as a $4-a-week bookkeeper for a Cleveland dry-goods merchant, and from the numbers learnt about commerce. He set up his own produce business with a $1,000 loan from his father when he was 19.

The 'black gold' rush began in 1859, when Rockefeller was just 20 years old. Lords are typically risk averse, and as prospectors flocked to the 'oil regions' of Pennsylvania and investors began buying up land for the risky game of oil prospecting, Rockefeller chose instead to refine the oil others had already found.

In 1864, at the age of 24, he set up a barrel-making operation at a small refinery he had established with friends, bringing the barrel unit cost down from $2.50 to 96c. Barrel-making led to oil refining. He brought in his brother to negotiate better prices with European end users and a partner, Henry Flagler, to negotiate lower rates with railroad operators.

Rockefeller's obsession with price and reliability gave him leverage to drive down raw material prices that others couldn't match. "Paint, Glue. We bought ours far lower than anyone else could, since ours was a steady demand for the largest quantities," he later said. Lords do not have an innate sense of timing, but are able to weather hard times as a result of their shrewd and intimate knowledge of their numbers. After the Civil War in 1865 many refiners were forced out of the industry by oversupply and overcapacity. Between 1865 and 1870 refined kerosene prices fell more than 50%, but Rockefeller was saved by his profit margin of 43c per gallon compared to the industry average of 19c.

When Rockefeller had driven prices down with suppliers as far as he could with his own capacity, he began buying up other small refineries. In 1872, he formed, and named himself the president of, the National Refiners' Association, to negotiate better terms on behalf of *all* member refineries.

By 1869, Rockefeller's oil refinery company, Standard Works had an output of 1,500 barrels per day. By 1872 this had risen to 10,000 barrels per day. In the 1870's, Rockefeller then began to bypass his highest cost – railway transportation – by buying up America's pipelines. In the 1880's, he bumped up margins further by cutting out the middleman and setting up his own gas stations.

It was a full 28 years after he entered and dominated the oil industry before Standard Oil bought its first oil field. By this time the oil industry was past the volatile phase that had driven out most of the early prospectors and had reached maturity. By 1891, Standard Oil was extracting 25% of all American crude.

In 1911, Standard Oil had such a grip on America's oil industry, with a 64% market share, that the Supreme Court ordered it to be broken into 34 new companies. These included companies we know of today as ConocoPhillips, Chevron and Exxon Mobil. Today, ExxonMobil is the largest company in the world by revenue, and these three companies have a combined market cap of $650 billion.

Rockefeller ended his reign of America's oil industry with a $900 million fortune. Having given 10% of his earnings to charity from his very first day of work, he went on to become one of the century's greatest philanthropists. The Rockefeller Foundation grew to assets of over $1 billion. It revolutionized medical research, public health services and sanitation standards in America. It went on to pioneer the green revolution around the world, saving the lives of an estimated one billion people in developing countries over the last century.

JEAN PAUL GETTY
"The Oil Baron"

Like Rockefeller, Getty built his fortune in the oil industry. Getty graduated from Berkeley and Oxford in 1914 before joining his father on his oil fields in Oklahoma. Getty, together with Trump, are the only two entrepreneurs in this book to have millionaire parents. Getty's father paid him $100 a month to seek out prospecting land to buy. Getty toured around in a Model T Ford for a year, without any luck, before he finally spotted a promising piece of land. With a limit on the amount he could spend, and heavy competition at the auction, Getty tried a ruse. He got a prominent bank vice-president to bid without revealing who he represented. The other bidders assumed it was a major oil company with deep pockets and kept out of the fight and Getty got the piece of land for "the astoundingly low price of $500". From this first move Getty, like all Lords, showed his ability to make calculated moves while remaining in the background.

Getty struck oil within a month and within the year he had made a million dollars. Getty promptly retired, saying later, "I lacked the maturity to grasp what – to play loosely with Emmanuel Kant – might be termed a categorical imperative. In order for it to have substantive meaning, wealth must be regarded as a means. The true measure of any wealthy person is shown by the broader ends toward which he directs the means. And so, snug (and not a little smug) with my million, I stopped working. Completely."

Getty was 23 years old and, without a purpose to strive for, headed to California. It was three years before Getty decided he would strive for a purposeful life. He returned to work, determined to carve out a niche separate from his father. As he began, he kept his finances tight, so when the 1929 stock market crash came, "Neither my father nor I had succumbed to the stock-speculation madness of the twenties; the Wall Street crash caused us no direct personal losses."

Following his father's death in 1930, Getty found himself flush with cash in a bargain basement market. He began to buy into Tidewater, a refining company, with the objective of getting into the matured oil refining market. Like Carnegie and Rockefeller, Getty built his fortune by understanding the numbers and maximizing efficiencies through vertical integration, controlling assets financed by others. Getty bought into the entire oil delivery process, controlling the oil wells, storage facilities, refineries, pipelines and supertankers to ship the final product. By 1948, Getty had won control of the oil concession on Saudi Arabia's undivided half-interest in the "Neutral Zone" between Saudi and Kuwait. The oil from this zone, which flowed through a series of Getty-controlled companies, turned Getty into a billionaire.

As the Getty empire grew, Getty became disillusioned with the American Government, saying, "US federal expenditures in 1900 were less than $500 million; fifty years later, they were closer to $50 billion… By 1974 they topped $300 billion. During the same period, the population of the United States increase less than threefold, from 76 million in 1900 to an estimated 212 million in 1974. Thus, federal spending rose over two hundred times more than the population. The insane overspending by federal, state and local governments is literally devouring the future of our society."

Getty's base became Europe, and his home became Sutton Place in England. It is here that Getty's thrift became legendary. Accumulators are known for watching their pennies but Lords take it to an art form. Despite being a billionaire, Getty installed a coin-box phone for guests to pay for their own calls. He stayed out of debt and economized wherever he could. He was reported to have waited ten minutes at a box office to save five shillings on a show ticket at the standby price. Getty dedicated a section of his autobiography to defending his decision, writing "I make no apologies for the reasoning in the situation. If I have ample time on my hands, the weather is clement and a ten-minute stroll will save ten shillings – well, why not wait and save the money?"

While Getty abhorred wasted capital, he was generous in his philanthropy, saying he would prefer to give his money than to waste it on himself. His response to his critics was to say, "I was brought up in an era when thrift was considered a virtue…People lived within their means, saved for rainy days – and swallowed no tranquilizers and had far fewer ulcers."

LAKSHMI MITTAL
"The Richest Man in England"

Lords like to stay in the background. Getty was only noticed when Forbes Magazine announced he was the World's Richest Man in 1957. Lakshmi Mittal was only noticed when he was revealed as the mystery buyer in England's most expensive house purchase, for £70 million in 2003. Mittal, today's modern-day Carnegie, has lived up to his namesake – Lakshmi, the Hindu Goddess of Wealth. Today he is known as the richest man in England, and the fifth richest in the world, with a net worth of over $27 billion.

Born in 1950, Lakshmi Mittal was brought up in Sadulpur, India, in a house built by his grandfather. Graduating from St Xavier's, Kolkata with a commerce degree in 1969, Mittal discovered early a passion for numbers, and applied it to good use in his family steel business. In 1994, he took over the international side of the business.

Mittal made a name for himself when he took over a steel company in Trinidad and Tobago in 1989 that was losing $1 million a day. By cutting costs and maximizing margins, he doubled the output and made the company profitable. By 1992, Mittal had bought up Mexico's third largest steel producer, Sicartsa, for $220 million. Saying, "I realized that life is too short to build a steel company from scratch", he made acquisitions in Canada, Germany, Irelend, and Kazakhstan, often buying state-owned steel plants and turning around their operations. Mittal ended up privatizing and turning around fifteen different government operations.

Mittal's was clear in his focus, saying, "Management teams need to become more bottom-line driven. As management, we need to be aware of all of the opportunities existing for further consolidation, restructuring and forming new alliances...Within ten years we are likely to see a handful of truly global players accounting for 80 – 100 million tons each, and with a footprint in all the major regions." This he said when such production capacities were unheard of.

In 1997, Mittal listed his group, Ispat International, on the New York and Amsterdam stock exchanges, continued with his strategy of acquiring and overhauling, and then in 2004 merged his two companies Ispat International and LNM Holdings. Mittal also added to his group by merging with an Ohio company, ISG. His management style was commented on by an ISG executive who said, "I had to make six reports a month. With Mittal, it was sixty-six – how much oil we were using, how many units of electricity per hour, how much time for repairs, in minute detail at every step."

The newly named "Mittal Steel" became the largest steel producer in the world by 2005. Still not satisfied, Mittal made his most audacious move in January 2006, launching a hostile bid to take over his nearest competitor, Arcelor for $33 billion. Like all Lords, Mittal had little interest in sweet talking Arcelor's executives once he had made a bid, letting the numbers do the talking. Arcelor's board unanimously rejected the bid and Arcelor's chief executive, Guy Dollé, dismissed Mittal as a "company of Indians".

Luxembourg-based Arcelor's management opposition was joined by a string of European governments, who saw Mittal's bid as a threat to their national interests. Mittal persisted. Rather than waste time on deal making and negotiations, he kept out of the limelight, lobbying governments in the background, and changing his bid until it became irresistible to Arcelor's shareholders.

By June 2006, the Arcelor Board approved a merger, leading to the creation of the largest steel company in the world by a long stretch, Arcelor Mittal. The new company combined Mittal's output of 63 million tons with Arcelor's 47 million tons. This compared to the nearest competitor, Nippon Steel, at 33 million tons. Mittal's control stretches far beyond the steel output, with controlling interests in mines, power, oil, transportation and shipping covering every aspect of the production process.

Like Carnegie before him, Mittal has risen to dominate the steel industry. The steel industry that Mittal has risen in, however, is on an entirely different scale. While Carnegie reached annual output of 3 million tons, Mittal to date has reached output of 110 million tons.

SERGEY BRIN
"Do No Evil"

Lords create their wealth once a market has become established and resources can be consolidated through ruthless efficiencies. While the steel industry took 120 years to churn through two cycles of creation, fragmentation, percolation and consolidation, the Internet has sped through a full industry cycle in ten short years.

Out of the carnage of the dotcom crash, Sergey Brin, together with Larry Page, have emerged as the present victors, aggregating global online traffic through Google, and taking a slice of each transaction as they go. By 2006, at 33 years old, Brin is the youngest entrepreneur in this book, with a net worth of $13 billion.

Born in Moscow, Brin moved with his family to America in 1979. With an affinity for computers and mathematics, Brin took a masters degree in Computer Science at Stanford University. There, he got interested in data-mining and pattern extraction and met Larry Page. The two of them started "Backrub" in 1996, a search engine based on ranking sites based on the back links to them from other sites. This then changed to "Google", named after "Googol", the mathematical term for a 1 followed by 100 zeros. Working out of Page's dorm room, the two tried to find a buyer for their system without luck.

Their luck changed when they met Andy Bechtolsheim, co-founder of Sun Microsystems. Brin recalls, "We met him very early one morning on the porch of a Stanford faculty member's home in Palo Alto. We gave him a quick demo. He had to run off somewhere, so he said, 'Instead of us discussing all the details, why don't I just write you a cheque?' It was made out to Google Inc. and was for $100,000."

The cheque sat in a drawer as the pair set up a company, bank account, and realized they had a business on their hands. The search site was now attracting 10,000 searches a day, and others began to see the same potential as Bechtolsheim. Friends and family added to the first cheque and Google Inc launched in 1998 with $1 million. Within a year, the site was up to 500,000 searches a day and the team grew to eight staff. Taking advantage of the dotcom frenzy, Brin and Page raised $25 million from Sequoia Capital and Kleiner Perkins Caufield & Byers, giving them the funds they needed to grow. The deal also secured them the expert help and network they needed in Mike Moritz and John Doerr, two venture capitalists who had the expertise and track record to support them.

By 2000, the site had risen to an incredible 100 million searches a day, and Brin and Page hired ex-Novell CEO, Schmidt to take over the management of the business, with Brin becoming head of technology and Page becoming head of products, suiting their natural Lord and Mechanic profiles. Google was still looking for a revenue driver that could leverage this burgeoning traffic. Display ads were not the answer, as they slowed down the searches. Finally, the team found the magic elixir: AdWords. Simple links paid for by advertisers on a pay-per-click, results-based model, AdWords didn't even need a sales team to grow, with advertisers tailoring their campaign and paying for their usage online.

By now, it was clear that Google was aggregating content and viewers at a pace that enabled it to entirely dominate online search – without users even needing to visit the Google web site. The Google

Toolbar allowed viewers to search without visiting the site; Gmail gave users free email storage in return for featured AdWords; and AdSense enabled website owners to earn income by featuring targeted AdWord links on their sites. The combination of AdWords and AdSense meant Google was now controlling searches – and profiting from each one – throughout the Internet, by effectively becoming the 'toll collector' of sponsored search traffic between sites.

With revenue continuing to grow, Google's IPO took place in 2004 raising $1.67 billion and giving Google a market cap of more than $23 billion. Today Google runs over 450,000 servers in data centres around the world, with a 54% market share of online searches: over one billion search requests every day.

While Carnegie consolidated the steel market and Rockefeller consolidated the oil market – both through control of flow through out the industry, how is Google achieving this on the Internet? Google is creating an unbeatable aggregation of global content. In addition to Google's online search of content, images and videos, "Google Earth" aggregates all global information geographically; "Google Maps" aggregates all local street information; "Froogle" aggregates products from online shopping websites; "Google Groups" aggregates the archives of online discussion groups. 2005 profits reached $1.4 billion on revenue of $6.1 billion.

In Google's prospectus, the pair stated a company mission of, "Don't Be Evil", adding, "We believe strongly that in the long term, we will be better served — as shareholders and in all other ways — by a company that does good things for the world even if we forgo some short term gains."

The Google story is far from over. In a 2006 interview with Time, when asked how their wealth was affecting them, Brin replied, "You always hear the phrase, money doesn't buy you happiness. But I always in the back of my mind figured a lot of money will buy you a little bit of happiness. But it's not really true. I got a new car because the old one's lease expired." Page added, "If we were motivated by money, we would have sold the company a long time ago and ended up on a beach."

LORDS IN A NUTSHELL

Dominant Wealth Frequency: Steel

Action Dynamic: Introvert

Thinking Dynamics: Intuitive / Sensory

Wealth Creation Key: Controlling cash generating assets

Secondary Profiles: Accumulator, Mechanic

Strengths: Controlling; cautious; organized; detailed; analyzes every situation; sees distinctions others miss; only comfortable once all bases are covered; able to list out every detail

Weaknesses: May excessively value tasks over relationships; little patience with social niceties; often involved in excessive organizing; can struggle in presenting complex ideas; can get absorbed in the data; often misses the big picture; often misses the big party

Successes: When focused on the back end, and freed of the front end, Lords rule. Once systems are in place to control business processes, Lords will run a tight ship and continually find ways to improve the bottom line.

Failures: When Lords are put in situations where they need to create and motivate, their dictatorial style can easily rub people up the wrong way. If they do not have the resources to access the data they need to operate effectively, they quickly become frustrated.

Lords need a controlled environment to operate. Yet this need for control often results in micro management, which can soon work against them. In fast growth industries, Lords can be left behind. As with every profile, choosing the right industry at the right time is a major factor in their success, and Lords excel when they are finding efficiencies within a consolidating industry.

THE LORD STRATEGY

1. BUILDING YOUR WEALTH FOUNDATION

You are happy enough on your own and with those that you are close to, but by being so you are closing the door to your wealth. You must open your mind to the wealth waiting for you, and find the mentors who can guide you.

This does not mean you need to be knocking on doors. Find yourself a Supporter who will be your front man to a network of opportunities and resources. Also look for Deal Makers to seek out the best cash flow streams for you.

2. MOMENT OF WEALTH CREATION

Your time has to be invested in selecting and financing the assets that will generate the cash flow you want. Internally, you need to invest in your ability to calculate and measure the cash flow that you will receive net of cost of financing given different scenarios with the market and interest rates. Invest time in learning the skill of seeking low asset prices from sellers that you can convert to high cash income via tenants or customers.

3. VALUE CREATION

The value that you want to create is largely internal, building your know-how of the financing industry, and understanding the supply and demand dynamics of the assets you are creating cash flow from: whether these are rental products, rental properties, natural resources or other cash generating assets.

4. VALUE OWNERSHIP

The key to the Lord profile is understanding that you do not have to own the asset at all. You simply need to own the right to the cash flow that it is generated from the asset. This is most apparent to someone who chooses to start a licensing agency, or a photo library, where cash flow is created without owning the intellectual property rights of the assets that are being leased or licensed out.

5. LEVERAGE

You will create leverage by multiplying your assets through the same leasing system. The management you need will not grow at the same speed as that at which your car leasing or property rental company grows, and so you leverage on your knowledge, your history and your system. This, in turn, allows you to leverage further by financing more assets to create further cash flow.

6. SECURE CASH FLOW

Unlike other wealth profiles, your job is made simple in that what you own is the cash flow, and so your cash flow is already secured. However, you do not have control over interest rates and future asset purchase prices, so control over cash flow also means the ability to control the amount that you are charging, whether it is the lease on the property or the overnight rental price from your video stores.

Once you have begun to create cash flow – whether it is a vending machine or a steel plant, begin to leverage on economies of scale by multiplying the flow, turning your trickle into a river.

LORDS TO LEARN FROM

John D Rockefeller (Standard Oil), Jean Paul Getty (Getty Oil), Andrew Carnegie (Carnegie Steel), Lakshmi Mittal (Mittal Steel), Sergey Brin (Google), Hank Greenberg (AIG), Frank Lowy (The Westfield Group)

CHAPTER TWELVE

THE MECHANIC

*"Most everything I've done
I've copied from someone else."*
- Sam Walton

A WELL-OILED MACHINE

The Mechanic is an enigmatic character who has the ability to control and manage many people without needing to demonstrate any charismatic leadership qualities. His creative thinking and systems focus leads to a knack for duplication and replication, which leads to a well-oiled machine that manages for him.

Where a Star endears, a Mechanic endures. What they build tends to be built to last. The endless perfectionist, the Mechanic will keep finding ways to improve his system, making things simple and smart, whatever the product – whether it is an process to make computers, cars or burgers.

PERFECTING THE SYSTEM

Mechanics tend to come late to the party. That's because they are better at perfecting what is there than coming up with something new from scratch. Successful Mechanics give Creators a run for their money in the business celebrity stakes. High profile Mechanics out there include Sam Walton, Ray Kroc, Ingvar Kamprad and Michael Dell, who expanded Wal-Mart, McDonald's, IKEA and Dell.

Mechanics often take over from Creators as businesses mature, and they are capable of starting global, system-based businesses that multiply around the world. Mechanics can be found behind most franchise and multi-outlet businesses, and in all manufacturing, distribution, construction and logistics businesses where all creative focus is on the systems rather than the products.

Mechanics rely on people less than any other profile – because the system takes on the work. When Henry Ford was criticized for the mindless tasks his workers had to perform on his production lines, he retorted, "I have heard it said … that we have taken skill out of work. We have not. We have put a higher skill into planning, management, and tool building, and the results of that skill are enjoyed by the man who is not skilled."

As a result, successful Mechanics expect – and factor in – a high turnover of staff. While Supporters and Deal Makers develop people and happily change processes, Mechanics develop processes and happily change people.

Mechanics like to take things apart and put them together again. They are up to the challenge of changing the wheels on a moving car and as a result they are continually challenging the status quo on the way things are done. This can be very stimulating for some, and very frustrating for others.

Mechanics who never got started are likely to have seen their sensitivity to systems as more of a curse than a talent. They are the first to notice when systems break down, and they are the first tasked to repair processes once the damage is done. For many Mechanics that never found their wealth, they found the comfort of a large, structured multi-national too inviting to resist, and became forever swallowed in a comfy armchair of middle income.

Successful Mechanics have overcome their need to be involved with everything, and have focused all their efforts on the engine of the business, while others look after the styling and upholstery. As they pass over people management to others and focus on efficient operations, they find their flow. After all, it's easier to fix a process than to fix a person.

HENRY FORD
"So Long as it is Black"

Henry Ford's role model was Thomas Edison, one of this century's great Creator profiles. Having an illustrious Wealth Creator as your mentor can be counter-productive – if they have a profile different from your own. Ford, like all of us, followed his profile naturally as a child. When his father gave him his first pocket watch, he took it apart and by the age of fifteen he had built a reputation as a watch repairman. Yet choosing Edison as a role model meant that it was only in his forties that Ford found his flow.

As the automobile industry took off in the 1880's, Ford worked for the Edison Illumination Company (later to become General Electric) while trying to invent his own car. In 1899, he convinced a group of investors to back his efforts, and he set up the Detroit Automobile Company. With Ford insisting on trying to perfect the design, the company went bankrupt. He tried a second time, forming the Henry Ford Company and raising $28,000 from investors. Again, he failed.

His early models were expensive and had limited success in an increasingly competitive market. Ford struggled in the early years to out-innovate the market, and by 1905 he had decided to change his approach. By now, the industry was thirty years old, and he was 42, with a history of limited success.

His new approach was to be inventive with the system of production rather than the car itself. In short, he switched from a Creator strategy to a Mechanic strategy. He discovered a new, cheap and reliable steel alloy from France and in 1908 produced the "Model T". The true innovation of the Model T was the production process, with the cars roped together to move through the production process at a constant speed, and tasks broken down for each man to follow.

Like so many Mechanics who succeed by lowering prices and increasing accessibility to a maturing market, Ford made his Model T the vehicle for the common man. In 1980, the Ford Model T was launched at $825. Ten thousand sold in the first year.

He reinvested the profits in a new production facility at Highland Park. America's first tailor-made 'production line', called by John D Rockefeller "the industrial miracle of the age."

When Deal Makers get into their flow, their deals *grow* in price. When Mechanics get in their flow, their products *fall* in price. Production increased from 19,000 in 1910 to over 78,000 in 1912 – now selling at $575. In 1913, Ford pioneered the moving assembly belt and by 1916 the price had dropped to $360. Sales reached 472,000.

With a team of engineers focused on efficiency, Ford fine-tuned every aspect of the production process to bring down prices. As black paint dried the fastest, all Model T's were black, leading to his famous phrase, "Any customer can have a car painted any color that he wants so long as it is black." The Model T went on to take 48% of the US auto market. By 1924, the ten millionth Model T Ford had rolled off the lines.

Henry Ford's story is a classic story of a Wealth Creator who resonated with his time. As cars became commodities, and price and reliability became paramount, Ford was there to deliver. His story is, unfortunately, also the story of how a winning formula becomes a losing formula as the industry moves on.

By the 1920's, at the height of the Model T's success, Ford's staff tried to persuade him to innovate the base product – the car. Ford refused. As irony would have it, his earlier company, the Henry Ford Company, would end up being his undoing. When he left the company, the investors continued with it under the management of Henry Leland. The company was renamed Chevrolet, which was then absorbed into a new company, General Motors. As Ford persisted with the Model T, a new spring was beginning in the industry. GM began to offer innovative Chevrolets with the same price and reliability as the Model T, but with an electric starter, three gears and other fancy features. By 1926, Model T sales had plummeted and in 1927, Ford discontinued production and closed Highland Park.

Ford had revolutionized America's industrial production process, but he had no second product to take over for the Model T, which had remained largely unchanged for 14 years. If his son, Edsel, had not been quietly working on a replacement, Ford as a company may not have continued as it has until today.

Even so, 75 years later, Fortune magazine named Ford Businessman of the Century, beating out runner-up Bill Gates. Today, Ford Motor Company is run by Bill Ford Junior, Ford's great-grandson, has revenues of $178 billion and, along with the Ford brand, owns Aston Martin, Jaguar, Daimler, Land Rover, Lincoln, Mazda, Mercury and Volvo. The Ford Foundation continues to donate over half a billion dollars each year to reduce poverty.

RAY KROC
"The Hamburger King"

While Ford had to wait until he was 43 before he found his path to wealth, Ray Kroc had to wait until he was 52 before he even spotted the garden gate. In his words, "I was 52 years old. I had diabetes and incipient arthritis. I had lost my gall bladder and most of my thyroid gland in earlier campaigns, but I was convinced that the best was ahead of me." Kroc was an aging milk-shake machine salesman when he met the McDonald brothers at their San Bernardino hamburger stand in 1954. Curious as to why one outlet would want to order eight of his Prince Castle Multimixers when most only needed one or two, he decided to visit Maurice and Richard McDonald's golden arches fifty-five miles east of Los Angeles.

Finding a crowded 'hamburger production line' with burgers selling for fifteen cents, Kroc quickly saw that he could make a lot more by multiplying these outlets than by selling milk-shake machines. Like all successful Mechanics, whose greatest 'a-ha' moment comes when they see the opportunity to revolutionize an existing industry, Kroc said, "When I saw it working that day in 1954, I felt like some latter-day Newton who'd just had an Idaho potato caromed off his skull. That night in my motel room I did a lot of heavy thinking about what I'd seen during the day. Visions of McDonald's restaurants dotting crossroads all over the country paraded through my brain."

Kroc set up a model franchise, drafted the first operating manual to multiply the outlet through franchises. Commenting on his Mechanic profile, Kroc said, "There is a certain kind of mind that conceives new ideas as complete systems with all of their parts functioning. I don't think in that 'grand design' pattern. I work from the part to the whole, and I don't move to the large scale ideas until I have perfected the small detail." Within two years, Kroc had perfected the small details, and was ready to franchise.

A popular story today is that McDonald's makes more money today from real estate than from hamburgers. This is a typical story of the dynamic balance of value and leverage, when a Wealth Creator continues to find new value, and leverages that value to find new value again – often taking them to an entirely different destination than they could have imagined.

In Kroc's case, he began by persuading the McDonald brothers in 1954 to allow him to sell franchises for $850. He kept 1.4% of sales and the brothers kept 0.5%, with him doing all the work. In 1955 he set up his first model franchise in Des Plaines, Illinois. Kroc then rolled out the franchises. By 1960, Kroc had franchised 200 outlets and grossed $75 million - but still made only $159,000 profit.

With little profit and less cash after six years, Kroc's break came in 1960. Deal Maker, Harry Sonneborn approached Kroc with an idea: to lease land on a subordinated basis, get a mortgage, then build and franchise with the franchisee paying rent to cover the mortgage and deliver a profit. With no capital, Kroc now had a way to create money from nothing, with the income they made from lease payments soon outstripping royalty payments.

To finance the properties, Kroc couldn't get bank financing, so he got financing initially from his suppliers, then later found a source of funds in insurance companies. In 1960, he sold 22.5% of the business to three insurance companies, giving him a $1.5 million loan secured against the equity. Kroc recalls, "That loan could be called the lift-off of McDonald's rocket-like growth in the sixties." Sonneborn was Kroc's Deal Maker, keeping an open conduit to financing as Kroc multiplied the system, keeping relentlessly focused on four principles: "If I had a brick for every time I've repeated the phrase QSV&C (Quality, Service, Value and Cleanliness), I think I'd probably be able to bridge the Atlantic Ocean with them."

Kroc's real estate model enabled him to create the profit model and asset base to secure financing, which in turn gave him a model to finance growth. In 1961, Kroc bought out the McDonald brothers for $2.7 million, financed entirely by a New York investor sourced by Sonneborn.

Soon, McDonald's was joined by plenty of competitors, but Kroc kept a step ahead by staying in his flow, saying, "My attitude was that competition can try to steal my plans and copy my style. But they can't read my mind; so I'll leave them a mile and a half behind." While he focused on the systems, new products appeared to fill the system. Kroc pushed his suppliers, saying to one, "Don't wine me, don't dine me, don't buy me Christmas presents… I want nothing from you but a good product."

He also found products by luck through the system – for example in 1962 a struggling franchisee in Cincinnati, Louis Groen, came up with a fish sandwich to compete with the competition in a Catholic-dominated community. When Kroc heard this he said, "Hell no! I don't care if the Pope himself comes to Cincinnati. He can eat hamburgers like everybody else. We are not going to stink up our restaurants with any of your damned old fish!" He changed his mind when his product team came back with an innovation – a slice of cheese. His response: "Of course! That's exactly what this sandwich needs, a slice of cheese. No, make it half a slice." The Filet-O-Fish was born.

Growth continued and by 1965, McDonald's had grown to 710 outlets and $171 million in sales but, as Kroc recalls, "What none of the stories mentioned, and I wasn't about to tell anyone, was that even though our stores were booming…we had no cash. We were barely able to meet our payrolls in corporate headquarters." Kroc solved his cash flow problems by continuing to work with his suppliers and investors to fund his growth until taking McDonald's public in 1966.

By 1970, Kroc had created a $500 million fortune, starting with nothing more than the enthusiasm, knowledge and network of a 52 year old. Kroc died in January 1984, 81 years old, thirty years after discovering McDonald's and ten months before McDonald's sold its fifty billionth burger. Today, McDonald's is the world's largest restaurant chain, serving 50 million customers every day.

SAM WALTON
"Made in America"

Like all successful Mechanic profiles, Sam Walton, who founded Wal-Mart and went on to become the richest man in the world in the 1980's, had an insatiable appetite for hands-on tinkering and testing.

Walton learnt about systems by first buying a Ben Franklin franchise on the advice of a friend. This practice of learning through the systems of others is one of the fastest ways for Mechanics to get started. When the landlord refused to renew the lease, Walton was forced to find a new location and in 1951 set up the "Walton Five and Dime" in Bentonville, Arkansas. Over the next ten years Walton opened a further eleven Ben Franklin franchises, pioneering the use of check-out counters near the exits, and profit sharing for staff. By 1962, Walton and his brother Bud owned sixteen stores, and Walton was ready to branch out on his own.

Walton's manager Bob Bogle, who was in charge of buying the signage for the Ben Franklin stores, was asked to come up with a name for the new store. He came up with "Wal-Mart" – as there were only seven letters in the name and so not "so many letters to buy". The focus of the store was price, with Walton saying, "What we were obsessed with was keeping our prices below everybody else's. Our dedication to that idea was total." Walton was happy to promote 'loss leaders', marketing items at ridiculously low prices to drive customers to the store, who would then buy more.

Walton focused on improving his systems at every opportunity, stopping at competitors' stores over the weekends with his yellow legal pad, taking notes and finding talent. Walton later said, "I did something I would do for the rest of my run in the retail business without any shame or embarrassment whatsoever: nose around other people's stores searching for good talent."

Walton funded his growth through his suppliers, managers, and individual investors in each outlet: "By 1970, we had seventy-eight partners invested in our company, which really wasn't one company, but thirty-two different stores owned by a combination of different folks. My family owned the lion's share of every store, but Helen and I were also in debt up to our eyeballs – several million dollars' worth."

To solve the issue, like Ray Kroc, Walton went to the stock market, listing Wal-Mart in 1970 and raising $1.8 million. Wal-Mart's "saturation strategy" was based on mapping out the area within a one-day drive of each distribution centre, and planning a Wal-Mart within each area that held between 5,000 and 10,000 population.

Walton would leverage on his love of flying, taking regular flights in his plane over new expansion areas: "I loved doing it myself. I'd get down low, turn my plane up on its side, and fly right over a town. Once we had a spot picked out, we'd land, go find out who owned the property, and try to negotiate the deal right then." In this way, Walton built his first 120 stores and kept ahead of the competition. He added, "I guarantee you not many principles of retailing companies were flying around sideways studying development patterns."

This strategy enabled Walton to launch in areas ignored by the larger discount stores, giving him uncontested markets in which to grow his business. By 1980, Wal-Mart had grown to 276 stores with revenue of $1.2 billion. With a growing empire, Walton devised a new system to stay on top of things. Connecting all his stores by satellite, Walton received real-time information from them, giving him information on sales by store and region on every one of the 80,000 products on sale. This became powerful information that vendors wanted, giving him additional leverage over price negotiations with them.

This paradox of focusing further on detail the bigger you get is reflected in Walton's statement, "The bigger Wal-Mart gets, the more essential it is that we think small." A second paradox was Walton's insistence that the more rigid their communication system, the faster creative ideas would flow. Without fail, every Monday his eighteen regional managers flew out of Bentonville in Wal-Mart's fleet of planes. They would come back on Thursday, tasked with finding at least one idea that would pay for their trip. On Friday morning they would attend a merchandising meeting and share their ideas. The best were implemented by phone to all stores by the afternoon. Every week, week in, week out, for thirty years.

Wal-Mart president, David Glass, comments, "Our Friday merchandising meeting is unique to retailing as far as I can tell… Once we've made that decision on Friday, we expect it to be acted on in all stores on Saturday. What we guard against around here is people saying 'Let's think about it'. We make a decision. Then we act on it."

This system built innovation into the entire Wal-Mart empire on a weekly basis, and was scalable with the company's growth. By 1985, Forbes ranked Sam Walton as the richest man in the United States. He kept this rank until he split his shares between his children, and the Walton family held five spots in the top ten rich list for the next fifteen years.

Walton died in 1992. If he was alive today with his family assets consolidated, he would continue to be the richest man in the world, with twice the wealth of Bill Gates. Today, Wal-Mart is the world's largest retail chain, with 1.8 million employees, 6,500 stores and revenue of $312 billion.

INGVAR KAMPRAD
"The Swedish Scotsman"

Like so many Wealth Creators, Ingvar Kamprad's fortune did not come from a grand plan, but from innovations arising out of necessity as he followed his natural path. Kamprad's redeeming quality was to commit that, no matter how difficult things got, he would not work for others but would stay true to his path. As a result, beginning with nothing, he became the richest man in Europe.

Born in Smland, Sweden, he started his company at the age of seventeen: by joining the "IK" from his initials, the "E" from Elmtaryd, the farm he grew up on, and the "A" from Agunnaryd, his home village, he came up with his company name, IKEA. Going door-to-door, he got started by selling products from stationery to picture frames, watches and wallets.

After finishing his national service, Kamprad went full time on his business in 1946. Tired of selling door-to-door, he began advertising and delivering to the home, experimenting with different products. After two years of trial and error, he tried furniture in his ads in 1948. He soon worked out his returns on furniture were the best, with fewer trips to make higher profits. Soon after, Kamprad discovered that a catalogue was a far more efficient way to get word of his furniture products to his customers, and, within four years, Kamprad had found his niche as a catalogue-based, furniture home delivery company. Kamprad was 24 years old.

A full eight years after starting his business, still struggling to make a profit and with a furniture price war taking place, out of desperation Kamprad decided to change his model by letting his customers touch and see the furniture. He bought a local joinery in Almhult that was about to close and turned it into an exhibition venue that doubled as a warehouse. An overwhelming 1,000 people turned up on the first day, Kamprad cut his costs throughout the process. By customers driving to the warehouse, he was able to cut transportation costs. By providing food at the store, customers stayed for far longer, giving him a higher yield per customer.

Then in 1955, Kamprad had another setback. Competitors, feeling threatened by his growing success, grouped together and pressured suppliers to stop supporting him. Unable to source supplies and banned from trade fairs, Kamprad's sales were drying up. He responded by buying his own exhibition centres, creating different furniture exhibits to give visitors choice – even though every exhibit was owned by him. The IKEA store was born.

Flat packing was introduced in 1956; self-service stores were introduced in 1965. By 2006, 235 stores had opened and the IKEA catalogue had reached 160 million copies, the greatest print run of any book, far exceeding the Bible. By continuing to focus on his flow and multiplying the result, Kamprad is now worth $28 billion.

Like Walton, who drove the same old, red pick-up even after becoming a billionaire, Kamprad has also made a name for himself for his thrift, with reports that he flies economy, saves wherever he can, and encourages IKEA employees to write on both sides of the paper. Even so, his charity foundation is the second largest in the world, with a value of $36 billion in 2006.

MICHAEL DELL
"Direct from Dell"

Here we are, at the 38th and final entrepreneur in this book. Appropriately, it is the same entrepreneur I came across in my 20's as I struggled with his ex-executives to find a stream to match his mighty river. Not only did I do a disservice to Hand Technologies by trying to follow a Mechanic strategy when I was a Creator profile, but I spent years out of my flow. Some of us are so busy doing what we are doing, we have forgotten who we are! Dell, on the other hand, was having a ball: a billion dollar ball.

On Michael Dell's 15th birthday, his parents bought him his first computer. To the dismay of his parents, the first thing he did with it was take it apart. A typical Mechanic profile, Dell had to see how it worked. By 19, while studying at the University of Texas he had started a business - PC's Unlimited – which was soon selling between $50,000 and $80,000 of upgraded PC's, upgrade kits and add-on components every month.

The difference of a Mechanic and Creator profile can be seen by comparing the way Dell came up with his first PC compared to the lengths Steve Jobs went to perfect his machines. Eight months after starting PC's Unlimited (later renamed Dell Computer Corporation), he called his local Intel salesperson and said, "Tell me who in this town can design a 286 computer." He got the name of six or seven engineers, called them up and said he wanted a computer designed.

One engineer, Jay Bell, replied, "I can do it in about a week, week and a half, for $2,000." "That doesn't sound like a lot to lose," Dell said. "I happen to be going out of town for a week. I'll give you $1,000 now and another $1,000 when I come back." By the time he returned, Jay Bell had built Dell's first 286-based PC.

Steve Jobs later acknowledged the entirely different approach Dell took to the PC production process, saying, "Pretty much, Apple and Dell are the only ones in this industry making money. They make it by being Wal-Mart. We make it by innovation."

Dell began selling his PCs from his dorm room in 1985, custom assembling each order, cobbling components together and keeping costs down. Demand was instant. By 1986, he hired Lee Walker, a venture capitalist, as president. Through his contacts, Dell got the financing he needed to grow the company and to then take the company public in 1988. The listing raised $30 million, and within three years of launch, the Dell Computer Corporation had turned from a one-man operation to an $80 million company.

As Dell focused on delivering low cost, customized PCs, a series of crises allowed him to evolve his system. In 1989, five years of hyper growth caught up and prices plunged. Dell relates, "We were suddenly stuck with too many chips that nobody wanted – not to mention the fact that they had cost us a ton of money." Dell had to sell off the inventory and said, "To our stunned disbelief, we had quickly become known as the company with the inventory problem." Dell put his mind to work on a system that would avoid a similar situation in the future.

Like Ford before him, Dell understood that it came down to 'inventory velocity' – the number of 'inventory turns' he could achieve by increasing output and reducing stock. While Stars will slow down their asset cycle – retaining brand equity for as long as possible, Mechanics will speed up their asset cycle – aiming to increase their inventory velocity. Dell's realization was, "The quality of your information is inversely proportional to the amount of assets required, in this case excess inventory… If you have great information – that is you know exactly what people want and how much – you need that much less inventory." With the support of suppliers and customers, Dell began to minimize inventory, leading to unbeatable pricing.

A crisis in 1993 helped to focus the system further. Dell had grown beyond its ability to finance growth. Dell said, "We had grown too quickly. We realized our priorities had to change. We needed to focus on slow, steady growth, and liquidity." Liquidity, profitability and growth became the cornerstones of Dell's systems and he said, "Once we established clear metrics and measurements, it was easy to see which businesses were performing or not, and to change the strategy accordingly. For example, we changed our information systems so that a salesperson could see the level of margin for a product literally as he or she was selling it on the phone."

Dell weathered the storm of 1993, and formalized three tenets out of these crises, which have since become Dell's Three Golden Rules: disdain inventory; always listen to the customer; never sell indirect.

Dell had now become a huge company. Saying, "My high school didn't teach any courses in how to manage a $3 billion company," Dell brought in more outside help. As with every profile in this book, nothing can happen without a team. Dell explains, "When you're the leader of a company, be it large or small, you can't do everything yourself. In fact, you can't do much of *anything* by yourself." He adds, "One of the challenges you face as a company grows is that you tend to get a little too close to your own strengths and weaknesses, and it's hard to be objective. I've heard this referred to as 'believing your own press,' but I prefer to think of it as 'breathing your own exhaust.' It doesn't sound healthy – because it isn't."

Dell brought in Bain & Co to advise on the changes they would make. Bain consultant, Kevin Rollins came on board to support the effort. With the arrival of the Internet, customers were able to customize their machines, purchase online and receive delivery of their purchase to their door. Dell's revenue began another upward trend, culminating in 1999 when Dell overtook Compaq to become America's largest seller of PCs.

As the IT industry enters a new cycle, will Dell go the same way as Ford as the industry moves on? In anticipation, Dell changed its name to "Dell Inc" in 2003, and looked beyond their IT market to the electronics market, applying their direct model to home entertainment, TVs and multimedia, and the anticipated convergence of appliances, electronics, the Internet and mobile networks.

In 2004, Dell promoted Rollins to President and CEO, while he remained as Chairman. In 2005, twenty years after Dell sold his first PC, Fortune Magazine named Dell at first place in their global ranking of "Most Admired Companies". In 2006, Dell was worth $17 billion. I, in the meantime, had gotten over my frustrations and was following my flow on the other side of the planet.

MECHANICS IN A NUTSHELL

Dominant Wealth Frequency: Steel / Dynamo

Action Dynamic: Introvert

Thinking Dynamics: Intuitive

Wealth Creation Key: Creating a better system

Secondary Profiles: Lord, Creator

Strengths: Innovative; perfectionist; detail-oriented; completes things well; able to quickly fine-tune; spots inefficiencies in the system; able to simplify and replicate

Weaknesses: Can seem aloof and removed; can cause friction with their communication style; often very structured and inflexible; internal focus can miss market shifts; focus on perfection can lead to slow willingness to change.

Successes: Mechanics are at their best when they can get hands-on with business processes and find ways to consistently improve. When they are tied up with people issues and have little freedom to change things they soon become frustrated. Mechanics don't take things at face value, and so excel when given the freedom to take things apart.

Failures: Mechanics are often mistaken for Creators, and so are left to map out plans and strategies, which they have difficulty doing. While Creators can quickly come up with a half-baked idea that will change as it grows, Mechanics won't be satisfied until they can present the fully-baked solution: a prototype, the ingredients, a comprehensive recipe and a pre-heated oven.

Without the right product and team attraction, and without the right environment to operate in, a Mechanic will soon struggle to get into their flow, as they will be distracted with imperfections and inconsistencies that they will want to change.

THE MECHANIC STRATEGY

1. BUILDING YOUR WEALTH FOUNDATION

You are dynamic, yet with an introverted tendency, so are likely to pick your friends carefully. That's OK, because now it's time to also pick your wealth network carefully. The people around you will attract the market to your natural talent at perfecting processes.

Your greatest catalysts to wealth will come from those who have created the products or businesses that you will now distribute or franchise, and those who can connect you to your markets.

2. MOMENT OF WEALTH CREATION

You need to maximize the time invested in innovating and perfecting the systems and processes in the business you have chosen to become involved in. This includes the constant process of stress testing, refining and measuring performance, and continuously looking for ways to extract even more value from the system.

3. VALUE CREATION

The value creation activities that are important to you include the documentation of all systems and processes, and all checks and measures. This becomes embedded value that endures not just with the venture you are involved in now, but the next one as well, and the one after that.

4. VALUE OWNERSHIP

Ownership must be in the systems that you create. If you approach a Creator with a one-outlet business, and you systematize the business, find the financing and multiply that business to further outlets. You don't need to own the outlets. You do need to own the operating system. Make sure you own it before you multiply.

5. LEVERAGE

You need to leverage through a system of your own creation. Whether it is a license, or a franchise, ensure that the leverage is at the lowest common denominator. The more idiot-proof the system is, the greater your ability to leverage will be.

In the event that your system is a distribution or retail system, such as Wal-Mart, your leverage also comes from your product partners. The more products that are attracted to your system, the more the market gets attracted to your system. Every new product or customer means additional revenue leveraged off the same system.

6. SECURE CASH FLOW

Your cash flow will come from the value you deliver with your system. That means ensure you have the right franchise, license or distribution agreements in place that will allow you to create an ongoing source of cash flow from your system.

As you tinker with your system, with your head under the bonnet, you are leveraging the value of the other profiles. Become a master of perfecting process, and those with products, financing and connections will find their way to you.

MECHANICS TO LEARN FROM

Henry Ford (Ford Motor Company), Ray Kroc (McDonald's), Sam Walton (Wal-Mart), Ingvar Kamprad (IKEA), Michael Dell (Dell Inc), Jeff Bezos (Amazon.com), Larry Page (Google), Fred Smith (FedEx), Alfred Sloan (General Motors), Lee Kuan Yew (Minister Mentor, Singapore)

PART THREE

Leaving Your Legacy

CHAPTER THIRTEEN

FINDING YOUR FEET

"Make the most of yourself, for that is all there is of you."
-   Ralph Waldo Emerson

A FRAMEWORK FORWARD

How do we chart a course between those high performing entrepreneurs who have found their flow, and those of us who are just getting our feet wet?

The coming chapters map out a process that takes us from action to attraction: from path to purpose. We will lay out the framework of your flow, and we will link this framework to established reference points left from the legacy of others. Your first step is to be clear on exactly what your Wealth Dynamics profile is. There are a number of ways to find out, and you can find them in the special section on page 293. Your Wealth Dynamics profile is important for setting you on the right track but remember, it is only the first step!

TURNING ON TRACTION

"Even if you're on the right track,
you will get run over if you just sit there."
-   Will Rogers

Have a look at a five lane expressway. The flow of traffic is all in the same direction, yet it's obvious the cars zipping along on the outside lane are moving faster. If you're parked on the hard shoulder, and you aspire to be in the outside lane, there is a process to get you there. You don't start in the outside lane, you start in the inside lane. You don't start in fifth gear, you start in first gear.

The key to this process is traction. On our path to wealth, we begin with action and we end with attraction. Traction links the two together – and not just literally:

ACTION

TR-ACTION

AT-TR-ACTION

If the wheels and gears of your car lost traction, you would lose grip and lose momentum (or crash).

Any one not living in traction does not apply what they've learnt, does not measure their momentum, and does not sense when they are over-revving their engine or when they are about to stall. As a result, they often find themselves in the wrong gear, or in neutral…

When you are living with traction, you become aware of your momentum and the flow of traffic around you. You can feel when it's time to change gears, and when it's time to change lanes. You gain the ability to move into your flow one step at a time.

How do you turn traction on? You turn it on by deciding to increase the value of time. The more you value your time, the greater your traction becomes. You spend less time saying "I'll think about it" and less time in 'neutral'. Successful Wealth Creators have a grip on reality where they are quick-to-learn and quick-to-apply. They live in the present, applying themselves fully to playing the game. They don't miss critical moments, and they recognize luck when it happens. Successful Wealth Creators don't waste their time, and they won't waste other people's time either.

As Ingvar Kamprad said, "You can do so much in ten minutes' time. Ten minutes, once gone, are gone for good. Divide your life into ten minute units and sacrifice as few of them as possible."

The grip you need at 120kph flow is quite different from the grip you need at 10kph. That's fine, as you will learn to pick up traction as you increase your flow. The more you play the game, the sharper your clarity, the stronger your connections, and the faster you can access the resources around you as opportunities arise.

Once you choose to live in traction and wasting time is no longer an option, the next step is to understand how to change gears, and to know what gears are in your gear box.

FOLLOWING A DYNAMIC BALANCE

The wealth equation, value x leverage, is not a static balance. It is a progressive, dynamic balance. The I Ching describes a dynamic balance as an oscillation between two opposites. Our lives revolve around a dynamic balance of day and night, sun and moon, male and female, yang and yin.

When we learn to walk, we learn that walking is a dynamic balance between our left and right feet. The art of failing forwards is not a linear progression, but an oscillating zigzag path between these two polarities. We master this dynamic balance when we understand intuitively that balance comes from forward momentum.

Wealth creation is a dynamic balance of creating value, leveraging that value, which creates new value, which we then leverage, which creates new value and so on. There is a hierarchy of ten values that we can leverage, and understanding this hierarchy allows us to see the journey of great Wealth Creators through a clearer lens. Each began at the bottom rung of the ladder and worked their way up the hierarchy, increasing their flow as they progressed.

THE TEN LEVELS OF VALUE

The good news is, without exception, that no Wealth Creator in this book began with money. They simply began with their time – and the first series of values they leveraged were free of charge! Of the ten values, six of the values are internal values, which means each of us already possesses them. The other four values are external values. All money on this planet flows as a result of the four external values.

These ten values can be grouped as five pairs: five lanes of the same expressway. Each pair is a complementary pair of yin and yang. Each of the Wealth Creators in this book has progressively stepped through these values on their way to the outside lane, increasing momentum and attraction as they go. Once you have understood these ten values, reflect on your own situation and decide what you need to work on to make the next shift.

INTERNAL VALUES #1 & #2
PASSIONS & TALENTS

What value did Warren Buffett leverage before he had the money to start an investment fund? What value did Arnold Schwarzenegger leverage before he had his big break? We all have six internal values that we can leverage to create attraction. In fact, you can notice the wealth of someone who leverages these internal values without ever seeing their bank account.

The first two internal values, our passions and our talents, are our *core values*. These are the values that Edison and Disney leveraged to attract financing. They are the values that Oprah Winfrey and Martha Stewart leveraged to attract their teams.

Value One: "Passions" – Your passions are the starting point on the value hierarchy. If you are pursuing wealth outside of your passions it is only a matter of time before you come sliding all the way back down. Passion is what makes you jump out of bed in the morning. When we leverage our passions by living our passions, we attract the people, resources and solutions we need to open our flow. Your first step is to identify and step into your passion. Your passions are your pilot light.

Value Two: "Talents" – While your passion sparks you (and others), your talents guide your time. Wealth Dynamics is based on identifying your talents – what you do well naturally without having to think about it. Creators naturally create, Accumulators naturally accumulate. Seeing your value through your talents gives you a place in your passion. Every great team needs to have people with the same passion, but different talents.

How to unlock your passions and talents: These two values are the "yang" and "yin" of our core internal values. We access them through rediscovery. As children we easily and openly access both, and then through our culture and schooling we condition ourselves away from both, focusing on what feels like "hard work". We coast on our strengths and work on our weaknesses.

If you got an 'A' and a 'C' at school, you were more likely to focus time on the 'C'. This is the entire opposite of wealth creation, where you would focus on the 'A', and give the 'C' to someone who was getting an 'A' in the same activity. We unlock our passions and talents by investing time with the teams that we resonate with, enabling us to 're-synchronize'.

These core internal values attracted IBM to Bill Gates, Benjamin Graham to Warren Buffett, Freddie Laker to Richard Branson, the McDonald brothers to Ray Kroc. Each leveraged these first two values to move up to the second two.

INTERNAL VALUES #3 & #4

KNOWLEDGE & NETWORK

The second two internal values, our knowledge and our network, are our *mid values*. Unlike our core values, we do not rediscover these, as we were not born with them. We acquire them over time.

Value Three: "Knowledge" – Anyone who has spent their life building their resume knows that the more knowledge they have, the more attractive they become. The problem arises when your knowledge moves further and further from your passions and talents. Knowledge only contributes to your flow if it is knowledge based on your passions and talents. As Donald Trump's knowledge of New York real estate grows, so does his attraction.

Value Four: "Network" – While knowledge is what you know, network is who you know. Every great Wealth Creator has an awesome network, but a network based around their passion and talents. As you build the right network, you access the resources you need and magic begins to happen, enabling a computer techie to become Disney's largest shareholder without paying a cent, and a Hollywood star to become Governor of California without flexing a muscle.

How to build your knowledge and network: While the first two we leverage at point blank range, the second two we leverage at a distance. People notice our passions and talents when they meet us. However, people we know will tell people we don't know about us if we have built valuable knowledge and networks. The two mid values operate two steps removed, where we begin to attract people we don't know, who seek our knowledge or our network.

INTERNAL VALUES #5 & #6
CHARACTER & PURPOSE

Wealth, however, does not occur two steps removed, but three steps removed. The best opportunities that Wealth Creators attract do not come from people they know speaking to people they don't know, but from people they don't know speaking to other people they don't know: three steps removed.

When Kmart came to Martha Stewart with her first million-dollar opportunity, they didn't know each other. When Randolph Fields came to Richard Branson with the idea for Virgin Atlantic, they were strangers. Their reputations preceded them. We don't find fruit on the trunk of the tree, or even on the limbs, but out at the end of the branches: three steps removed. Our first two base values provide the trunk. Our second two mid values move us to the limbs. Our third two key values get us out to the branches. They are called the key values, as they unlock our wealth. They open the doors to our true flow and attraction.

Value Five: "Character" – When choosing what businesses to invest in, Warren Buffett has said, "After some mistakes I've learnt to go into business only with people whom I like, trust and admire. We've never succeeded in making a good deal with a bad person." Your character is your personal reputation in your market. Can you be trusted? Do you have integrity? Do you deliver? Your character is determined by your conduct: your day-to-day actions as seen by others. You can master the first four values, but if you send out the wrong message through your conduct, you will still find few resources and opportunities are attracted to you.

Value Six: "Purpose" – While character is determined by conduct, purpose is determined by contribution. Contribution is not a measure of what you get, but of what you give. Purpose is the highest of your six internal values, yet many of us are out seeking to get before we have determined what we want to give. A river with no outlet will attract little flow; water will naturally choose an easier path down the mountain. Your cause in life will be your greatest attractor.

How to build your character and purpose: Conduct and contribution is not something you plan for. You start it today. What is your conduct today? What is your contribution today? Your actions - no matter how small – are already leaving tracks.

These two key values have a longer frequency. They reach further and last longer. Think of the most inspiring individuals that you have heard of or read of. It is likely that it is their character and purpose that stand out in their achievements. Your passions are your pilot light with a short frequency that needs to be reignited daily. Your purpose is your glowing embers, outliving your businesses and outliving you. Wealth is what you're left with when you lose your money. By building these six internal values, you begin to attract the resources, talent and opportunities to grow your flow daily regardless of the money. Is Nelson Mandela wealthy? Was Mother Theresa wealthy? If they needed a million dollars could they click their fingers and have it? Even if you lost your business or your money, when you build your internal values, you still have ongoing attraction from the strength of your knowledge and network. Opportunities continue to flow to your passion and purpose. On your journey you may drop out of the fifth lane, but you will never find yourself on the hard shoulder again.

A MILLION DOLLARS A SECOND

"When spring comes the grass grows by itself."
- Tao Te Ching

Once we have built a foundation of wealth through our internal values, it's time to see how these internal values lead to the four external values. *All* money flow on this planet is the result of leveraging the four external values.

Last year the Gross Domestic Product (GDP) of the world's nations exceeded thirty-five trillion US dollars. That means the amount of goods and services physically produced and exchanged on this planet every week was about $700 billion - about $100 billion every waking day.

This is simply the value of goods and services exchanged for money. It excludes wealth creation from the capital growth of our property and assets, or from the wealth exchanged in the flow of our global money markets and stock markets

Even so, this phenomenal rate of value transfer works out at $4 billion every hour – *more than one million dollars every second.*

In the last minute, sixty million dollars of new value has been exchanged for cash. Within ten hours, the entire net worth of the world's richest man will have come and gone. Within a day, the capital value of the world's largest company will have flowed right by.

How hard can it be to make a million dollars if a million just flew by in that last second?

Sitting on the hard shoulder, this can seem a little overwhelming, but from the third lane, moving to the fourth lane becomes a simple maneuver. As with the six internal values, we can split these four external values further into pairs, with each pair attracting a different 'quality' of money flow. By understanding the four external values, this flow becomes more understandable.

EXTERNAL VALUES #7 & #8
THE TWO RETAIL VALUES

The more visible values that we see exchanged for money are the two 'retail' values. When you buy these two values, you view your money as being 'spent'. You buy dinner, you eat dinner, and your money is gone. You buy a pair of shoes, you get the shoes, and the shoe shop gets your money. The two retail values are what we see when we walk down the high street or turn on the TV:

Value Seven: "Fulfilling a Need" – Value seven fulfils a need, be it food, water, shelter, education or transport. This value is a commodity, which means where the money flows is largely a matter of price: the lower the price, the greater the flow.

Value Eight: "Fulfilling a Want" – Value eight fulfils a want, which means we don't need it, but we want it. In today's consumer society, we spend far more on what we want than what we need. Where the money flows is not a factor of price, but of desire. We may *need* transport, but we may *want* a Ferrari, and as a result we will pay a huge premium for what we want.

As we figure out what value we can deliver that people will spend money on, keep in mind that less than 5% of the money flow around this planet moves as a result of the retail values. The other 95% moves as a result of the wholesale values. In fact, no one ever became a billionaire from retail values. Every one of them moved up the ladder to the two wholesale values.

EXTERNAL VALUES #9 & #10
THE TWO WHOLESALE VALUES

The 'quality' of money flow is entirely different for the two wholesale values. Whereas the money that flows for retail values is seen as "money spent", the money that flows for wholesale values is seen as "money invested". We may think twice about spending $500 on a meal, but rush to invest $10,000 in the next hot IPO. We may 'um' and 'ah' over a $5,000 holiday, but have no hesitation in putting down a $50,000 deposit on a new home. At wholesale value, the dollars aren't *spent*, they are *invested*. In retail value, the more we spend, the more we lose. In wholesale value, the more we invest, the more we make.

Value Nine: "Component Value" – Value nine requires money investment plus additional creation to deliver a return on investment. Bill Gates made far more selling his software to PC manufacturers than to general consumers. The PC manufacturers see the money they invest for each piece of Microsoft software giving them a return, as it enables them to sell their PCs for more. The more they buy, the more they make. Ray Kroc made far more selling franchises for McDonald's than by selling the burgers themselves. The franchisees see the money they invest in a franchise giving them a return when they add in their own effort in running it.

Value Ten: "Investment Value" – Value ten requires money plus timing to deliver a return. When we buy a property, stocks or commodities, we invest money on the expectation of future returns that evolve simply through time. If Bill Gates had not listed Microsoft, he would not be the richest man in the world today, as his wealth does not come from his pay check, but from his listed shares.

The process of leveraging retail value to wholesale value, and of leveraging component value to investment value, is a fundamental key to wealth creation. Martha Stewart began her business at retail value operating in the scale of hundreds of dollars. She then leveraged this into wholesale component value through Kmart, operating with contracts in the scale of hundreds of thousands of dollars. By leveraging the media and Kmart's suppliers, her wholesale component value escalated into endorsements in the millions of dollars. Then, with the help of Sharon Patrick, she moved up to wholesale investment value and made a billion dollars.

Each of the Wealth Creators in this book went through a similar process to move to the outside lane. As a result, a hamburger company can end up in the real estate business and a search engine that lets you search for free has made over a thousand millionaires.

The dynamic process takes traction, perseverance, and a little luck.

XL VISION VILLAS – A CASE STUDY

Within our network of entrepreneurs in Asia, there are many stories of how people have built momentum through this dynamic balance, and we document this every month in *XL Magazine*, covering the stories of local entrepreneurs alongside features on many of the same entrepreneurs that appear in this book.

Amongst these stories, I occasionally add my own. Here is a current and personal example of a speedy escalation of value x leverage that led to one of my life dreams being achieved in a short period of time.

Since I was eighteen, I had a dream of owning and running a tropical resort. Not terribly original, but I spent my childhood in Papua New Guinea, and I grew up loving the tropical lifestyle.

Ten months ago, in September 2005, I moved to Bali with my family. My wife, Renate, had spent her childhood on the beaches in Mexico, and we both wanted our three children, Kathleen, Theresa and Luke, to experience the same childhood in paradise that we had lived. We arrived in Bali with no knowledge or network, so decided to lease a villa while we familiarized ourselves with the island.

Of course, we also talked about having our own resort in the future, but with our busy lives this remained just a dream. Little did we expect that, through luck and application, we would have our own resort within a matter of months.

Step One: Follow Your Flow

When we arrived in Bali, Renate was in the middle of a Masters Degree in Radiography, specializing in CT scanners. To complete her degree she needed hands-on use of a CT scanner. She could only find two CT scanners on the island, and both were out of access to foreigners. At a dinner party we went to two weeks after arriving, someone asked Renate, 'What will you be doing in Bali?'. Having given up on finding a scanner, Renate replied, 'I'd like to contribute to the people here, but I'm not sure how yet.' The person replied, 'With your medical background, you should meet John Fawcett.'

John Fawcett set up the John Fawcett Foundation twenty years ago, and has given over 22,500 Balinese a new life of sight through cataract surgery and his mobile eye clinics. Renate visited John the next day, and was so moved by the photos and letters from the people that John had touched, she said she would help him in whatever way she could. Her worries over finding a CT scanner were a million miles away.

John then took her around his clinic, and said, "Well, we do need help. We get plenty of donations but can't always use everything we get." He led her into a room and said, "For example, the Australian government donated this big and very expensive piece of equipment and we don't have the expertise to use it." Renate took one look and her eyes popped. It was a CT scanner.

Step Two: Listen to Luck

The next day, as Renate was telling me the story, we were out hunting for a villa that would suit our family. We couldn't get hold of the real estate agent we were using, so I said, "Let's just hop in the car and go find her." While waiting for our agent at the real estate office, I stumbled across photos of what looked like a neglected resort, twenty minutes drive away.

In Bali, resorts advertised for sale are rare, and resorts advertised for lease are almost unheard of. Within half an hour we were walking around the most wonderfully enchanting boutique resort, practically abandoned. It retained a skeleton staff and an owner in Europe who had shut down operations after the first Bali bomb in 2002.

We were both savvy enough to know that nothing ever looks as good as it seems, and we had heard plenty of stories about the pitfalls of investing in Indonesian real estate. Yet here was a resort that had just appeared as if by magic. Two pieces of luck sealed our decision.

The first was a connection between the resort and John Fawcett. Sitting by the pool, we came up with the idea of calling the resort "Vision Villas", making it a place where people would come to get vision, and to give vision. It would operate as a workshop retreat for entrepreneurs, trainers and groups to get vision, and for each person who stayed, the resort would make a donation to the John Fawcett Foundation to fund an eye operation, to give a life of sight.

The second piece of luck was when we asked the cost of leasing the property. We had set our budget for our home, and expected the resort to be far in excess of this. Erika, our real estate agent, came back with a figure. Absurdly, the amount was exactly the same as our budget.

Step Three: Fail Forward

Defining the downside of any decision is the key to taking action at critical moments. If we go ahead, what is the worst that can happen? We calculated the cost of involvement. We calculated the cost of renovating the resort, and the value that might add to it. Taking a cue from Branson's decision-making process, we called the people we had met in Bali who were in the resort industry and asked for their feed back. We learned of the break clauses we should add into the contract. Within two days we had made a decision to limit our exposure to a two-year lease with an option to buy, and made our offer, which was accepted. We moved in to the resort three months after arriving in Bali.

Step Four: Leverage Your Internal Values

As a Creator profile, I know I should not spend a moment trying to run the things I start, and my first focus was to find the right people to manage the renovations and run the resort. I was traveling across Asia and Renate was supporting John Fawcett during the week, so we leveraged our time on the weekend. Using our passions and talents, we spread word-of-mouth about our exciting venture, and we soon attracted fabulous referrals to people who could support us and that we could trust.

Lalu Suratman became our contractor with a team of fifteen to renovate the resort, Wayan Suarma became our resort manager and built a team of 28 staff to run the resort. I had calculated the cost of offsite retreats and training that my various companies already spent each year, and had worked out that by redirecting these retreats to our new resort, we would not only break-even on the resort's set-up cost, but we would save money for each of my companies.

When we moved into the resort in December 2005, we celebrated with the kids over champagne and 7-Up. We began to leverage our new-found local knowledge and network to equip the resort. We publicized our new project to our network of entrepreneurs across Asia, and had Desley Truscott fly in from Australia to oversee the interior design, Abu Hanifah from Success Shop in Singapore supply educational CDs and Gautam Gangali from Right Selection in Dubai supply leadership books for the resort library.

We leveraged our key values to our network, attracting over 150 people from 12 countries to the launch event in April and donations to John Fawcett from guests and visitors that far exceeded the donations we were already giving to John from room night stays.

Step Five: Leverage Your External Values

By tapping into the flow of training expenses already being spent in my other companies, Vision Villas was profitable from its first month.

Within the first two months of operation, we held our first training workshops, we hosted our first wedding, and we proudly entertained my parents, with dad educating his grandchildren on the various rare birds nesting in the gardens and mum running a Reiki workshop for a group from Australia and Singapore. Flow leads to flow, and in the first month we were up to 68% occupancy against a Bali resort industry average of less than 30%.

We kept occupancy high by leveraging on wholesale component value, leasing to workshop organizers who bought at wholesale rates to mark up and resell to their attendees, rather than relying on the retail value of the tourist trade.

By June 2006, we decided to accelerate the purchase of the resort, and put an offer in, which after some negotiation was accepted. We are now leveraging at wholesale investment value, structuring the ownership of the resort into shareholdings bought by ourselves and trusted investors from within our network.

With no prior knowledge of how to structure such an arrangement, we borrowed from the extensive knowledge and contacts of close connections we had now made in Bali, who had plenty of experience in structuring Bali property investments. We set a 12% annual rate of return for our investment group, and profit targets for the resort management team to achieve.

Within a year, we are well on the way to becoming the proud owners of our own Bali resort, and the owners of a profitable resort management company, already building a reputation for itself within our network as the workshop retreat specialist. We have achieved this with little risk and little additional investment – we simply redirected flow from elsewhere within our river. We noticed luck when it happened, and redirected our wealth – our existing momentum and resources – to take advantage of it.

Step Six: Secure Your Value and Cash Flow

With value x leverage, the dynamic balance always continues. By playing the Creator game, I keep focused on my value being in the businesses I create. As a Creator, the key value that has grown within this adventure is the resort management company, XL Vision Villas. This has now attracted resort owners and investors in Fiji, Thailand, Malaysia and New Zealand who would like to work with the resort management company to set up their resort as a workshop retreat marketed under the same concept and brand. By seeing the value in the resort management company, and not the one resort, the value can continue to leverage and grow.

Renate, on the other hand, is playing the Accumulator game, and keeps her focus on the investment value created from this adventure. She is becoming an expert on the land prices and trends within the area of Bali around the resort. She has become connected to the 'inside knowledge' of the area, opening up an entirely new universe of opportunities for land investment, attracting investors interested in this knowledge, and helping us to find the perfect plot for our future home. As we play the game and run the race, our luck continues to grow. As Ray Kroc said, "Luck is a dividend of sweat. The more you sweat, the luckier you get."

THE EIGHT STAGES OF ENTERPRISE GROWTH

As you move up your own personal value hierarchy, your business or investments are also passing through a cycle. Understanding this cycle adds another layer of complexity to your journey. The Wealth Profile Square passes through four seasons in every cycle. As an enterprise moves through the eight profiles, the value carried within the enterprise evolves. Like pass-the-parcel, the value changes as the parcel changes hands. Every great Wealth Creator understands intuitively what part they play in the cycle. Each receives value at one level, and passes it on at another.

Wealth creation is about both effective receiving and effective giving. It is about understanding how value grows from an idea into a commercial, tradable commodity through this transfer. It is also about understanding how every evolutionary process has a natural path of least resistance.

Many entrepreneurs, even after understanding their profile, do not follow this process, and try to 'short-cut' it. For example they might try to raise financing before proving their concept, or try and set up a franchise system before building a profitable pilot. With your car, you start in first gear and once you have momentum, you move to second, then to third. If you try and start a business in fifth gear it will, like the car, be almost impossible to get moving.

Below are the eight stages of business evolution, and how they relate to the eight wealth profiles:

Stage One – Proven Concept (Creator)

First gear in any business is not just to come up with an idea, but also to prove it in the market. That means having proven commercial demand where someone in the market has bought or committed to buying whatever it is you are selling, at the price you are selling it. What do you do if you cannot afford to deliver a proven product until you have the team and financing? You do what Edison and Gates did, and forward-sell the product into your market, using your customer's money to deliver the product they want you to deliver.

With XL Vision Villas, only by demonstrating to our new industry contacts in Bali that we had a niche willing to pay for a workshop destination at the prices we set (and showing them forward orders to prove it) did they overcome their initial skepticism about 'just another resort in Bali'. Money flows as a result of a particular proven commercial concept.

Stage Two – Brand Attraction (Star)

Second gear is to build relationships with customers that will return to buy again – not just the existing product but other products under the same niche or brand. Once you have achieved first gear, second gear is a natural progression. What if you need the team to deliver this ongoing value? You forward-sell the promise of forward value to those who will benefit most from it, as Oprah and Martha did.

The key activity in stage two is creating brand attraction, where you establish repeat business on the basis of future as well as present value. Wayan Suarma, our Resort Manager at XL Vision Villas, has twenty years experience in the industry. He was attracted on the basis of the brand promise. At stage two money flows as a result of your brand promise.

Stage Three – Operating Team (Supporter)

Once you have ongoing customer transactions, it is far easier to attract the world-class team you need to succeed. Attracting the team on just an idea is far more difficult. By the time you reach this third gear, the value has grown from the idea to the relationship to the operating team. In fact, as Eisner and Welch show, the value in the operating culture becomes strong enough that you can change products, services and markets entirely yet the value remains.

The key activity in stage three is creating an ongoing commercial operation by building a team that can execute. Money flows as a result of your ability to repeatedly deliver.

Stage Four – Market Connections (Deal Maker)

Trying to do deals with just a concept (especially an unproven one) is very difficult. Doing deals with profitable, operating teams is far easier. Fourth gear sees the value in the business grow from the team to the partnerships the team has within the market – its suppliers, strategic alliances, market partners. These players, already actively profiting from their market, will see value in a business once it has built an operating enterprise that will not live or die off one idea.

The key activity in stage four is entrenching the business in the market through effective market connections. Once XL Vision Villas was an operating resort, creating links to training companies, event organizers and travel agents became far easier. Money flows as a result of the value you give to, and receive from, market partners.

Stage Five – Tradable Entity (Trader)

If you are looking to sell part or all of your company, it becomes far easier to do so when your business is entrenched in its market. In fifth gear, value progresses from market connections to the value of the business itself. The business now becomes the product. It can change products, brands, even the management team running it, and it can still increase in value. Traders like Soros understand this, and will never speculate on unproven concepts outside the market.

The key activity in stage five is creating short-term tangible market value in the business. Once we had proven the XL Vision Villas resort as a profitable enterprise, we set up a corporate structure to own the resort that would enable shares to be bought and sold easily without the resort needing to change hands. Money flows as a result of being able to trade parts of your company's asset value.

Stage Six – Bankable Asset (Accumulator)

Many entrepreneurs attempt to start their business in sixth gear – to raise finance before they even have a proven concept. None of the entrepreneurs in this book attempted that strategy. Investors will put their money in businesses that are tradable far faster than into businesses with no easy exit. That means sixth gear becomes easy to get to once you have built momentum in fifth gear. Value now has moved from transient money (traders increase their wealth by accelerating the speed of their money flow) to long-term money (accumulators increase their wealth by decreasing the speed of their money flow).

The key activity in stage six is creating long-term, lasting value in your business. Money flows as a result of being able to 'mortgage' part of that value, where you no longer need to part with any ownership, but simply leverage your value as security. While we could have attempted to buy the resort straight away, if we wanted other investors to buy it with us, we would have struggled to prove our case in a plan. It was far easier to attract the investors once we had a track record, a plan and a structure to deliver lasting value.

Stage Seven – Cash Generating Infrastructure (Lord)

While at stage five, traders will demand a piece of the pie that they can trade, and at stage six, accumulators will be content with a piece of the pie that they can simply hold, at stage seven value has grown due to the constant dividends the pie creates. By stage seven, it's no longer about owning the pie. It's about owning the cash flow. Rockefeller made his fortune in oil without owning a single oilfield. At this stage of your business development, you really can have your pie and eat it too.

The key activity in stage seven is creating stable cash flow from your ongoing operations. Money flows as a result of owning the flow – which can be the flow of an entire market – as in the case of Rockefeller's Standard Oil, or Sergey Brin's and Larry Page's Google. Value is now in the flow.

Stage Eight – Licensable System (Mechanic)

Once a business has developed a cash generating infrastructure, it can sell a license for others to use the same system. It only becomes easy to sell a franchise when you already have a proven cash generating system. At this stage of the business, you can change your products, branding, management team, market partners, bankers and investors, and the business can still grow in value. Selling a license for others to make money – without giving away any ownership of your products or shares in your business – is a good way to make money! But start from first gear and work your way up.

The key activity in stage eight is creating a license system around your flow. As in the case of Walton's Wal-Mart, or Kroc's McDonald's, money flows as a result of being able to 'rent' rights to your river. XL Vision Villas is several years away from this stage, but once we have a series of workshop retreat destinations that are delivering constant cash flow, this next step is a natural progression. Of course, when it happens, the management team at stage eight will be quite different from the one that got it started.

Build momentum at each stage, and get the order right. Stay in your flow, and let your businesses and investments stay in their flow. If you get order wrong, even the best business will stall or burn out, just as yanking the gears will stall or burn out a finely-tuned racing car.

THE I CHING

"I was born not knowing
and have had only a little time to change that here and there."
- Richard Feynman

The flow of time is the factor that connects the frequency of the eight Wealth Profiles with the frequency of the eight steps of enterprise change. While Wealth Dynamics may appear a relatively new system, this connection of time flow with states of change dates back to the beginning of written history. These steps have a parallel in an ancient system documented in what is believed to be the first 'book' in China. This book was a curious set of codes called the "I Ching" which was 'written' by a mythical figure five thousand years ago.

According to Chinese mythology, China was originally ruled by three mythical sovereigns. The first of these, "Heavenly King" Fu Xi, is credited with developing the I Ching, which became China's Oracle and translates to 'the Book of Changes'. While Fu Xi was mythical, the I Ching became very real. It evolved over four dynasties to become the basis for China's two central philosophies, Taoism and Confucianism in 600BC. These have widely influenced our lives to this day, providing us with the foundations of everything from Chinese medicine, astronomy, yoga and meditation to our formalized family, military, government and legal systems.

> *"In the beginning there was as yet no moral or social order. Then came Fu Xi who looked upward and contemplated the images in the heavens, and looked downward and contemplated the occurrences on earth. He united man and wife, regulated the five stages of change, and laid down the laws of humanity. He devised the eight trigrams, in order to gain mastery over the world."*
>
> — From the *I Ching*.

The I Ching is based on the idea that everything flows from a dynamic balance of opposites and that the nature of time changes as a result of this flow. Within these ever-changing tides there is an immovable, ultimate path for each of us. These opposites are known within the I Ching as "Yin" and "Yang", which make up the famous circular image of the Taiji. This symbolizes the perpetual interplay of yin and yang, night and day, male and female.

Yin and Yang combine in eight three-lined 'trigrams' to make up the building blocks of the I Ching, which correlate to the eight profiles within Wealth Dynamics. Throughout history, these eight trigrams formed basis of Chinese strategic thinking. Each has a different symbolic representation that gives us a sense of the energy within the eight paths (and eight gears):

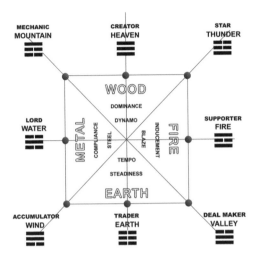

Trigram	I Ching Description	Yin / Yang	WD Profile
Heaven	Originating, creating	Supreme Yang	Creator
Thunder	Arousing, inciting	Young Yang	Star
Fire	Spreading, dependable	Middle Yang	Supporter
Valley	Playful, courting	Mature Yang	Deal Maker
Earth	Nurturing, yielding	Supreme Yin	Trader
Wind	Equaling, penetrating	Young Yin	Accumulator
Water	Adapting to difficulty	Middle Yin	Lord
Mountain	Completing	Mature Yin	Mechanic

Within the I Ching, these eight 'trigrams' combine into sixty-four pairs of 'hexagrams', creating a map of time - a map similar to the map of DNA. Once the 64 codons of DNA were identified in the 1990s, we had the building blocks to decode the genetic sequence of all living things. So too, when the I Ching mapped time 5,000 years earlier, it gave Chinese masters a comprehensive system to decode time. The I Ching also related energy to matter through the five elements. The Hexagrams of time (and energy), interplay with the five elements of place (and matter): wood, fire, earth, metal and water.

According to the I Ching as we are born from energy to matter, we take on varying qualities of the first four elements, and it is this combination that defines our differences. The universe was seen as in constant flux, and we have the choice to live in resonance with this flux by understanding it and following our path within it, or to be in a constant battle against it.

In the Chinese system, the five Chinese elements are not elements at all, but states of change. "Fire" does not refer to fire, but the state that fire is in when it glows. "Wood" does not refer to the wood in trees, but the state that wood is in when it grows. The five could more accurately be described as: Grow (Wood), Glow (Fire), Slow (Earth), Know (Metal) and Flow (Water). While western culture became rooted in a Newtonian world based on cause-and-effect (until the advent of general relativity and quantum mechanics), Chinese culture has always focused on states of change, where nothing is static and where we experience entirely different realities in the context of our state of change at any moment in time.

Wealth Dynamics refers to these five states as "frequencies". When we tune in to our frequency (and we all have a dominant frequency), we experience a different reality, and we begin to attract the right people, resources and opportunities, as if by luck. Many people call this our 'flow'. Flow is what we find in water, the fifth element. As we follow the strategies to resonate with our natural frequency, we increasingly tune into and experience flow.

Flow is not an ethereal concept in Wealth Dynamics, but an achievable state, reached through a natural step-by-step path that each of us can tread - because many have trod the path before us. The end goal of Wealth Dynamics is not just to know your profile. It is to identify your path, tune in to your flow, and fulfill your true potential. Following your flow allows you to create poetry in motion.

"You will find poetry nowhere unless you bring some with you."
- Joseph Joubert

CHAPTER FOURTEEN

A BRIEF HISTORY OF FLOW

"Be not merely good, be good for something."
- Henry David Thoreau

WHERE'S YOUR FORTUNE?

In June 2006, newswires around the world carried the headlines "Warren Buffett to give his fortune to Gates Foundation". Bill Gates, the wealthiest man in the world, decided to give his fortune away some time ago, setting up the Bill & Melinda Gates Foundation with his wife and father. With the June press announcement, Buffett, the second wealthiest man in the world was now giving away his fortune as well.

What is this fortune? Do you have a fortune? Is it yours to give away?

In today's money-driven economy, it is easy to relate 'fortune' to 'money' and leave it at that. Yet within history's deeper meaning of the concept of 'fortune', we find a link between the temporary nature of our life, the permanent nature of our legacy, and the strange phenomenon of 'luck'. This historic understanding gives a deeper insight into how your flow leads to your fortune. Fortune has evolved over the centuries into a word with four separate, yet related meanings:

for·tune (fôr'chən) n.

1. **Luck:** The chance happening of events (fortuitous, fortunate)
2. **Success:** Especially when at least partially resulting from luck
3. **Fate:** A foretelling of one's destiny (fortune-telling)
4. **Wealth:** A large sum of money or possessions

According to the Chinese, your fortune is your luck. The symbol for good fortune, 'fu', is also the symbol for good luck. The word fortune in English, originated from the Latin *'Fortuna'*, the Roman Goddess of

Luck. Throughout history, our ancestors saw fortune and luck as one and the same thing. If you had good fortune you attracted your luck, and if you had good luck you attracted your fortune. From this definition, fortune evolved to mean the result of luck as well as the cause of it. Coming across 'fortuitous' events would make you more 'fortunate'. Your 'fortune' then evolved further to mean more than your chance. From fortune-telling, fortune became your destiny.

Bill Gates has a fortune. Warren Buffett has a fortune. But their fortune is more than the dollars they give. It is their luck, and it is their legacy. Do these fortunate fellows see themselves as lucky? Actually, they see themselves as super-lucky. As Gates said at the press conference announcing Buffett's $31 billion philanthropic gift, "I think the key thing is to get more people who are super-lucky to think about giving back."

> *"Only learn to seize good fortune,*
> *for good fortune is always here."*
> - Johann Wolfgang von Goethe

Your fortune already exists, and it is simply waiting for you to follow your flow. Living in your flow is living a life of good fortune. Exactly *where* it exists though, is an entirely different story – and a story worth telling.

A BRIEF HISTORY OF FLOW

Fortune follows flow. So why are we not already following our flow? Should we blame the government? Our schools? Our Victorian work ethic? Or is there a more deep-rooted reason that flow is not more commonly accessed in our society today? Over the last five thousand years, there has been an intimate relationship between flow, our 'frequency' and the power of attraction. It has only been in the last eighty years that this relationship has suffered a break in connection.

Understanding the history of this relationship gives us answers to the state we find ourselves in today. In the following pages, we will take a journey through the history of flow: the history of the five frequencies, and the location of the fifth element - the location of our fortune.

This journey is a surprising one, and may appear bizarre at times. Read the following account on this history of flow and you will end up with some startling conclusions! As Mark Twain said, "Truth is stranger than fiction".

Lao Tse, and the Five Frequencies

In the last chapter, we touched on the I Ching, the Chinese Book of Changes. According to Chinese accounts, Lao Tse integrated the I Ching's structure of flow into the Tao Te Ching in the sixth century BC, giving birth to Taoism (translated as 'The Way').

> *"The Way gave birth to unity,*
> *Unity gave birth to duality,*
> *Duality gave birth to trinity,*
> *Trinity gave birth to the myriad creatures.*
> *The ten thousand things carry yin and embrace yang.*
> *They achieve harmony by combining these forces."*
> - Lao Tse, 500 BC

Like Confucianism, Taoism began as a 'school of philosophy' based on the I Ching, but not in the narrow sense that we would think of as philosophy today. A Tao Master would be versed in philosophy, cosmology, medicine, music and meditation. All disciplines were based on the interplay of yin and yang, with the flow of all matter and energy transitioning through the five frequencies of wood, fire, earth, metal and water.

The five elements became integrated into all aspects of Chinese understanding of the universe. In cosmology, they related to the five visible planets. Yin and yang related to the moon and sun. In medicine, they related to organs of the body, through which *Qi,* or our "life force" would flow. The elements related to the seasons of the year, the directions of the compass, and all aspects of Chinese culture.

The Chinese categorized people according to the five elements, the night sky, and the twelve animals of the zodiac, with astrology providing both a chart of personalities and a calendar of time.

In Feng Shui, earth was seen as the centre, with the other four elements making the four points of the compass. In the annual cycle, the seasons began in wood (spring) and ended in metal (winter). Flow was seen as a natural process that changed frequency as it progressed. Flow has a creative cycle (where water creates wood, wood creates fire, fire created earth, earth creates metal and metal creates water). Flow also has a controlling or destructive cycle (where water controlled fire, fire controlled metal, metal controlled wood, wood controlled earth and earth controlled water).

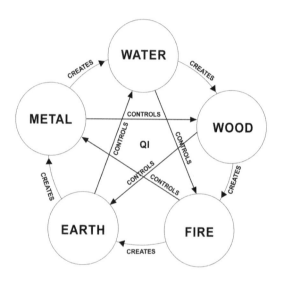

The overlay of the circle of the constructive cycle and the pentagram of the destructive cycle became the pentacle symbol of creation within the Chinese study of flow. The Tao study of flow was interested in how, by mastering flow in our changing, material world, we could transcend to a unchanging, higher world.

As Taoism developed, this study of flow became a discipline in its own right: a study of methods to transcend and transmute matter and time. This study of flow became known throughout the next 1,500 years of human history as "alchemy".

The Famous Five Flow West

Today, many people have come to think of alchemy as a quirky quasi-science that preceded chemistry and physics, with a misconception that the main objective of alchemy was 'turning lead to gold'. Taoist alchemy (the earliest recorded form of the discipline) had two components: external alchemy and internal alchemy. Both had the objective of discovering mastery of matter and time, with the ambitious objective of achieving immortality. Throughout history, immortality has been the primary goal of alchemy in all its forms.

Wai-tan (external alchemy) was a study of drugs, herbs and chemicals, and has led to the basis of traditional Chinese medicine, which remains in use throughout China today. *Nei-tan* (internal alchemy) was a study of our internal *Qi* and has led to today's disciplines of yoga and meditation. Both were a study in flow, utilizing the five elements as definable frequencies of change.

The five frequencies, which became the five 'alchemical elements', found their way to India, to Persia, then on to Greece. In India, they became known as the 'Pancha Mahabhuta' (the five great elements), dividing the five into four primary elements and one 'quintessence'.

Like the Chinese, the Indians defined the five elements as various frequencies of vibration from which all matter and energy is formed. The four primary elements evolved to *vayu* (air), *agni* (fire), *aap* (water) and *prithvi* (earth). Alchemical processes focused on moving the flow of these four elements to the fifth, *akasha*. *Akasha* in Sanskrit means 'space', but refers to a dimension outside of the other four. It sits in a different dimension and from this element the other four are derived. *Akasha* was seen as the 'binding substance', 'life force' or 'soul' that pervades our universe. It became known in the West as 'quintessence'. The word 'Quintessence' comes from the Latin *quinta essentia*: the fifth element.

Over the centuries, Indian culture evolved the concept of the five elements, which made the first five of the seven 'chakra' energy centers in the body. With the sun and moon, they related to the seven days of the week, the seven colors of the rainbow and the seven notes on the musical scale.

Like the Chinese, the Indians had an internal and an external form of alchemy. The internal tradition of finding flow and reaching *akasha* continues today through yoga and meditation. *Akasha* is synonymous with 'spirit', which derives from the Latin *spiritus*, meaning 'breath'.

Aristotle Adds Aether

By 360BC, alchemy was being practiced widely within Persia, Egypt and Greece. Aristotle (384 – 322 BC) became the first to take the five alchemical elements and formalize them within a system in Ancient Greece. He differentiated the four base elements as the interplay of two pairs of polarities: hot and dry, and wet and cold. As in India, the four base elements were: fire (hot and dry); earth (cold and dry); air (hot and wet); and water (cold and wet).

As in India and China, the four base elements were related to the seasons: air was spring, fire was summer, earth was autumn and water was winter. In Greek medicine they were related to the 'four temperaments' and 'four humors'. The fifth element, 'quintessence', Aristotle named 'aether'. This he called the 'divine substance'.

Aristotle was the first to study and define the notion of 'causality', which then became a central theme in the history of flow. What caused flow? He differentiated the four base elements from aether by saying the four moved in straight lines and so had to have been set into motion by a 'cause' while aether moved in cycles, and so had no beginning or end. Differentiating between a plane with 'cause and effect' – with a defined cause of flow - and a fifth element of eternal motion – with eternal flow – was a convenient distinction, allowing him to define the universe as a series of celestial spheres made of aether, rotating eternally around the earth, which sat at the centre.

While terrestrial phenomena had 'prime movers' that could be identified, he thought that the eternal celestial spheres must have an eternal 'prime mover'. Unfortunately, this distinction led to a separation in the West between the four base elements and the fifth element, that embedded itself in Western culture over the following 1,800 years.

Christianity and the Catholic Church adopted Aristotle's model of the universe, with the 'prime mover' being God, and the outermost celestial sphere being the Christian Heaven. There the model stayed until Galileo (1564 – 1642) invented the telescope and declared to the Church's surprise that the earth was not at the centre of the universe after all. For his efforts, Galileo was called before the Pope, tried for heresy, ordered to recant his claims and placed under house arrest.

During these 1,800 years, it wasn't only Galileo who was getting in trouble for pursuing a clearer understanding of the flowing world around us. Alchemists were seen as practicing magic and also charged with heresy. The pentacle became a symbol of witchcraft and the devil, and the understanding of flow – still alive and well in the East, was largely lost in Europe's 'Dark Ages'.

Leonardo da Vinci Gets Physical

Flow re-emerged as a subject worth studying during Europe's Renaissance. Leonardo da Vinci (1452 –1519) was fascinated with the human anatomy, astronomy, optics and hydrodynamics – the study of water flow. He collected his observations on water flow in one notebook, including his thoughts on the flow of water in rivers, how sea fossils ended up on mountain tops, how these ideas were related to erosion, astronomy and celestial light.

This notebook became known as the Codex Leicester after it was bought by the 1st Earl of Leicester, Thomas Coke, in 1717. The five-hundred year old notes on flow remain the only notes of da Vinci's in private hands. Today the notebook belongs to Bill Gates, who bought it for $30.8 million in 1994.

In da Vinci's work, the internal alchemy of the East resurfaced, famously symbolized in the Vitruvian Man drawing: a naked man in the position of both a cross and a pentacle, superimposed on a circle and a square. Da Vinci saw the human body as a *cosmografia del minor mondo* (cosmography of the microcosm), where each of us are anatomically and spiritually a living embodiment of the universe. This famous diagram combined man within our material world (square) and our spiritual world (circle) and between the symbol of the church (cross) and the symbol of alchemy (pentacle).

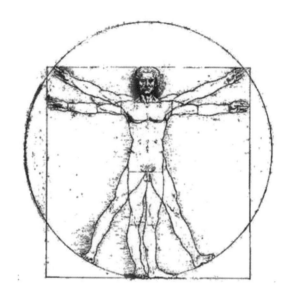

Isaac Newton becomes the Father of Flow

It would be a century later before all elements of flow connected within the mind of one man. The elements of flow, attraction, alchemy and fortune linked in the life of Isaac Newton (1643-1727).

Admitted into Trinity College, Cambridge in 1661, Newton set to work on a variety of subjects. He invented the reflecting telescope, and was the first to decode white light into the colors of the rainbow at the age of 24. To calculate the flow of planets, he invented an entirely new mathematical technique to measure 'flux', which he called 'fluxion'. This later became known as calculus.

Newton's Principia explained the flow of the planets and of all objects through his Three Laws of Motion. As with Aristotle before him, Newton was intrigued by causality. His deduction that all planetary motion was the result of gravity became a major breakthrough, leading Einstein to comment two hundred years later:

"It was, no doubt, especially impressive to learn that the cause of the movements of the heavenly bodies is identical with the force of gravity so familiar to us from everyday experience. Newton succeeded in explaining the motions of the planets, moons, comets, down to fine details as well as the ebb and flow of the tides and the precessional movement of the earth—this last a deductive achievement of particular brilliance."

Although Newton was able to explain that gravity was the result of mass, he could not explain how this gravity was created. If mass was the cause of gravity, and gravity was the cause of mass, what was the cause of both? He turned to books and experiments on alchemy, as a way to understand aether, eternal motion and immortality.

Throughout his life at Trinity College, Newton also had problems reconciling the religious basis of the Trinity with his own personal views of one God. He kept this a secret together with his extensive work on alchemy, which was frowned on by both Church and College.

When he left Cambridge in 1696, he packed his thoughts and unpublished alchemical works in a box, where they remained for 240 years before being collected and revealed to the world by English economist, John Maynard Keynes.

"Newton was not the first of the age of reason. He was the last of the magicians, the last of the Babylonians and Sumerians, the last great mind which looked out on the visible and intellectual world with the same eyes as those who began to build our intellectual inheritance rather less than 10,000 years ago."
- John Maynard Keynes, written on Newton's 300th birthday

Ironically, whilst being last of the magicians, Newton put the first hammer in the temporary coffin of aether. By coming up with the Law of Universal Gravitation to explain the heavens, the idea of 'aether' began its slippery slope out of our modern scientific vocabulary. In the coming years, alchemy moved on to chemistry, metaphysics moved on to physics, and the idea of 'spirit' separated from 'science' for the first time in history.

Meanwhile, in London in 1670, Newton was appointed Master of the Royal Mint. As irony would have it our intrepid alchemist, having spent previous years attempting to transmute base metals into gold, spent the rest of his life minting money as the guardian of England's monetary system.

James Maxwell Mixes It Up

With the release of the da Vinci Code, there has been plenty of speculation that while in Cambridge, Newton was part of a secret society. Although there is no evidence that he was, there is evidence that James Maxwell was. Like Newton, Maxwell (1831 – 1876) went to Trinity College, Cambridge, where his work was described a hundred years later by Albert Einstein as the "most profound and the most fruitful that physics has experienced since the time of Newton."

Maxwell studied philosophy at Edinburgh University and then mathematics at Cambridge. At Trinity College, he became part of the Cambridge Apostles, a secret society supposedly made up at any one time of the twelve smartest students at Cambridge. His work on flow led to major advances in thermodynamics and the kinetic theory of gases. Maxwell progressed Newton's work by showing that the universe's attraction had far more to do with flow than with mass.

In 1864, he presented his "Maxwell's Equations" to the Royal Society, linking magnetism to electricity, and linking electromagnetism to light. The *Maxwell* is today the unit to measure magnetic flux. Maxwell's work gives us a wonderfully, poetic Taoist phenomenon where yin creates yang, and yang creates yin. Electromagnetism works on the basis that a changing magnetic field creates an electric field, and a changing electric field creates a magnetic field. The process of changes in flow of both the electric and the magnetic fields have the effect of creating attraction.

Maxwell's work progressed the work of Newton by relating attraction to electric and magnetic flow, and identifying light as an electromagnetic wave which, when it changed frequency, changed through the colors of the rainbow.

Attraction Becomes Flow's Final Factor

Maxwell's work laid the foundation for Einstein's theory of Special Relativity in 1905. In his paper "On the Electrodynamics of Moving Bodies", which featured his famous equation $E=MC^2$, Einstein directly linked matter and energy as two forms of the same thing.

Einstein's theory of General Relativity, published in 1915, unified Special Relativity with Newton's Law of Universal Gravitation, explaining gravity as a product of mass-energy and momentum of spacetime. Einstein's theories entirely dismantled Newton's classical laws of motion. Between Maxwell and Einstein, a new understanding of electrodynamics, in which fields had effects outside of visible cause, lead Einstein to comment: "Many physicists maintain, not without weighty arguments, that in face of these facts not only the differential law but the law of causality itself—hitherto the ultimate basic postulate of all natural science—fails."

Motion and flow could no longer be explained in terms of Newtonian, mechanical cause and effect. General relativity relied on a fourth dimension, variable time, and attraction based on a spacetime curvature we couldn't see, but where the greater its flux, the greater its curvature. While Newton's gravity grew with mass, Einstein's gravity grew with *the flow of spacetime*.

Einstein, like Newton before him, made enormous steps forward in providing the world with an understanding of how to measure our universe. But he, too, agonized over the lack of a first cause. If gravity was caused by the flow of spacetime, what caused this flow? If current laws explained that gravity attracts, what was keeping the stars in our galaxies and electrons in our atoms in perpetual motion?

Einstein believed that an 'aether' must exist that had a force that balanced the force of gravity. He added this aether into his equations as a 'cosmological constant' in 1917, which was an all-pervading constant in the universe that worked as cosmic 'anti-gravity', and as such held the universe in perpetual flow.

When astronomer Edwin Hubble proved that the universe was expanding according to Einstein's equations, without the need for the cosmological constant, Einstein famously declared this to be the "greatest blunder" of his life.

Aether was swept into the recesses of science, and modern science became focused entirely on studying what could be measured, intent on separating itself from 'ethereal' and 'intangible' concepts that muddied the waters. Our education system and modern economy moved in the same direction, preferring Newtonian causality (where every 'cause' has an 'effect') to explain everything from the grades we get to the money we make.

Ironically, from scientific discoveries made in the last twelve months, it is looking like Einstein's "greatest blunder", and the concept of a cosmic aether has made a very large return to modern science.

Carl Jung Steps In

It was in the years between his two theories, between 1909 and 1913, that Einstein met psychoanalyst Carl Jung over a series of dinners in Zurich.

"Professor Einstein was my guest on several occasions at dinner... These were very early days when Einstein was developing his first theory of relativity, [and] it was he who first started me off thinking about a possible relativity of time as well as space, and their psychic conditionality. More than thirty years later, this stimulus led to my relation with the physicist Professor W. Pauli and to my thesis of psychic synchronicity."

- Carl Jung

These dinners led to a crossover between the disciplines of matter and mind. Einstein discussed a theoretical world where cause need not precede effect, leading Jung to a view of time, space and causality as three dimensions that rule the material world of traditional physics, hiding a further 'acausal' dimension, which he termed the 'collective unconscious'. Jung's ideas were a breakaway from his mentor's, Sigmund Freud, and while Freud had groomed Jung to be his understudy, the two soon split, leaving Jung alone and in angst over the nature of consciousness and personality. A breakthrough finally came, however, in 1920 when Jung met with German missionary and scholar, Richard Wilhelm.

By a stroke of luck, Jung was approached by Wilhelm on the scholar's return from China, where he had befriended Chinese Sage, Lao Nai-Hsuan. Lao had decided in his wisdom to make the ancient knowledge of China available to the Western world, and had worked with Wilhelm for seven years – starting in 1913 – to translate the I Ching into German. Lao died as soon as the translation was complete and Wilhelm returned to Germany looking for a publisher. After being inaccessible to the west for four millennia, in 1920 the I Ching finally found its way to the Western world and onto Carl Jung's lap.

The I Ching had a profound effect on Jung. It articulated the same flowing and interchangeable world of energy and matter that Einstein had described, and the same duality of a causal and acausal reality. He ended up writing the introduction to the book and helped to get the I Ching published. From the I Ching and his conversations with Wilhelm, Jung gained a new clarity into the nature of our consciousness and personalities:

"For the first time this profoundest work of the Orient was introduced to the West in a living and comprehensible fashion. What he told me, out of his wealth of knowledge of the Chinese mentality, clarified some of the most difficult problems that the European unconscious had posed for me." – Carl Jung

Then, with the revelations and distinctions he got from the I Ching, in 1921 Jung published 'Psychological Types', which introduced the world to the interplay of opposites and the four base frequencies.

Yung took the nature of opposites in the first four Chinese elements: wood/spring, fire/summer, earth/autumn and metal/winter, and translated them to the psychoanalytical polarities of: introvert and extrovert; intuitive and sensory; thinking and feeling; and judging and perceiving. These insights led to Jungian psychological typing, which subsequently gave birth to psychometric testing models such as Myers-Briggs and DISC profiling.

As Luck Would Have It

Jung then began to look for the connections between the idea of a conscious, temporary world and an unconscious, eternal world. Through his studies, he became one of the 20th Century's most avid scholars of alchemy. Using the symbolism he found within alchemy, Jung began to identify the connections between our conscious, 'causal' world (which has time and place) and our unconscious, 'acausal' world (which has no time and place). He turned his attention to the fifth element, in an attempt to understand the collective unconscious. In his biography, "Memories, Dreams, Reflections", Jung described dreaming and its acausal nature. In dreams, time merged, and dreams appeared to be full of alchemical symbolism.

Jung then coined the term 'synchronicity', inspired by the 'meaningful coincidences' on which the I Ching was based, Like dreams, Jung saw synchronicity as an emergence of the unconscious into the conscious world – a sign of the fourth dimension. 'Luck' was an acausal product of the unconscious. Jung used the term 'synchronicity' for the first time in 1930 at the memorial address for Richard Wilhelm in which he gave an explanation of the I Ching.

"Think of a flat carpet hovering one meter above the ocean. Think of an observer walking along the carpet and call this his conscious world. As the tips of the waves penetrate the carpet, they appear as distinct events. As a wave rolls along, it appears like a chain of events. So far, so good. But when two waves break at the same moment, he thinks it is a coincidence. This is an acausal event. One wave did not appear to cause the other. For the observer to comprehend that the waves were connected, he would have to comprehend an entire ocean that he cannot see."

This ocean is what Jung called the collective unconscious and the emerging waves of coincidence were the best indication of flow.

"These coincidences, which Jung termed synchronicity, are sure signs you are in the flow. Flow is a harmony of being that has been sought after through the centuries in the spiritual traditions of the world. In the East, it has been linked to the Tao, the underlying interconnectedness of the universe. In our lives, flow is obvious in those times when things happen effortlessly, everything falls into place, obstacles melt away, and our timing is perfect. In those times, we feel a deep sense of harmony and underlying order. We know we are in the right place, at the right time, doing exactly the right thing."

- Charlene Belitz & Meg Lundstrum, The Power of Flow

So how to access the collective unconscious? Jung saw the process of alchemy as the way. Unlike Newton's obsession with external alchemy, however, Jung's focus was internal alchemy. Richard Wilhelm, as well as translating the I Ching, translated "The Secret of the Golden Flower", which was a pivotal book in Taoist internal alchemy. Jung saw internal alchemy from a psychoanalytical perspective: internal alchemists aimed to achieve immortality by accessing a timeless state by flowing from the four base elements of causal consciousness to the fifth element of acausal, timeless unconscious.

From here, our history of flow diverges into three streams: our modern global economic system, modern mythology, and the state of modern science.

John Maynard Keynes Turns it On

As Jung was studying alchemy in Zurich, another member of the Cambridge Apostles was applying the principles of flow to the monetary system. John Maynard Keynes followed in the footsteps of James Maxwell as a member of Cambridge's secret society.

He became the self-appointed guardian of Newton's collected works in Cambridge, and while Newton had spent thirty years literally making money for the British economy in the seventeenth century, Keynes spent his lifetime advising governments on how to circulate that money in the twentieth century.

Keynes studied the flow of money and credit in economies, and became the founder of macro-economics, advising the government on how to increase the flow and supply of money to stimulate and manage the economy.

Keynes' theories on money flow led him to a primary role in influencing the British and American governments through the Great Depression. He was responsible in 1945, as Chairman of the World Bank Commission, for founding the International Monetary Fund, which oversees the entire global monetary system today, and the World Bank, charged with increasing economic growth in developing countries and reducing world poverty.

Before Keynes, there were no formalized global money markets, and government spending and taxation were at a fraction of their levels today. Now, we take it for granted that it is the government that can determine the health of our economies and takes responsibility for righting imbalances and inequities. There is a popular belief that in some way the government is responsible for our own wealth, and for the poverty that we, or others, experience.

Yet we operate within a history of fortune-making which is already five thousand years old, and a global monetary system which is only sixty years young.

May the Force Be with You

The history of flow has led us to our modern global economic system, and to a $20 billion Hollywood franchise. Jung's interest in internal alchemy led to a renewed interest in mythology during the 20th Century. American scholar, Joseph Campbell (1904 – 1987), spent his life studying eastern and western mythology, influenced heavily by Jung. His thread of common themes and archetypes that have resonated across different cultures throughout history became the subject of his most famous books, "The Hero with a Thousand Faces" and "The Masks of God."

In turn, during the 1970's, George Lucas took the enduring themes of Campbell's mythology to create the movie 'Star Wars'. The same themes of yin and yang, the interplay of opposites, following your path, the stages of the hero's journey and the 'quintessence' are all covered in the modern-day myth. In Star Wars, the mysterious energy field called 'the Force' is described by Jedi Master Obi-Wan Kenobi as "An energy field created by all living things. It surrounds us, penetrates us, and binds the galaxy together."

> *"My ally is the Force, and a powerful ally it is.*
> *Life creates it, makes it grow.*
> *Its energy surrounds us and binds us.*
> *Luminous beings are we."*
> \- Yoda

If Hollywood science fiction was not strange enough, science itself began to take some bizarre twists that were far stranger than fiction…

Wolfgang Pauli goes Quantum

Shortly after Richard Wilhelm died, Carl Jung met Wolfgang Pauli, who became his patient. Wolfgang Pauli taught at the Federal Institute of Technology in Zurich, Switzerland where Jung was a Professor of Psychology. By the time they met, Pauli was already a leading figure in the new science of quantum mechanics. He had discovered the exclusion principle, a quantum mechanical principle that underpins our understanding of chemistry and the fundamental properties of matter today.

Pauli's work led to a quantum understanding of attraction. Magnetic mass was shown to be a result of quantum mechanical spin and Pauli's exclusion principle. The principle, stated in its simplest form, was that "no two identical fermions may occupy the same quantum state simultaneously". (In quantum mechanics a fermion is any particle with anti-symmetric wave function – which includes all electrons, protons and neutrons, amongst others.)

By showing that the base materials in matter, which are wave functions, cannot occupy the same quantum state, Pauli laid the basis for understanding how matter can be 'solid' when it is simply made of oscillating energy. His work conceptualized how these different solid states make up our modern periodic table of 116 elements.

Pauli's deep thoughts led to disturbing and bizarre dreams, and he became one of Jung's best patients. Jung documented Pauli's dreams in his book "Psychology and Alchemy", which contains over 400 dreams. Between them, these two leading thinkers in psychology and science developed a link between our physical and psychical worlds. In 1932, Pauli had a dream of a "world-clock", which gave him a sensation of "sublime harmony". Jung documented the dream and compared this to the medieval concept of "*anima mundi*" or "world soul", which connects us all in one unity, or "*unus mundus*".

In 1934, Jung documented a dream that Pauli had in which a man who looked like Einstein said to him that quantum physics was but a one-dimensional part of a deeper reality. Pauli and Jung delved deeper into the nature of synchronicity, and how it related to the quantum world where Newtonian cause and effect no longer applied, and where determinism was replaced by probability.

In a letter Pauli sent to Jung in December 1950, he wrote: "A process of transmutation of an active centre, ultimately leading to a stable state, is accompanied by self-duplication ('multiplying') and expanding phenomena, associated with further transmutation that are brought about through an invisible reality."

Pauli struggled to reconcile this apparently unscientific notion of a world soul with his physics pedigree. In 1952 he wrote to Jung saying that the future challenge must include finding "that other, more comprehensive coniunctio" (union of opposites), that transcends the artificial separation of psyche and matter.

Pauli went on to receive the Nobel Prize in Physics for his "decisive contribution through his discovery of a new law of nature, the exclusion principle or Pauli principle." He was nominated by Einstein.

David Bohm Adds a New Dimension

As the first Star Wars film hit the cinemas, the history of flow took a further step forward in modern science. While quantum mechanics gave an explanation as to how energy waves created solid objects, like Newtonian physics and relativity it still did not explain why gravity existed. Pauli and Einstein believed quantum science was an incomplete and first step towards a deeper understanding of our universe. A quantum theory of gravity was still out of reach, and the sciences of quantum physics and general relativity contradicted each other.

David Bohm (1917-1992), a quantum physicist who worked with Einstein at Princeton University, attempted to create a model that would reconcile quantum physics with general relativity. He came up with the terms "implicate order" and "explicate order" in 1980. He theorized that what we see around us in our material world is an "unfolding", "explicate" order, which derives from an "enfolding", "implicate" order, in which space and time are no longer the dominant factors. Through this theory, in a nutshell, Bohm believed that flow was not the result of our material world, but our material world was the result of some unseen flow.

"The new form of insight can perhaps best be called Undivided Wholeness in Flowing Movement. This view implies that flow is, in some sense, prior to that of the 'things' that can be seen to form and dissolve in this flow".
- David Bohm, 1980

Quantum mechanics was a necessary tool to understand why electrons continue to flow and orbit in atoms when Newton's laws would suggest they should collapse in to the middle. Bohm, however, saw it as a mistake to see this flow as isolated. He gave the example of a vortex of water in a stream. The water constantly spinning in the vortex could only be properly understood by seeing that the vortex (explicate order) was the result of the stream (implicate order).

In the case of the spinning electrons, we could see the explicate order, but we cannot see the implicate order that created it. He saw this theory as a way to reconcile quantum mechanics and relativity, saying "…in relativity, movement is continuous, causally determinate and well defined, while in quantum mechanics it is discontinuous, not causally determinate and not well-defined. Each theory is committed to its own notions of essentially static and fragmentary modes of existence (relativity to that of separate events connectible by signals, and quantum mechanics to a well-defined quantum state). One thus sees that a new kind of theory is needed which drops these basic commitments and at most recovers some essential features of the older theories as abstract forms derived from a deeper reality in which what prevails is unbroken wholeness."

Bohm was, effectively, suggesting a world we could not see – a hidden dimension that was affecting our four dimensions of space and time. Bohm went on to connect his theories on the workings of the universe with the workings of our brains. Bohm saw the universe as being essentially a hologram, and proposed that our brains operate in a similar way. His work laid the foundation in neuro-psychology for the 'holonomic brain theory', in which our conscious thoughts are a holographic projection of our unconscious.

Although Einstein was a fan of Bohm's, and wanted him as his assistant at Princeton, the American government was not. During the McCarthy "witch-hunts" in 1950, Bohm was brought up in front of the Un-American Activities Committee and arrested, and although he was later acquitted of being a communist, Princeton University had already suspended him and he moved to Brazil.

Bohm became one of a number of scientists who were opening the door to a strange universe of hidden, multiple dimensions. As particle accelerators became more sophisticated, leading to the discovery of an ever-increasing range of sub-atomic particles, the idea of multiple dimensions grew in vogue within the scientific community. In the 1990's, string theory became fashionable as an attempt to describe the many sub-atomic particles being found in high-energy collisions of atoms. String theory explained that the particles we encounter in our material world are simply multi-dimensional 'strings' that vibrate at different frequencies in various other dimensions. As a string changes frequency, the particle we encounter magically changes. Change frequency, and you change form.

By the late 1990's, it was becoming accepted from the data appearing from increasingly accurate measurement at a quantum scale and at a cosmic scale, that we live in a very strange universe indeed. Cause and effect were appearing to be more the exception than the rule. In string theory and modern cosmology, there appeared to be more that we did not understand than we did understand.

To spiritual gurus, yogis and mystics, working on age-old models based on spiritual wisdom, the universe appeared to make perfect sense. Yet for western scientists focusing strictly on what could be measured, the universe was becoming curiouser and curiouser.

Aether Makes a Rather Large Reappearance

To make matters worse, the scientific measurement mindset of the 20th century spilled over into the industrial and corporate models of the west. The machine age made predictable and dispensable machines for living in, driving in and working in. The machine age made predictable and dispensable machines out of its citizens.

The mystery and magic of flow had no business in our education or in our economy. The idea of science and spirit separated. The idea of progress and purpose divided. The idea of making money and making a difference split in the 20th century. Even so, like a glowing ember, the fifth element was never discounted entirely by modern science – and in fact it now appears to be making a rather large reappearance.

In the 19th century, Maxwell believed that light, as an electromagnetic wave, was able to travel by moving through 'luminiferous aether'. This concept of aether as a transmission medium continued with Einstein, who said in 1920, "According to the general theory of relativity, space without aether is unthinkable; for in such space there not only would be no propagation of light, but also no possibility of existence for standards of space and time."

Einstein created the cosmological constant to take account of this state of affairs in his calculations. Yet scientists saw little reason for an aether as it did not seem to be needed for calculations in general relativity or quantum mechanics. As no one had ever seen it or measured it, aether was dropped from 20th century science as a redundant concept. Or so it seemed.

In the last five years, evidence has grown that the rate of expansion of the universe is actually increasing, in a way that could only be explained by the existence of some kind of "antigravity". This became known as 'dark energy'. Then, in March 2006, NASA's WMAP satellite made the disturbing discovery that only 4% of energy in the universe is visible. 22% is thought to be composed of 'dark matter' and the remaining 74% composed of 'dark energy'.

"When you teach undergraduates, and they say, 'Well, what is dark matter?' Well, nobody's really sure. 'What is dark energy?' We're even less sure. So you have to explain to a student, that 90 percent of the universe, 95 percent, is in two ingredients that nobody really understands."
- Richard Ellis, Caltech astronomer

What, exactly, this dark energy is remains a mystery to modern scientists, other than it is spread evenly throughout the universe and is accelerating the expansion of the universe. But the most prevalent theory today within the scientific community is that dark energy is, in fact, Einstein's cosmological constant. The element that Einstein believed was his "greatest blunder" is now thought to make up three-quarters of our universe. We can't see it, we can't touch it, we can't taste it, but we know it's there. Scientists today are calling this dark energy *quintessence* - the fifth element.

YOUR LIFE PURPOSE

"I know that this defies the law of gravity,
but you see, I never studied law."
- Bugs Bunny

Perhaps in our lifetime we will see a unifying theory that takes into account an understanding of both our conscious and our unconscious worlds. Perhaps the natural alchemical process understood by past generations will provide a link for connecting the science of what we can measure with the spirit of what we can sense. Perhaps we are already there, and today's Wealth Creators – such as the ones in this book – are our modern magicians.

The process by which your path and purpose lead to your flow and fortune, is not a step-by-step route, but an unfolding process. As David Bohm articulated, our fortune is an *enfolding purpose* and our path is an *unfolding process*. Your path will be full of mistakes and learning. But it will also be full of luck and magic. Fortune is about quality, not perfection. As Michael Eisner said, "Quality – and this is something I learned from George Lucas – does not mean perfection. The cost of perfection will drive you out of business. What you are striving for is magic, not perfection."

Your fortune is timeless. It is in your unconscious, so you cannot 'think' your way to it. It will open as you unfold, through the cycles of your life. Earl Nightingale, in his message "The Strangest Secret" in 1956, explained to the world that the key to success is "the progressive realization of a worthy cause". Play the game with awareness – that there is a purpose to your life, which is for you to realize your own worthy cause, and to leave your own legacy.

"Our real gift to life is an awareness of its purpose. When we are aware of life's purpose, the light of the soul shines in our life, and its secret hidden within the world comes alive. And the light that is within us is within everything; it is "at the centre of all things." When our light comes alive within us, it comes alive within all of creation. It reveals to creation its true purpose."
- Llewellyn Vaughan-Lee, Anima Mundi: Awakening the Soul of the World

CHAPTER FIFTEEN

TURNING ON

"The universe is full of magical things,
patiently waiting for our wits to grow sharper."
- Eden Phillpotts

MAKING MAGIC

Rather than believing that our fate and fortune are in the hands of others, how do we harness the principles of flow to realize our own fortune? Armed with these five alchemical elements, how are we equipped to make magic? What follows are some absolutely essential distinctions within the frequency of the five elements. When we understand and apply these distinctions, we soon experience an entirely different level of flow.

The Online Wealth Dynamics test measures our four base frequencies. The four base frequencies match the four base elements: dynamo is wood/spring; blaze is fire/summer; tempo is earth/autumn; and steel is metal/winter. The fifth element, spirit is water/transition.

We each have a predominant frequency, and it is the mix of our predominant frequencies that will determine our Wealth Profile.

Imagine now, that the Wealth Dynamics Square is simply the base of a pyramid. These four frequencies make up the four sides of the base, and the fifth element, water, is at the apex of the pyramid. It sits on a different dimension. Imagine now, that each learning cycle that we go through is a cycle that takes us through these four seasons, and ends at a different level of consciousness. Each learning, learnt well, takes us to another level of awareness in playing the game.

AN ANSWER TO EVERY QUESTION

There is an answer to every question, yet depending on which frequency is our strongest, we have a natural question we are more likely to ask. The cycle of five frequencies gives us a sequence of five questions that arise in every learning cycle.

Dynamo asks "What?" - Dynamo frequencies are tuned to the question "What?". At critical moments, they are most likely to ask "What should I do?". When brainstorming they will ask "What's a better way?", "What's a better product?", "What should I do next?". The question "What?" sparks innovation.

Blaze asks "Who?" – Blaze frequencies more naturally ask "Who?". At critical moments, they ask "Who do I need to call?", "Who can help me?", "Who knows the answer?". On 9/11, Rudy Giuliani didn't start by asking "What should I do?". He started by asking "Who do I need here now?". He got them together, and then the plan emerged.

Tempo asks "When?" – Tempo frequencies naturally ask "When?", which is why they are so good at timing: "When should I act?", "When should I sit tight?", "When is the right time?". Every trader makes the most money at those critical moments when they just 'know' the time is right, having stayed on the frequency for long enough.

Steel asks "How?" – Steel frequencies naturally ask "How?", which is why they are so good with systems. While the question can disable someone just getting started, as they get bogged down in the detail, it is the right question to ask once you know the what, who and when.

These four base elements take us through a cycle of four seasons, yet the learning only comes when you transcend the plane in which your journey took place, and then ask the question "Why?".

Spirit asks "Why?" – The fifth element, your entrepreneurial spirit, asks "Why?". "Why did that failure occur?", "Why did it work out that way?", "Why am I even doing this?". Asking "Why?" takes you to a higher level of consciousness, by injecting meaning into your journey.

The more cycles we pass through, the more times we complete, gain awareness, and then embark on the next cycle; the more we fail forward. As a result, the learning cycle is not a two-dimensional rotation, but a three-dimensional spiral taking us to ever-increasing levels of distinction in playing the game. As the Zen saying goes, "To know and not to do is not yet to know."

> *"The significant problems we have cannot be solved at the same*
> *level of thinking with which we created them."*
> - Albert Einstein

Knowing that each of these questions relate naturally to the frequency of each element allows us to do three things. It allows us to follow a five step question and answer process for every problem-solving process: what, who, when, how, why, with the last question taking place at a different level to the first four. It allows us to know what questions others of different frequencies answer most easily, so we don't waste time trying to get a Supporter to answer "How?", a Mechanic to answer "Who?" or a Creator to answer "When?". It also allows us to know what the company focus should be depending on the phase of growth cycle it is in.

ATTENTION TYPES

Even before we begin working with our teams, our frequencies give us away. In fact, the first few minutes when we meet someone new are the critical moments when understanding frequencies can be very useful. Your success in building rapport will come from noticing the frequency of others, and changing your frequency to their frequency: re-tuning from your radio station to their radio station.

> *"You can make more friends in two months by becoming*
> *interested in other people than you can in two years by*
> *trying to get other people interested in you."*
> - Dale Carnegie

A Neuro-Linguistic Programming system called VAK (Visual, Auditory, Kinesthetic) categorizes us by the senses we are most likely to use to form our learning and first impressions (sight, hearing, touch). As a general rule (with exceptions), the four base frequencies fit an extended attention and learning model based on your most natural form of mental processing:

Dynamo frequencies are more "Visual" – Dynamo frequency tunes in to "the big picture". As the highest frequency, Dynamo looks for the aerial view of a project or idea, where it can be summarized in a page, and most effectively if it comes with images! You get the attention of Dynamo by giving them a snapshot of your objectives. Dynamo learns effectively by "visualizing" the project or process.

Blaze frequencies are more "Auditory" – Blaze frequency needs to talk things through. Blaze makes talking a form of "active listening" where their impressions and decisions come through the conversation. Learning and decisions will come more slowly than in Dynamo, but they will come more collectively. For this reason Blaze frequency is more social than Dynamo or Steel.

Tempo frequencies are more "Kinesthetic" – While Blaze may be satisfied through hearing what they need to hear, Tempo frequency needs a better "feel" before forming a decision or making a clear impression of a person or an idea. Tempo will conduct market research where Dynamo will make an impulse decision. Tempo looks for a comfort level where it all "makes sense" before acting.

Steel frequencies are more "Analytical" – Steel frequency takes the longest to decide, as it needs all the data. Have you wondered why cars and computers come with such thick manuals? They are for the Steel profiles! Steel will analyze the details: the terms, conditions and small print before taking action.

Knowing the attention style of each frequency is useful for a number of reasons. It helps us to know how to get our message across in a way that they can receive effectively and in the manner that they enjoy the most. There is nothing worse than trying to force a Dynamo frequency through excessive small print, or putting a Steel frequency through excessive small talk.

It also helps us to know how to form our business presentations and structure our training in the way that will be most effective, by suiting the person we are presenting to or training. We have a wonderful exercise in one of our Wealth Dynamics workshops where we divide the room by frequencies, and then ask each team to decide if money was no object, what car would they drive and why. You would be surprised by the answers, and it explains why we have so many different types of car on the market!

We then ask each frequency if they had a day to learn how the engine of the car works, how they would choose to learn. Of course, the answers again vary from frequency to frequency, from seeing the big picture, to talking it through, to taking it apart, to reading the manual. The final part of the exercise is a decision-making challenge, where each team is given a simulated business crisis to resolve in a short period of time. Again, the solutions to the issue are entirely different for each frequency, as each looks at the issue from a different perspective. Not surprisingly, the most effective solution comes when the four different sides are brought together.

When we pay attention, learn and communicate with an awareness of the frequencies, our traction from moment to moment increases tremendously.

What about the Spirit Frequency? – The fifth element is a fifth avenue for input, which opens through the activity of the other four. As we will see in the final chapters, as you play the game, your awareness grows, and the process by which information flows and is processed through the fifth element is called "gratitude".

LEADERSHIP TYPES

There are many books out there explaining how to be a "good leader". The truth is, each frequency has a leadership style that comes naturally. If you try and adjust your style to something different, it will not only be uncomfortable, it will feel like hard work, and at critical moments you will snap back to your natural style.

Dynamo is Task-based – Dynamo leadership is based on driving forward the new idea or project, and knocking over the tasks to move ahead. People, analysis, timing, all take second place to action. As Richard Branson said, "I believe in benevolent dictatorship provided I am the dictator." If you want to get things moving, put a Dynamo leader in place. But once things are moving, move him on to the next project and appoint a new leader!

Blaze is People-based – Blaze leadership is based on motivating people to perform at their best. Not the most important thing if you do not yet have the value in the market, but once that's in place, collective communication and collaboration become key. In the words of Jack Welch, "In leadership you have to exaggerate every statement you make. You've got to repeat it a thousand times and exaggerate it."

Tempo is Activity-based – While Dynamo is about creation and Blaze is about collaboration, Tempo is about consultation. When Woodrow Wilson said, "The ear of the leader must ring with the voices of the people," he was talking about Tempo leadership. A Tempo leader will check themselves and their teams against their activity relative to the market. Don't expect a creative plan from a Tempo leader. Do expect what needs to be done to get done on time.

Steel is Data-based – While Tempo is about consultation, Steel is about calculation. Whereas a Blaze leader can assess his sales team by being out on the field with them, the Steel leader will know just by looking at the numbers. When entrepreneurs such as Getty and Rockefeller are criticized for their aloof style, it is that style which enables them to lead from the back, rather than from the front or side.

Having great leadership around you does not come from trying to mould leaders into a particular style. It is about understanding what cycle your businesses are in, what leadership is needed, and then putting in place the leader whose frequency resonates most effectively. Leaders change markets and markets change leaders based on this cycle of resonance.

What about the Spirit frequency? – The fifth element also has a leadership style. While the four base frequencies are based on creation, collaboration, consultation and calculation, the fifth frequency is based on contribution. The fifth element, water, is the key to flow. Flow is based on not just effective receiving but more importantly on effective giving. Knowing "why" we are doing what we are doing – to give it back – leads us inevitably to our fortune.

EFFECTIVE OPERATING ENVIRONMENTS

As we embark on our journeys, we are often disabled by the conditions around us – or we create conditions that disable others. We each have a different operating environment which suits our frequency best, and if we lose that environment, we soon choose to move on. When we take away the environment that our team members, family members or friends need, we can cause unexpected – yet inevitable – results.

American psychologist, Abraham Maslow, in 1943 described five levels of need, which became known as Maslow's Hierarchy of Needs. At a base level were biological and physiological needs, such as air, food, drink and shelter. Then safety needs, such as security, law and order. The third level was love needs, such as family and relationships. Fourth was esteem needs, such as independence and achievement, and fifth was self-actualization needs, such as personal growth and realizing potential.

American motivational speaker, Anthony Robbins, takes this hierarchy and explains that many emotional conflicts occur because of the opposing nature of our emotional needs. In his 'Six Human Needs', he compares certainty to variety: we need certainty but the more certainty we have, the less variety we have. We want variety, but the more variety we have, the less certain we become. He compares Maslow's third and fourth needs: connection and significance. We want connection, but the more connected we are, the less significant we become. We want significance, but the more significant we are, the less connected we become. He adds two needs to Maslow's fifth need: growth and contribution.

These emotional needs link to our five frequencies:

Dynamo needs Significance – Take away significance, esteem or independence from their operating environment and Mechanics, Creators and Stars will soon leave if they can. Provide an environment that gives them the freedom to grow, and they will work at their best. A Dynamo's greatest stress comes from a loss of independence and a loss of any prospect to individually shine.

Tempo needs Connection – Tempo frequency does not need this same independence. However, take away their connection or comfort and they will soon react. While Dynamo needs to fly, Tempo needs to be grounded. When a project is moving too fast, Tempo will want to slow it down. If connections with customers or staff become strained, a Deal Maker, Trader or Accumulator will want to re-connect before progressing further.

Steel needs Certainty – Steel frequency strengthens with certainty. Invite Steel to a wild party, and they will be the first to take a rain check. Take away certainty, and discomfort sets in fast. Performance comes from predictability. Force an Accumulator, Lord or Mechanic to perform without preparation in front of something as unpredictable as people, and you will experience how cold winter can be!

Blaze needs Variety – Blaze frequency, on the other hand, burns brightly out and about. Variety is about people and places. Put Blaze in a back office with a spreadsheet, and the flame soon goes out. Lock a Star, Supporter or Deal Maker in a fixed plan with no variety, and don't expect them to shine. Get them out and about, however, and watch them ignite.

Understanding the need for an effective environment in which to operate gives us an insight into why those around us react to change. Change their environment, and it changes their performance and comfort. It also gives us the chance to communicate more effectively. I am a Creator profile and Renate is an Accumulator profile. In the past, when I outlined a new plan, if it sounded like it meant less connection and certainty for her, she would react negatively to it. I, on the other hand, would see her reaction negatively, as a sign that she didn't want me to have any independence or significance.

Now, if I'm thinking of any new plan that turns me on, I also question how it can also lead to more connection and certainty, so it will turn her on too. When she thinks of a new plan, she does the same. As for our children, when Kathleen, our ten year old daughter, recently took her profile and found out she was a Star, the entire opposite of her mother, she said "Oh, well that explains a lot."

Spirit needs Growth and Contribution – The fifth element flows on growth and contribution. As our water element grows, our need for each new learning cycle to provide growth and contribution grows as well. The more water, the better the garden grows. This is, however, a choice. Some of us have chosen to ignore this process of growth and contribution. Some of us go from day to day without asking 'Why?'. We do not grow, we do not contribute, and flow eludes us, as does our fortune – our wealth, our luck, and our legacy.

FIVE ASPECTS OF VISION

We are each made up of a percentage of each frequency, and the Wealth Dynamics profile identifies how much of each base frequency we have. Recently, one of our Life Members asked, "I can see what percentage of the first four frequencies I have, but what about my percentage of water?"

Of course, over 60% of our body is water. Water is the one element essential for all life. Water is all around us, but spiritually we still choose our own percent of the fifth element. 70% of the earth's surface is covered by water, yet you might still find yourself in a desert. Water is seen within all the world's major religions as the great purifier. Water clears our vision. The higher our fifth element, the more clearly we can see.

Each frequency provides a different aspect of vision, and understanding these five aspects allows us to see why we often end up with different points of view, depending on our frequency.

Dynamo provides Perspective – Perspective is related to depth of vision. Perspective gives a deeper view of what is possible. Perspective focuses light and sparks the flame, yet this focus can miss the elements on the periphery. Dynamos are great at providing perspective, but often at the expense of the peripheral issues.

Tempo provides Perception – Perception is related to breadth of vision. Peripheral vision gives a wider view of what is there. Perception includes more distinction on what already exists, grounding experience in place and time, yet can miss what might be. Tempos see the wood for the trees, but often miss the bigger picture.

Steel provides Clarity – Clarity is related to the detail of vision. Clarity can see in black and white, and can pick up detail that others will miss. Clarity can clearly distinguish between the different elements of a situation, yet can miss the fun in the moment. Steels see every detail, but often at the expense of the people involved.

Blaze provides Color – Color is related to drama of vision. Color can make our vision come alive with variety and vibrancy. Color allows us to see the rainbows in light, and gives us a chance to dance, yet with color we lose clarity, and can easily miss the detail. Blazes see the excitement, but often miss the detail.

Spirit provides Insight – The fifth element offers the fifth aspect of vision, insight. Insight transcends our two eyes, and is seen through what different cultures have termed the 'third eye'. Insight relates our outer world to our inner knowledge, or in Jungian terms, our 'conscious' to our 'unconscious'.

Perspective gives us vision through time, and perception gives us vision in time. Clarity gives us detail in our vision, and color gives us drama in our vision. Insight links our seeing to a higher level of knowing. All five form our vision, and by knowing which frequency to turn to see more clearly, we can choose the right teams, and choose the right journeys, to cycle to higher and higher insight.

When we understand how we and the people around us fit into the four base frequencies, and how all of us experience flow through the five alchemical frequencies, we begin to equip ourselves for the journey ahead. Knowing that every learning cycle, relationship cycle, team cycle, business cycle and industry cycle passes through each of the five frequencies, and knowing that we have a natural strength in only one of the frequencies, brings knew meaning to the proverb, "No man is an island".

When we bring together the right team, we build the power of great vision. Through vision, we can turn our thoughts to action.

With great vision, we can turn great thoughts to great action. We can turn dreams to reality.

Making magic is a team sport.

CHAPTER SIXTEEN

TUNING IN

*"Carl Jung said our conscious minds use only
five percent of our brain power for daily functioning.
If we can learn to tap into that unconscious,
subconscious, and dormant ninety-five
percent, the results can be amazing."*
- Donald Trump

IT'S ALL IN YOUR HEAD

How do we tune in to the rhythms around us? How do we synchronize our frequency with the changing frequencies in time?

While the five elements have been around since the beginning of time, it has only been in the last twenty years that modern scanners and experimentation have taken neuroscience to a level where we can now know with more certainty what cognitive functions are taking place in which parts of the brain.

The four sides of the Wealth Dynamics Square match the 'four sides' of the brain: our frontal lobes (located on the front and top of the brain) are the centre of our creative thinking and intuition; our parietal and occipital lobes (located at the centre and back) are the centre of our sensory function; our left hemisphere is responsible for analysis, with one input at a time; and our right hemisphere is responsible for our relationships, with multiple inputs at a time.

*"The brain is simply a collection of neurons and other cells,
gathered together in one place to simplify the wiring."*
- Helen Phillips, New Scientist

If our brains are all so similar in size, and if wealth appears to have little to do with intelligence or talent (with fortune eluding many of the most intelligent and talented amongst us), what is the process by which our brain turns success into a habit?

All of our actions are based on either a conscious action, based on mental calculation, or unconscious action, based on reflex. Breathing is a reflex action, whereas intellectual argument is a calculated action. Yet when we see a great athlete in action, it is often a reflex action at a critical moment that wins the game.

> *"In the same way that I tend to make up my mind*
> *about people within thirty seconds of meeting them,*
> *I also make up my mind about a business proposal*
> *within thirty seconds and whether it excites me."*
> - Richard Branson

In 1997, researchers at John Hopkins and the University of Maryland using a PET scanner found that we all learn new skills through our outer cortex, but then in repetition these physical skills are stored and accessed through the inner brain, within the cerebellum.

Conscious thought operates on the outer layer of the brain. We are masters of pattern recognition and we experience the world by comparing our experiences to the patterns formed by our past history. This is where we conduct our conscious thought. Yet within the centre of our brains, we conduct our unconscious thought.

It was only in October 2005 that a study at MIT found the location where our habits are stored: the basal ganglia, located next to the cerebellum in the inner brain. They found through a series of experiments that at critical moments when a familiar situation was encountered, a lost habit could be automatically re-activated from within our unconscious.

Dr Ann Graybiel, Professor of Neuroscience at MIT's Department of Brain and Cognitive Sciences, said: "It is as though somehow, the brain retains a memory of the habit context, and this pattern can be triggered if the right habit cues come back. This situation is familiar to anyone who is trying to lose weight or to control a well-engrained habit. Just the sight of a piece of chocolate cake can reset all those good intentions."

Our actions are fired much faster by the more primitive, unconscious inner brain, responsible for our automatic actions, than by the outer, conscious brain, responsible for pattern recognition or memory. But to 'program' our habits at the centre, we need to first create patterns through our experience. To know and not to do is not yet to know.

We learn to drive a car consciously by using our cerebral cortex, until it becomes an unconscious process accessed through the cerebellum and basal ganglia. A footballer learns through practice but scores in the game through instinct and habit. We gain our greatest learning through conscious thought, but at our critical moments we achieve our greatest actions through our unconscious thought.

> *"We are what we repeatedly do;*
> *excellence, then, is not an act but a habit."*
> - Aristotle

Tuning in is a process of conscious learning, leading to unconscious habit. The more we play the same game, the better we get at that game. Where do we experience flow? Is it a pattern or a habit? Is it conscious or unconscious? Hidden in the very centre of our brains, (above the cerebellum and the basal ganglia) lies the pineal gland - about the size of a pea. The pineal gland, which controls our melatonin levels, looks after our sense of rhythm with nature, synchronizing our internal biorhythms with nature's cycles.

This tiny pea in the unconscious, automatic part of our brain has been recognized for thousands of years as the doorway to our flow.

Oddly enough, despite being wrapped away in the unconscious centre of our brain it is light sensitive. In Taoism, Hinduism and Buddhism, since long before the medical function of the pineal gland was known, it has been referred to as the "third eye". Indian tradition links the *ajna chakra* (sixth chakra) to the pineal gland. *Ajna* translates in Sanskrit to "command". Whereas the base *chakras* each relate to a different element, the sixth *chakra* relates to time, and insight through 'higher knowing'.

The Ancient Greeks believed the pineal gland was our connection to higher thought; Descartes called it "the seat of the soul." The "third eye" became a sign of divinity, or "heavenly eye" in China, the "eye of Shiva" in India, the "eye of Ra" in Egypt (the Sun God - the sun symbolizing gold in alchemy). Combined with the pyramid, a symbol of the trinity and the divine, it became the "all-seeing eye" which we now find on the back of every American dollar bill.

IT'S ABOUT TIME

How do we know when we are in the flow? On the one hand, flow is our path of least resistance. At a deeper level, flow is a well-known state that people who become totally immersed in an activity they have mastered, whether a sport or their passion, can find themselves in. When we are in our life flow, we can access this flow state more easily. When we are in it, we change the way we experience time.

The conscious brain experiences time, while the unconscious brain appears to take little notice of it. Jung observed that dreams occur outside of time, with no past, present or future. When we operate in our unconscious, time appears to disappear.

When we are in our flow, we experience time quite differently. On the one hand, time seems to fly, as we operate largely from our unconscious. Yet we can also slow time down almost at will, as our conscious mind is freed up to live entirely in the moment. When we are in our flow, quite amazingly, it feels like we can control time.

"Wealth is controlled time."
- Buckminster Fuller

We have all had an experience when "time flies". This is when we are doing something we love, our unconscious mind is operating and our conscious mind is at rest. We have also all had the experience when we can "slow time down" – especially at critical moments when you are entirely in the moment, and are able to recount every step of the instant. What exactly is it that makes time appear so relative?

Deepak Chopra, in his book "Synchrodestiny", recounts: "The physical world is made up of nothing but information contained in energy vibrating at different frequencies. The reason we don't see the world as a huge web of energy is that it is vibrating far too fast. There is an analogy that illustrates this point. Scientists know that it takes a snail about three seconds to register light. So imagine that a snail was watching me, and that I left the room, robbed a bank, and came back in three seconds. As far as the snail was concerned, I never left the room. I could take her to court and she would provide the perfect alibi. For the snail, the time that I was gone from the room would fall into one of those gaps between the frames of flickering existence. Her sense of continuity would simply not register the gap.

"So the sensory experience of all living beings is a purely artificial perceptual construct created in the imagination. There is a Zen story in which two monks are looking at a flag that is waving in the wind. The first one says, "The flag is waving". The second one says, "No, the wind is moving." Their teacher comes over and they pose him the question, "Who's right? I say the flag is moving. He says the wind is moving." The teacher says, "You are both wrong. Only consciousness is moving." As consciousness moves, it imagines the world into existence."

Time is a phenomenon of the conscious. Flow is a phenomenon of the unconscious. When we are in the flow, we have plenty of space to slow time down. In the words of Ayrton Senna, one of Formula One's most successful motor racers: "When I am competing against the watch and against other competitors, the feeling of expectation, of getting it done and doing the best and being the best, gives me a kind of power that, some moments when I am driving, actually detaches me completely from anything else as I am doing it. I can give a true example of this - Monte Carlo 1988, the last qualifying session. I was already on pole and I was going faster and faster. One lap after the other, quicker and quicker and quicker. I was at one stage just on pole, then by half a second and then one second and I kept going. Suddenly I was nearly two seconds faster than anybody else, including my teammate with the same car. And I suddenly realized I was no longer driving the car consciously.

"I was kind of driving by instinct, only I was in a different dimension. It was like I was in a tunnel. I was just going and going, more and more. I was way over the limit but still able to find more. Then suddenly something just kicked me. I kind of woke up and realized that I was in a different atmosphere than you normally are. My immediate reaction was to back off, slow down. I drove back to the pits and I didn't want to go out any more that day. It frightened me because I realized I was well beyond my conscious understanding."

> ### *"Time is an illusion. Lunchtime doubly so."*
> - Douglas Adams

Fritjof Capra, in his book "The Tao of Physics" explains: "To get the right feeling for the relativistic world of particles, we must *'forget the lapse of time'*, as Chuang Tzu says, and this is why the space-time diagrams of field theory can be a useful analogy to the space-time experience of the Eastern mystic."

Capra continues, "Although the physicists use their mathematical formulation and their diagrams to picture interactions 'en bloc' in four-dimensional space-time, they say that in the actual world each observer can only experience the phenomena in a succession of space-time sections, that is, in a temporal sequence.

"The mystics, on the other hand, maintain that they can actually experience the full span of space-time where time does not flow any longer. Thus the Zen Master Dogen: *"It is believed by most that time passes; in actual fact, it stays where it is. This idea of time passing may be called time, but it is an incorrect idea, for since one sees it only as passing, one cannot understand that it stays just where it is."*

"Many of the Eastern teachers emphasize that thought must take place in time, but that vision can transcend it. "Vision", says (Lama) Govinda, "is bound up with a space of a higher dimension, and therefore timeless." The space-time of relativistic physics is a similar timeless space of a higher dimension. All events in it are interconnected, but the connections are not causal. In the words of Swami Vivekananda: "Time, space and causation are like the glass through which the Absolute is seen... in the Absolute there is neither space, time or causation."

Professional archer, Tim Stickland tried to describe the process by saying, "Your conscious mind always wants to help you, but usually it messes you up. But you can't just set it aside. You've got to get it involved. The thing you have to do is anchor it in technique. Then your unconscious mind, working with your motor memory, will take over the shooting for you." Sports psychologist, Dr Costas Karageorghis, adds, "Flow state is an optimal psychological experience. It's when you're functioning on auto-pilot when everything clicks into place and goes right."

Bill Russell, one of American basketball's most prolific players, said in his biography, "At that special level all sorts of odd things happened.... It was almost as if we were playing in slow motion. During those spells I could almost sense how the next play would develop and where the next shot would be taken."

This may all sound quite fuzzy, so it is timely that we return to a quote by Albert Einstein, which he used to explain relative time: "Put your hand on a hot stove for a minute, and it seems like an hour. Sit with pretty girl for an hour, and it seems like a minute."

When you are outside of your flow, time passes slowly and it is all-too-easy to miss your critical moments. When you are in the flow, time passes quickly, yet appears to stand still. You have the space to notice the critical moments and to slow down time when they occur.

"You have the sight now Neo.
You are looking at the world without time."
- The Oracle, in the film "The Matrix"

RIDING THE WAVES

Wealth Dynamics is not a static model based on a static balance. It is an unfolding model based on a dynamic balance. As we begin to create value, providing leverage to others, and as they create value, providing leverage to us, we follow a cycle. But we must be mindful that this cycle relates to greater cycles in our relationships, our businesses, our industries, our countries and cycles on a global scale. Harnessing these greater flows give us far greater leverage, as a sailor harnesses the winds and a surfer harnesses the waves.

The flow of nature is not a constant stream, but an ebb and a flow, where our actions need to change as we pass through each cycle. As we each have a dominant frequency and profile, this is not a journey we can undertake alone. Success comes from moving ourselves and our team into the right place at the right time, so that each of us can stay in our own flow as the seasons unfold.

Some of us are terrible farmers, relaxing when the sales are coming in easily and then panicking and pushing the sales team when sales dry up, even though we have heard the sayings, "Make hay while the sun shines", and "Don't plant your seeds in the winter".

Understanding that there are specific activities we need to be focused on at every stage of the cycle, understanding that your ebb is someone else's flow, and that when your industry or country ebbs, another industry or country is flowing, are keys to sustained wealth.

> *"When someday I die, please tell those whom I know*
> *that I ebbed with the flow."*
> - Mihaly Csikszentmihalyi

TEAM CYCLES

Leadership of any business needs to evolve as the business evolves. As Henry Ford said, "Asking 'Who ought to be boss?' is like asking 'Who ought to be the tenor in the quartet?' Obviously the man who can sing tenor."

As the season of your business changes, ensure the right profile is leading the change. The leaders of the most successful new start-ups are always Creators and Stars with dynamo frequency. The leaders of companies that are acquiring market share and market presence in a consolidating industry are always Supporters and Deal Makers with blaze frequency. The leaders of the most successful companies who have already begun to dominate their niche are always Traders and Accumulators, and the leaders of companies consolidating mature markets are always Lords and Mechanics.

How do you know what season your business is in? Simply by seeing what season you have just passed through. If you have a great product that has proven itself in the market, you are out of spring and into summer, focusing on building your market. If you have many new customers and sales are coming easily, you are out of spring and into autumn, focusing on servicing your customers well. If your customers are happy and your staff settled, you are out of autumn and into winter, focusing on building the right systems for the next spring.

The biggest error that entrepreneurs make is when they hold on to their winning formula for too long, by which time the seasons have changed and their winning formula has become a losing formula. Another error is when they put the wrong people into the wrong position, basing the choice more on their qualifications and knowledge than their natural passions and talents.

Your choice of who should be where within your teams is as important as who should be leading your enterprise or projects.

> *"Talent wins games,*
> *but teamwork and intelligence wins championships."*
> - Michael Jordan

Your flow comes from following your natural path. Your team momentum comes from each team member following their natural path. Each frequency and each profile has a different role within the team where they can be most effective. Often the best team selection is not the person who can be most effective, but the person who enables the existing team to become more effective.

Creators – Creators are the best initiators, and although they can be quick to create chaos, they can also be surprisingly innovative at finding ways out of chaos. Always put them in charge of new projects, but move them on to the next creation once their job is done.

Stars – Stars are the best promoters, but need to lead from the front. Give them the chance to shine, and give them the space to deliver results without tying them down. Give them the systems and support to enable them to focus on building new business.

Supporters – Supporters are the best leaders, but don't expect them to come up with the plan themselves. Build a plan and set the goals with a Supporter, and then let them lead the team towards the plan. Let them set their own management style, and their own agenda.

Deal Makers – Deal Makers are the best peacemakers, and will leave everyone feeling good. Don't expect them to go out cold calling, as they thrive on building the relationships they have. Work with Deal Makers to nurture the customer and partner relationships you have.

Traders – Traders are your best negotiators. They will always get you the best price, in both what you buy and what you sell. They want to be given the parameters in which to work. Traders will have their ear to the ground in your market and your team.

Accumulators – Accumulators are your best ambassadors. They are reliable, get things done on time, and are not prone to making rash decisions. Accumulators make the best project managers, when a specific task needs to be delivered reliably.

Lords – Lords are your best analysts. Give them the space to study the detail, and to deliver the data. Don't ask them to go out and network, as they are strongest when focused behind the scenes.

Mechanics – Mechanics are your best completers. They will wrap up the process and find smart ways to do it better next time. Don't ask a mechanic to start from scratch, but do give them an existing process or product to improve on.

When we place a team member out of their flow, we really only have ourselves to blame for the result. Of course, when others are not set up to operate in their flow, it is only a matter of time before you are pulled out of your flow as well.

INDUSTRY & COUNTRY CYCLES

"Never cut a tree down in the wintertime. Never make a negative decision in the low time. Wait. Be patient. The storm will pass. The spring will come."
- Robert Schuller

All industries run through cycles, and different industries run through different cycles in different countries. Richard Branson invested time in Australia as the budget airline industry was in the spring, while in Europe the airline industry was in winter. Rupert Murdoch moved to America where the media industry is in the autumn, while in Australia it is in the winter.

Our connectivity today, both electronically and physically, allows us to connect and move easily between countries and industries, depending on our passion. Take the property industry as an example. In 2006 we have seen different property entrepreneurs in our Asia Pacific network moving countries and activities to match their flow.

Dynamo – You will find property developers most active in Macau, Vietnam, Perth, and parts of China and Thailand where the property markets are in the spring.

Blaze – You will find real estate agents most active in Singapore, Malaysia and parts of Southeast Asia, where the property markets have moved from spring to summer.

Tempo – You will find property traders most active in pockets of China, where the market has moved from summer to autumn, and in parts of New Zealand and Australia, where the property markets are in the autumn and moving to winter.

Winter – You will find land lords making their money in New Zealand and Australia, and land buyers accumulating land in India and Indonesia, where the property markets are consolidating in winter.

Every Industry Contains Every Profile

Every industry has its mix of Wealth Profiles: the more competitive the industry, the more pronounced and distinct the predetermined roles in that industry's ecosystem.

In the early 1900's, the first moviemakers set up base in the hills of Hollywood in California – mainly because Thomas Edison (who owned the rights to all movie-making equipment) was based on the east coast. Hollywood was far enough away from Edison that each time Edison sent agents to California, the movie makers would hear about it before the agents arrived, and would hide their equipment and escape to Mexico.

During these early times, the pioneers in the industry, including Cecil DeMille and Charlie Chaplin, had to be involved in all areas including creating, producing, directing, acting and distributing.

Today, on the other hand, the Hollywood ecosystem works by everyone staying focused on their strengths: the Creators focus on script writing and directing; the Supporters manage the support crew and casting; the Mechanics manage post-production; the Deal Makers are Hollywood's agents; the Accumulators are the producers; the Traders are the distributors; the Lords own the cinemas and video stores; and the Stars are, well, the Stars.

In the entertainment business, Steven Spielberg (Creator), George Lucas (Creator), Arnold Schwarzenegger (Star), Nicole Kidman (Star), Michael Eisner (Supporter), Mike Ovitz (Deal Maker), David Geffen (Deal Maker) and Paul Allen (Accumulator) have made their fortune from the same industry, but in entirely different niches that have suited their profile. Every industry, from education to property, hospitality to wellness, has the same structure to varying degrees. Your profile will not determine your industry – your passion will. Your profile will, however, determine your role in that industry.

Every Industry Cycles Through Every Season

How do you know what season an industry is in? By seeing what season it has just moved through, and which Wealth Creators have just risen with the wave. In the short space of ten years the Internet has gone through a full cycle, with Wealth Creators of each profile rising in wealth as their time came.

In 1995, when the first Internet companies, like Netscape and Yahoo! launched, it was the Creators who were making the most money. By 1997, it was Stars and Supporters who began making the money; you could get rich just by joining the right team in Silicon Valley. By 1999, we began to hear of venture capital companies and merchant banks, some of whom were making more money deal making than the owners of the companies they were dealing in.

By 2000 and 2001, it was the Traders who made the most money, as the market went up, and came back down. Everyone else lost their money. By 2003, it was the Accumulators making the most money, picking up Internet assets at their low point.

Knowing what not to do is even more important than knowing what to do as industries cycle. Bill Gates was criticized during the deal making hey-days of the Internet in 1999 and 2000 for not spending Microsoft's cash on more mega-deals. He kept focused on investing his time on creating, and Microsoft is today stronger than ever.

Warren Buffett was criticized during the trader days of 2000 and 2001 when the market was at its hottest, for not taking more risks with Berkshire Hathaway. Buffett kept focused on accumulating, and today he is stronger than ever, accumulating Amazon.com bonds amongst other investments two years after the crash.

By 2005, it was the Lords and Mechanics making the most, as cash flow came from services, with companies like Google and Amazon picking up 'rent' for their online real estate. Does this mean the Internet is heading for its next spring? With mobile devices, from phones to iPods, connecting with the Internet, spring is already arriving.

There are ripples, on waves, on currents, on tides in our global economy. Whilst it appears the Internet is heading for a new spring, Deal Makers are profiting in China as the local Internet market is in the autumn. Supporters are profiting in India as business process outsourcing is in the summer.

Being able to connect with the right people in the right country in the right way opens an entire universe of possibility, where there is only one thing stopping you from reaching your potential. That one thing is, of course, yourself.

> *"We must be willing to get rid of the life we've planned,*
> *so as to have the life that is waiting for us."*
> - Joseph Campbell

YOUR LEGACY

"A man's true wealth is the good he does in this world."
- Mohammed

THIS IS OUR TIME

We live in a magical world of flow. Your own flow is your own personal path to connect to this magic. Following your flow connects you to the life you are meant to live. Flow comes from resonating within your own frequency and from being in a state of fortune. You are in a state of fortune when you are feeling 'fortunate'.

You are already fortunate, but you may not be living in that state. To notice your good fortune is to notice your good luck. This occurs when you say "thank you" for what you already have. For example, if you could afford to buy this book, you are already far ahead of the billion people on this planet who live on less than a dollar a day.

That's already lucky.

The state of good fortune is the expression of gratitude, and to live in good fortune is to live in gratitude. Living in gratitude is more than just saying "thank you". It is living in awareness of your good fortune every day. As John F Kennedy said, "As we express our gratitude, we must never forget that the highest appreciation is not to utter words, but to live by them." This is the core reason for your existence.

You are here to live an extraordinary life: to maximize your power to create and your power to contribute. You are here to find your flow, to follow your fortune, to leave your legacy. Like the magicians that have come before you, you are here to make magic.

"This is our moment. This is our time."
- Bono

YOUR CHOICE, YOUR CAUSE

"Everyone has a purpose in life.
Perhaps yours is watching television."
- David Letterman

The greatest beauty of legacy is that you choose your own. The truth is, we will all leave a legacy whether we like it or not. We live in a consumer society, where our consumption is at an all-time high, and those of us who do not leave a legacy deliberately will leave one accidentally – we will leave a legacy through our consumption. We will be remembered by future generations not by what we gave, but by what we took.

You have a choice as to whether you leave a legacy accidentally through your consumption, or deliberately through your creation and contribution. You *will* leave a legacy. The only question is whether it is accidental or deliberate.

Wealth is not how much money you have, but what you are left with when you lose your money. When we leave this planet, we lose our money. We can't take it with us. If, when we leave this world, the next generation is less able to look after themselves, that's not wealth. If, when we leave this planet, our environment is in a worse state than when we got here, that's not wealth. As the Cree Indian saying goes:

"Only when the last tree has died and
The last river has been poisoned and
The last fish has been caught,
Will we realize that
We cannot eat money."

Being *wealthy* comes from being *worthy*. Being worthy comes from the progressive realization of a worthy cause. Like fortune, *cause* is a word worth reflecting on. Throughout history, great minds from Aristotle to Newton to Einstein have studied causality. What is the cause that creates the effect? What is *your cause*? What is your cause that will create your effect?

Many of us see our 'cause' as something we can think about later in life. Yet it is your 'cause' that will create your 'effect'. Water will only flow when you provide an outlet. You define your power to receive by first defining your power to give. It is your fortune (your legacy) that will lead to your flow, which will in turn lead to your fortune (your luck and wealth), and so the cycle continues. It is this unfolding cycle that begins with the very thing you may have been putting off – your cause.

THE AGE OF EFFECTIVE GIVING

Throughout history, it has not always been necessary to give in order to get. While flow creates equity, lack of flow creates inequity, and in the past Wealth Creators could take advantage of equity or inequity to create their wealth. Much like the difference between a river and a bucket, wealth through flowing value is far more sustainable than wealth through hoarding value. The latter only lasts as long as the inequity remains.

In the past, entire cultures have risen and fallen as a result of creating inequity. Yet as flow has grown in our world, this has become increasingly difficult to do. With the global flow of our money markets, our media, our communication, the Internet, anyone who tries to get without giving finds themselves losing attraction fast.

This is the age of effective giving, where the more effectively we give, the more effectively we receive. In fact, great Wealth Creators understand the power of flow to not just create greater equity, but to reduce inequity on a global scale.

*"When we decided to turn our attention to philanthropy,
we were determined to invest in ways that would make the biggest
possible impact on reducing inequity."*
- Melinda Gates

The opportunities to reduce inequity increase with global flow. With great challenges lie great opportunity, and we have the opportunity in our lifetime to see an end to poverty, global access to health care and education, a reversal in the degeneration of the environment, and the possibility that every individual will have the chance to participate in the global flow of wealth around this planet.

Solutions to each of these challenges do not come from creating new resources, as the resources already exist. Solutions come from redirecting and increasing flow.

Who is responsible for this? Oddly enough, many believe it is the world's governments. While they play a part, we forget that the world's governments have less than a hundred years experience at driving economies.

For flow to grow, governments do have the power to change the plumbing, but it is today's Wealth Creators who can turn on the tap.

In the United Nations' Millennium Goals, set in 2002, 191 nations committed to halving global extreme poverty by 2015 and ending poverty entirely by 2025. Within two years, one country had already achieved their 2015 target of halving poverty from its 1990 level. That country was China.

In 1990 over 300 million of China's people lived on less than $1 a day. By 2002, that had dropped to under 150 million. Every month over one million Chinese have moved out of extreme poverty, month after month, year after year, for the last ten years.

It was not the government that created this change. It was the entrepreneurs. The GDP of China has grown by 1,000% from its 1980 level. The flow of wealth led to a rising tide of enterprise, which led to 150 million people rising out of extreme poverty.

We are in an unprecedented age of effective giving – where the richest people in the world are pledging their fortunes to make a difference. We are in an age where entrepreneurs, such as Brin and Page, can start a company from scratch, such as Google, and within six years can commit a billion dollars to charity. Understanding how the thirty eight Wealth Creators in this book are contributing back will give you greater vision of effective giving: it will grow your perspective, perception, clarity, color and insight into your own cause.

LEGACIES TO LEARN FROM

Long before he had amassed any wealth, when John D Rockefeller began working in 1855 at the age of 16, he spent a dime on a small book called Ledger A. This became his most precious book, holding the record of his giving. In his first year of work he donated 6% of his earnings to charity. Three years later he increased this to 10%. Over the next forty years, he continued to increase his flow in, and his flow out. He became the richest man in the world, and by 1922 he had spent $475 million on charitable causes.

Rockefeller's focus was on relieving the poverty created by industrialization and education. He founded the University of Chicago, the General Education Board and, in 1913, he set up the Rockefeller Foundation, to "promote the well-being of mankind throughout the world." It was the work of the Rockefeller Foundation in international field research into hookworm, malaria and yellow fever that set the first global standards in sanitation and disease prevention.

The foundation's agricultural development program led to the modern green revolution, increasing crop yields throughout developing countries, saving an estimated one billion lives over the last century.

Andrew Carnegie followed a similar path declaring, "I propose to take an income no greater than $50,000 per annum! Beyond this I need ever earn, make no effort to increase my fortune, but spend the surplus each year for benevolent purposes!" In 1889, Carnegie wrote "The Gospel of Wealth", explaining how it was the responsibility of those who knew how to create wealth to circulate it back through effective philanthropy. From 1901, Carnegie dedicated himself to giving his money away. He funded over 2,800 libraries, in partnership with local governments, throughout Britain and America, and when he died he had given the vast bulk of his fortune, $350 million, away.

While Carnegie's visible legacy is the increased access to knowledge through his education and library endowments, his legacy lives on in today's personal empowerment movement through his theories of wealth creation. Carnegie believed that financial success came down to a simple concept that any one could follow. In 1908 he commissioned a 25-year-old newspaper reporter, Napoleon Hill, to interview over 500 millionaires to document the keys to their success. Hill interviewed Thomas Edison, Henry Ford, Charles Schwab and John D Rockefeller, amongst many others, and published "The Law of Success" in 1928.

In 1937, Napoleon Hill wrote "Think and Grow Rich", with a theme in the book being the "Carnegie secret". This was the same secret that Earl Nightingale explained in his recording "The Strangest Secret" in 1956, which went on to become the first recorded voice message to sell a million copies. Coining the phrase, "Whatever the mind of man can conceive and believe, it can achieve," Hill alluded to the secret throughout his 1937 classic: this was the power of universal attraction created through the frequency of our thoughts.

While Rockefeller's fortune led to today's green revolution, and Carnegie's fortune led to today's personal education revolution, Jean Paul Getty's fortune went to the growth of our culture. The Getty Foundation funded the British Library and National Gallery, as well as museums and galleries throughout America, with over $300 million in the last century. The Rockefeller Foundation has $3.2 billion in funds under management today.

Henry Ford's legacy on the other hand went towards reducing poverty and promoting democracy. Ford's foundation has become a lasting legacy, growing each year as 5% is donated and 95% is invested. By the end of 2004 the Ford Foundation had a total investment portfolio of $10.5 billion, giving out around $520 million in grants for the year.

From Lasting Legacies to Living Legacies

As Wealth Creators play their game, it becomes clear that the value they bring to their giving is far more than the value of their money. In June 2006, Bill Gates announced his departure from operational activities at Microsoft – from July 2008 – to focus entirely on the Bill & Melinda Gates Foundation. The Foundation had already received $31 billion of Gates' fortune. In July 2006, Warren Buffett announced he would be donating $37 billion of his fortune to the same Foundation.

Like the Rockefeller Foundation before it, the Gates Foundation focuses on fighting global inequity through education and disease prevention, with over $6 billion already invested in global health grants, fighting diseases such as AIDS, malaria and tuberculosis. It has invested a further $1 billion in helping to redesign the American education system, and in providing Internet access in all American libraries. Today, the Foundation has 240 staff and gets over 3,000 proposals for funding every month.

Buffett's $37 billion gift – which could amount to far more as it is in the form of Berkshire Hathaway shares – began in July 2006 with the first annual donation worth $1.5 billion, to be used by the Foundation within the year. When being interviewed on how he and his late wife saw his fortune, Buffett said, "We were totally in sync with what to do with it – and that was to give it back to society". His approach, though, of handing his fortune over to the Gates Foundation, is as different to Gates' approach as an Accumulator strategy is to a Creator strategy.

"Compare what I'm doing with them to my situation with Berkshire, where I have talented and proven people in charge of our businesses. They do a much better job than I could in running their operations. What can be more logical, in whatever you want done, than finding someone better equipped than you are to do it? Who wouldn't select Tiger Woods to take his place in a high-stakes golf game?"
- Warren Buffett

We live in an unprecedented era, when the two wealthiest people in the world are joining forces and their fortunes while their companies continue to generate flow. This, however, is only the beginning of what the Wealth Creators in this book are doing in leaving their legacy.

Ted Turner Turns Heads

The link between effective giving and effective receiving is a link that has been understood by Wealth Creators throughout history. In 1980,

Li Ka Shing set up the Li Ka Shing Foundation, to promote "a culture of giving" in Hong Kong society. Since 1980, the Foundation has given HK$7.7 billion to education and heath care projects. Having come from a poor family and gone on to become the richest man in Hong Kong, he wanted to spread the word of the power of effective giving, yet he chose to spread this word in a quiet way, with many people in Asia still not aware of his largesse and philosophy.

Ted Turner, on the other hand, as the founder of CNN, chose the power of the media to magnify his message. In 1998, he announced a pledge of $1 billion to the United Nations to support world peace and progress. He made his announcement in a press conference to the world media. Since the announcement, the United Nations Foundation (UNF), set up as a result of his pledge, has attracted over $400 million in donations in addition to his ten-year, billion dollar pledge, and has already donated $900 million to UN projects in 115 countries.

Turner's landmark announcement has led to a new era of effective giving, where Wealth Creators have realized that their words can be worth far more than their money alone. The publicity that the UN has received since 1998 through the UNF and the UNF's Better World campaign initiative has led to renewed support from the public, stronger partnerships and better PR. Today the UN's Millennium Declaration is better known to the general public than any other UN initiative in history.

> *"I know what I'm having 'em put on my tombstone:*
> *'I have nothing more to say'"*
> - Ted Turner

Profiles Leverage their Profile

In 1998, while Turner was announcing his UN pledge, Oprah Winfrey was setting up Oprah's Angel Network. Saying to her audience, "You get from the world what you give to the world", her charity encouraged others to use their lives to help others in need. Over the years, Oprah has given an estimated $250 million to charity, leveraging on her celebrity status to raise far more through her audiences for causes including AIDS, poverty relief in Africa, education and child protection.

In 1991, long before she became a billionaire, Oprah testified before the US Senate Judiciary Committee on the need to set up a national database of convicted child abusers, as part of the National Child Protection Act. In December 1993, President Clinton signed the "Oprah Bill" into law.

While political leaders build their legacies from within public office, Wealth Creators such as Arnold Schwarzenegger and George Soros, like Oprah, are creating their legacies alongside the policy makers. Long before becoming the Governor of California, in 1979 Schwarzenegger was part of the coaching team for the Special Olympics. The first Special Olympics for disabled sportspeople was set up by Schwarzenegger's mother-in-law, Eunice Kennedy Schriver, in 1968. Since his first involvement, Schwarzenegger has become a familiar face supporting the Special Olympics, which now has programs in 150 countries.

In America, Schwarzenegger's first political appointment was on the President's Council on Physical Fitness and Sports, from 1990 to 1993. During that time, he co-founded the After-School All-Stars, which gives school children after-school sports, life skills and academic support. Today Schwarzenegger is honorary chair of the program, which has been supported by the likes of Tiger Woods, Muhammed Ali, Andre Agassi and Shaquille O'Neal. While he is better known for his films, in the realm of making sports and fitness more accessible, Schwarzenegger has been one of the most influential figures in America over the last fifteen years.

Within an entirely different domain, long before he had built his fortune, George Soros was funding the cause of democracy. In 1979 he funded black students to Cape Town University in apartheid South Africa. In the 1980's he funded Eastern European dissidents in Poland and Czechoslovakia. By 1984, Soros had set up the Soros Foundation in Hungary, and today the Foundation funds institutions in 50 countries that promote open societies, with $400 million spent annually on education, public health and civil society development.

Soros has invested an estimated $4 billion of his fortune in his philanthropic work, and all of his time. In 1993, Soros launched the Open Society Institute, to promote open societies by working alongside governments around the world. Soon afterwards, Soros handed over the day-to-day operations of his Quantum Fund, and today travels the world as Chairman of the Open Society Institute, influencing the governments and institutions around the world to support greater democracy and tolerance.

Anita Roddick, founder of the Body Shop, worked for the United Nations before launching her natural cosmetics chain in 1976. The Body Shop became synonymous with environmental and social activism. Over time, Roddick's campaigning on environmental and social issues have departed from the work of the Body Shop. Like Soros, she has dedicated herself completely to her cause, saying, "The most exciting part of my life is now – I believe the older you get, the more radical you become. There's a Dorothy Sayers quote I love, 'A woman in advancing old age is unstoppable by any earthly force.'"

Are You Keeping Good Company?

While Wealth Creators such as Bill Gates, George Soros and Dame Anita Roddick have followed in the path of Carnegie and Rockefeller, by dedicating the second part of their lives entirely to giving back, other Wealth Creators are using their companies as the vehicles to create flow and contribute flow.

Ray Kroc set up his first Ronald McDonald House in 1974, 'homes' linked to hospitals for families to stay in while their children were in hospital. Each house raised funds from McDonald's customers at the fast food restaurants. By 2005, 250 homes had been opened in 27 countries providing 6,000 rooms each night. The charity, now run by 30,000 volunteers, has raised over $400 million and helped over 10 million families.

In 1987, while he was stretching his bank credit, Richard Branson set up the Virgin Healthcare Foundation together with Anita Roddick and Michael Grade. The foundation has lobbied for the campaign Parents Against Tobacco, which raised over £100 million to restrict tobacco advertising in sport. While each Virgin company is run separately, in 2004 Branson launched Virgin Unite, with the plan to connect all the Virgin companies, partners, suppliers and customers with the "best of the best" social entrepreneurial groups and charities: a "social dating agency" identifying the most effective ways to make a difference. In 2006, at the second Clinton Global Initiative, Branson pledged to give 100% of the profits of Virgin Atlantic and Virgin Trains over the next ten years to fund renewal fuels technology.

Sam Walton's Wal-Mart Foundation gave $197 million in 2005 to support over 100,000 local charities. This came from company and customer donations and mobilized 800,000 volunteer hours of support for projects in areas where a Wal-Mart store operated. The Wal-Mart Foundation is separate from the billion dollar Walton Family Foundation, set up by Sam Walton and his wife, Helen, which gives out over $100 million in grants for progressing education each year.

In 2004, Sergey Brin and Larry Page committed one percent of Google profits and equity to the Google Foundation. The foundation supports organizations from the Make-a-Wish Foundation to Doctors Without Borders, funding initiatives to reduce inequity and end poverty. By linking the income of the Foundation to the profits of Google, the founders are linking their living legacy with a lasting legacy. When making their announcement, Brin and Page said, "We hope that someday this institution will eclipse Google itself in overall world impact by ambitiously applying innovation and significant resources to the largest of the world's problems."

Making Effective Giving Everyone's Business

"We thought we had the answers.
It was the questions we had wrong."
- Bono

There are more billion-dollar charity funds set up by entrepreneurs in existence today than existed in living history. Yet it is not personal wealth that leaves the greatest legacies. It is the power to unlock flow. In December 2005, Time Magazine featured Bill and Melinda Gates, and Bono, as the joint Time Persons of the Year.

The way in which Bono and the Gates Foundation have contributed to reducing global inequity could not be more different, but each has leveraged on their own personal flow to unlock global flow in their own way. In 1984, six years after U2 was formed, Bono took part in Live Aid, organized by Bob Geldof to raise awareness of poverty in Africa. By 2002, Bono had set up his own organization DATA (Debt, Aids, Trade in Africa) with funding from Bill Gates and George Soros.

DATA was set up to hold western governments accountable for the pledges they had made as part of the 2002 United Nations Millennium Declaration to halve global extreme poverty by 2015 and eradicate it completely by 2025. In 2005, Bono took a leading role in the Make Poverty History campaign, convincing Bob Geldof to back a series of Live 8 concerts prior to the July G8 Summit in Scotland.

Without any billion-dollar fund, Bono applied his passion and talents – campaigning throughout U2's Vertigo tour that took them across America and Europe. By the end of 2005, western governments through the combined efforts of discussion, campaigning and public pressure, committed to an extra $48 billion a year in aid to developing countries by 2010, and proposed canceling up to $55 billion in third world debt. While the work to ensure these changes has only just begun, Bono has demonstrated that it does not take billions – or even millions – of dollars of flow to begin unlocking *hundreds* of billions of dollars of flow. It takes collective momentum towards a worthy cause.

Effective Giving through Social Enterprise

Bono generated momentum by getting his audience to join the ONE campaign from their mobile phones during his Vertigo tour. Other entrepreneurs have leveraged in other ways to magnify and multiply the effects they can achieve – through other entrepreneurs. Paul Newman, having already become one of America's leading social entrepreneurs with Newman's Own, set up the Committee to Encourage Corporate Philanthropy in 1999, appealing for greater corporate giving by America's largest companies and playing a part in the doubling of corporate giving to $7 billion by 2005.

Jeff Skoll, the first president of eBay and its second largest shareholder today, championed the launch of the eBay Foundation, and then went on to support social entrepreneurs. In 2003 he launched the Centre for Social Entrepreneurship at Oxford University, defining a social entrepreneur as "Society's Change Agent - A pioneer of innovations that benefit humanity". The Skoll Foundation, launched with $250 million of Skoll's eBay stock, supports social entrepreneurs today through its awards program and online network, socialedge.org. eBay founder, Pierre Omidyar, followed a similar route. With his eBay shares currently worth $8 billion, Omidyar left eBay and dedicated himself to giving his money back in the most effective way he could. He set up the Omidyar Network in 2004, with a $400 million fund to invest in social enterprises and promote "individual empowerment on a global scale".

"We exist for one single purpose: so that more and more people discover their own power to make good things happen.
We are actively building a network of participants,
because we know we can't do this alone."
- Pierre Omidyar, Omidyar Network

After leaving AOL Time Warner in 2005, Steve Case dedicated himself to his Case Foundation, which he started in 1997. With the aim of fostering entrepreneurship in non-profit organizations, Case joins an growing group of Wealth Creators, including Gates, Newman, Branson, Skoll and Omidyar, who are applying their expertise to increase wealth contribution through themselves and more importantly through the support and education of others.

From Passion to Purpose

Choosing a cause is not necessarily about 'changing the world'. Many of the Wealth Creators in this book have focused on just one cause that would create a lasting legacy in its own way. Ingvar Kamrad, who's Stichting INGKA Foundation owns the IKEA Group and has assets of $36 billion, is supporting the mapping of the world's forests through Global Forest Watch, and forest preservation through WWF.

Paul Allen, who launched his foundation in 1986, has given $815 million of his fortune to the advancement of education, science and technology. The foundation funds projects such as the Allen Institute for Brain Studies, which is attempting to create a groundbreaking brain atlas. Allen has also funded the future of public space travel, combining the technology of his 'SpaceShipOne' orbital transporter with Richard Branson's Virgin Galactic space travel company in 2004.

Some projects are even more specific. Walt Disney focused on funding the California Institute of the Arts (CalArts). Henry Kravis focused on causes in New York. Peter Lynch focuses on causes in Boston. Some projects are annual awards to encourage the recognition of others, from John Templeton's annual Templeton Prize, worth $1.4 million, to the Walton's Teacher of the Year Award, which has recognized over 26,000 school teachers.

Martha Stewart, Donald Trump and Amitabh Bachchan have all used their media exposure to promote charitable giving, and many of our Wealth Creators from Gates and Buffett to Ford, Getty, Edison, Jobs and Walton have seen their giving as a family affair, their contribution as a shared activity with those closest to them.

Even before his July 2006 announcement, Buffett already had four $100 million foundations run by his family. Each of these will also continue to receive part of his fortune: the Susan Thompson Buffett Foundation, named after his wife who died in 2004, focuses on health and family planning; the Susan A Buffett Foundation, chaired by his 52-year-old daughter, funds education; the Howard G Buffett Foundation, chaired by his 51-year-old son, funds nature conservation projects; and the NoVo Foundation, run by his 48-year-old son, Peter, seeks to reverse environmental degradation and uphold human rights. Wealth Creators soon realize that effective giving does not just bind communities; it binds families.

> *"The ones who are crazy enough to think that*
> *they can change the world, are the ones who do."*
> - Steve Jobs

WE ARE LIVING IN A SEA CHANGE

Everyone living with a sense of clarity and history can see that today we are in the midst of an historic sea change. We live in an age of personal empowerment, where any one of us can pursue our power to create, and pursue our power to contribute. We are more connected globally through our economies, cultures, communications and conscious thought than ever before. There are more people addressing and articulating our global issues than at any other time in history.

As your power of wealth creation has grown, so has your opportunity for wealth contribution. What will be your own personal area of focus? What will be your project?

Will it be education? At the World Education Forum in 2000, the Dakar Framework for Action was adopted by 127 countries to give all primary school-age children access to an education by 2015. This initiative, overseen by UNESCO, is now five years old. In 2003, the United Nations declared the next ten years the "Literacy Decade'. While there are 100 million children of primary school age still out of school, there are 860 million adults who remain illiterate.

Will it be the environment? The latest WWF Living Planet Report tells us that between 1970 and 2000, there has been a 40% fall in the number of species worldwide. The population of freshwater species has halved and tropical terrestrial species have fallen by 65%. In the last thirty years, two-thirds of the biomass of the bigger fish in the Atlantic has disappeared.

Since 1970, the global Ecological Footprint has grown by 70%. The footprint is the total area required to produce the food, fiber and timber that we consume, provide the space we inhabit, and absorb the waste we create. This was 13.5 billion global hectares in 2001. Earth's biocapacity – which is the total area it can sustainably offer for these functions – is 11.3 billion global hectares. Our footprint exceeded the earth's biocapacity in the 1980's, and by 2001 we were exceeding the earth's capacity to sustainably support our demands on it by 21%. By 2050, WWF calculates our consumption will exceed our planet's capacity to deliver by 120% per year, creating an ecological debt we have no means to service.

Will it be poverty? According to the World Bank, there remain 1.1 billion people living on less than a dollar a day, and 2.7 billion people living on less than two dollars a day. 50,000 people die every day as a result of poverty-related causes - 18 million every year.

Will it be health? UNICEF and the World Health Organization estimate there are over 2.5 million infant deaths each year from diseases against which vaccines already exist. At the launch of DATA, Bono said, "Twenty-five million Africans are HIV-positive and they will leave behind 40 million AIDS orphans by the end of the decade. This is really unacceptable. It's an everyday holocaust." At the same event, Bill Gates said, "There's this paradox that if a plane crashes, and a few hundred people are killed, that's news. But the fact that every day, 50 times as many children died of preventable diseases? -- it's not news that day, the next day or the next day."

It has been easy in the past for many to ignore those in need around them because they didn't know about them, or they didn't think their efforts would make any difference. We no longer have those excuses. We know the challenges that the world faces, and we know we have the power to make a difference. No one of us is too small to make a difference. As Anita Roddick said, ""If you think you are too small to have an impact, try going to bed with a mosquito".

Are we already making a difference? Are we making the world a better place? We are only just at the beginning of a new global conscience, but already our combined efforts are making a measurable change. Since 1990, the world's population in extreme poverty has fallen from 28% to 21%. Infant mortality has decreased in every developing region of the world, from 19% in 1960 to 8% in 2001. From 1950 to 1999, global literacy increased from 52% to 80%.

Flow continues to grow. The World Bank reported record private capital inflows to developing countries in 2005, up to $491 billion. In 2005, the economies of the developing world grew at a pace 125% faster that the percentage growth of the developed world.

The big trends are reflecting progress, but it is the small details in your own cause that will be the measure of your legacy.

CHOOSE YOUR CAUSE

As we've seen, your active intention is far more powerful that your bank balance. Your cause does not need to be about spending a billion dollars or saving a billion people. The cause may be right on your doorstep - right in your neighborhood.

In early 2006, we launched our XL Social Enterprise Accreditation (SEA) Program to provide certification to cause-driven enterprises. Within two months, we had attracted over 180 companies across Asia Pacific and over $20 million in pledges for a wide range of causes, from education to the environment, health, children, orphanages, micro-loans, technology and culture. Some companies participating are million-dollar multinationals. Others are seedling start-ups. No cause is too big, and no cause is too small.

Our program, the XL SEA Program has a target of reaching $100 million in annual contributions through social enterprises each year, tracking the most effective within our Social Enterprise 500 annual list. This is one of many initiatives that are now appearing to enable entrepreneurs to make a difference. Bill Drayton, the first to coin the term "social enterprise" in the 1980's, runs Ashoka, supporting social entrepreneurs worldwide. The Social Enterprise Alliance provides resources for entrepreneurs and non-profit organizations. Networkforgood.org, set up in 2001 as a joint venture between Yahoo! and Time Warner, lists over one million charities to choose from and has already attracted over $76 million in donations and 200,000 volunteer positions.

Choosing your cause is not the same as choosing your life cause. Anita Roddick originally chose Greenpeace to support, only to switch later to Friends of the Earth. Bill Gates began with technology in schools and libraries, only to move on to global vaccines. Warren Buffett began with supporting his family foundations, before extending his support to the Gates Foundation. If choosing the right cause is stopping you from starting, it's stopping your flow. Choose a cause you can support today, and support it.

THE THREE POWERS

When it comes to flow and fortune, there is an important phenomenon I should share. When you follow your flow, it is not just the power you deliver that changes. The power that drives you changes as well.

Why is it that people in their flow seem to have so much energy? Why is it that when we are in our flow, we need less sleep, we become sharper, we become healthier, we become more radiant? Why is it that when we flow, we glow? We drive ourselves with one of three powers. Each one has a different frequency and a different result. These three powers are related to your six internal values.

Elected Power

If you are trying to make it on your own, you are living on elected power. Like a wind-up radio, elected power is a generator you need to wind up to get started. Elected power comes from your passions and talents. It relies on you motivating yourself every day, and it has a very short frequency. You can wake up one day motivated, and run on elected power. But the next day, should you forget to wind yourself up, you soon lose momentum. Living off elected power is the most tiring way to live your life.

Connected Power

Once we begin to leverage our knowledge and network, we change our power. Once we begin to share our power with others, we begin to shift to connected power. Like an electricity grid, when you plug in, you have immediate access to connected power.

Some of us get this sensation when we connect with our colleagues at work. Some of us get this sensation when we connect with our family and friends. No matter what your elected power, when you connect and plug in, you have access to a power that drives you. Connected power has a longer frequency, but the moment you disconnect from your team, from your partner, from your children, the power goes. Once you disconnect from this planet, the power goes.

Reflected Power

When we have leveraged the two key values, our character and our purpose, we step into a new realm. This is when our power moves to reflected power. Like solar energy, you no longer need to plug in. The power of the thoughts of those whose lives you touch already drives you. Your attraction attracts your power. You are energized simply by the power of purpose. This is the power of what Jung called the collective unconscious. Like solar power, the power comes from a higher source. Like the sun, like alchemical gold, it is magical.

Reflected power has a longer frequency. In fact, its frequency has the power to outlive you. Why is it that the people we admire the most are often people we have never met? Why is it that someone who lived 2,000 years ago can have more influence on you today than your next door neighbor?

When you leave this planet – as we all will – if you have lived on elected power, you will be instantly forgotten. If you have lived on connected power, you will live on in the memories of those you connected with – and your memory will leave when they leave. If you have lived on reflected power, your impact will last far longer, and reach far further. Reflected power has a frequency that outlives us.

When we are in the flow, with a worthy cause, we access reflected power. We move at pace, yet we move with minimum effort. Our lives have the power to sweep us off our feet.

"Enlightenment is an accident,
but some activities make you accident prone."
- Zen saying

ALCHEMY ACCOMPLISHED

While academics continue to question how our world works, and as many of us struggle to get by, there are Wealth Creators amongst us who continue to turn flow to fortune, making money to give away.

Today I sat on the beach in Bali, watching the ocean ebb and flow. This ocean was here, ebbing and flowing, 5,000 years ago. It will be here, ebbing and flowing, in 5,000 years. The sun will continue to rise and set, the tides will change and the rivers will flow long after you and I are gone. Flow is eternal.

Each of the great magicians of the past searched for the ultimate goal of alchemy: immortality. Lao Tse, Aristotle, Newton, Einstein, Jung; each found immortality. Even though we never met them, we know of them today. Their lives live on in their legacy. Their contribution continues to resonate within our collective unconscious.

The Wealth Creators in this book are following a similar path. Their legacies are living on and will continue to live on through future history. Their legacy will not be what they got. It will be what they gave. In Winston Churchill's words, "We make a living by what we get. We make a life by what we give."

Each of our lives is such a brief instant within the history of time. Through our flow we have the opportunity to create a lasting fortune. Through our legacy we can transcend time. We each choose whether our lives will be a cosmic spark, or a cosmic sparkle.

Every one of us, like never before, has a chance to make magic. Through our own flow, we have a chance to shape history. This book provides a framework for you to follow your flow.

The rest is up to you.

This is your life, your legacy.

"In a gentle way, you can shake the world."
- Mahatma Gandhi

"Your work is to discover your work
and then with all your heart to give yourself to it."
- Buddha

YOUR WEALTH DYNAMICS PROFILE

"Knowing others is intelligence;
knowing yourself is true wisdom."
- Tao Te Ching

KNOWING YOUR PROFILE

There are five possible ways for you to know what your Wealth Dynamics profile is. Each is based on the fact that our frequency already gives ourselves away. Here are the five ways:

1. You have mastered your flow

When you have mastered your flow, you know your flow, and your frequency is quite obvious. The entrepreneurs in this book reflect their Wealth Dynamics profile in their actions. This does not apply to people who are *not* in their flow. On average, over half of people who are *not* in their flow guess their profile wrong. They judge their profile on the basis of their past activities, forgetting that their past activities have not created them wealth.

2. You have mastered the five frequencies

Once you gain a deeper understanding of how our frequencies already drive us, you can identify your profile and the profiles of others around you very quickly. At some of the workshops that I conduct, I will ask for volunteers from the audience, and through a number of questions will identify their Wealth Dynamics profile – not just from their answers, but from the way they answered, their posture, their eye movements, their hesitations, the energy they create in the room and a whole series of other signs. With these distinctions, the audience is soon able to identify the profiles along with me. The results are then verified by the participants taking the online Wealth Dynamics test.

The more clear you are of the distinctions between the five frequencies, the more natural it is to spot profiles. This comes from playing the game. A footballer who has played the game enough times can instantly spot the goalkeeper in the opposing team by his movements and posture – not just because he's wearing the big gloves.

3. Attend a Wealth Dynamics Weekend

At our Wealth Dynamics Weekends, you experience the contents of this book in action, in a way that applies to you. Everyone on the weekend takes the Wealth Dynamics profiling test online, and experiences, through a series of activities, flow in action. Anywhere between 150 and 250 entrepreneurs attend each event, and when each profile is grouped together, it becomes very clear how different our frequencies are. When you see a group of Lords together, you realize why they are called Lords. When you see a group of Stars together, you realize why they are called Stars!

As each of us has a value that is someone else's leverage, the opportunities exchanged on the weekend are phenomenal, with an average of 20 or 30 new businesses being formed from each. The Wealth Dynamics Weekends are facilitated by myself, with an international crew, and take place each year in: Gold Coast, Australia; Auckland, New Zealand; London, England; Las Vegas, USA; Bangalore, India; Shanghai, China; Jakarta, Indonesia; Singapore; and Dubai. The cost to attend varies depending on the location and capacity, but is usually between US$800 and US$1,000.

4. Work with an XL Wealth Consultant

The XL Results Foundation has over 1,000 Life Members who are able to utilize the Wealth Dynamics principles in their mentoring and coaching. Our Life Members are located in 18 different countries. Contact members@resultsfoundation.com to find a coach near you.

5. Take the Wealth Dynamics Online Test

This is the simplest and quickest way to find your profile. Over 20,000 entrepreneurs have now taken the Wealth Dynamics test within Asia Pacific, where the XL entrepreneur network has grown over the last five years. The online test is a questionnaire which will provide you automatically with your Wealth Dynamics profile, together with your percentage of each frequency, your primary profile, your secondary profiles, and a graph of your frequencies.

When you take the online test, you will receive, together with your results, a twenty-page guide to understanding your profile. The online test costs US$100, and can be taken at www.wealthdynamics.org.

MY WEALTH DYNAMICS PROFILE

Here is an example of a Wealth Dynamics profile, where the guinea pig is...me! The graph shows:

1. **My Primary Profile: Creator** – This tells me I need to follow a Creator strategy to follow my flow. From the accompanying guide, I can also see that my secondary profiles are Star and Mechanic, which means that I can and should leverage on these two in order to maximize my flow as a Creator.

2. **My Frequencies** – This tells me that, with 60% of my frequency as Dynamo, my flow is clearly when I have my head in the clouds! Blaze is at 16%, and Tempo and Steel are at 12%. That means that the more I can find strong Tempo and Steel frequencies to support me, the less time I need to invest out of my flow, and the stronger my team will be.

As explained in chapter 15: Dynamo relates to wood/spring frequency; Blaze relates to fire/summer; Tempo relates to earth/autumn and Steel relates to metal/winter. While our frequencies do oscillate throughout our lives, our primary Wealth Dynamics profile tends to remain the same. The more we focus on playing the game in that profile, the further we move into our flow.

MY WEALTH DYNAMICS PROFILE

Name : Roger Hamilton

WEALTH DYNAMICS PROFILE

Wealth Frequencies

Dynamo: 60%	Blaze: 16%	Tempo: 12%	Steel: 12%

Primary Wealth Profile: Creator

ACTION STEPS

"I do not try to dance better than anyone else.
I only try to dance better than myself."
- Mikhail Baryshnikov

FIVE SIMPLE STEPS

What next? Right at this moment, we are all at a different place in our flow. Some of us are well on the way, with successful businesses but with not enough time to achieve what we would like to achieve. Some of us are just getting started, with plenty of time but without knowing how or where to leverage it.

These five simple steps will enable you to move forward regardless of where you are, applying the principles in this book: set your standards; build your network; choose your playground; play your game; and leave your legacy.

SET YOUR STANDARDS

Setting your standards is the first step to playing the game. While your goals are what you reach for, your standards are what you settle for. Even the most ambitious footballer will never get in the first squad without the high standard of training every day.

Setting your standards is about making a commitment to yourself. How much time will you dedicate to following your flow? How much energy will you dedicate to ensuring you are on the right frequency? How much discipline will you have to ensure you are surrounding yourself with people in their flow? A lack of high standards leads to a lack of traction and a lack of perseverance, and, as Ted Turner said, "Winners never quit, and quitters never win."

BUILD YOUR NETWORK

Flow is far easier to fall into when you surround yourselves with others who are in their flow. These individuals are not the majority, but they are surprisingly easy to find. That's because they leave tracks, and they gravitate together.

Whether you have come across people who are achieving success through the calls you make, or the events you attend, invest time to question and understand the journeys of others. The stories in this book are only the beginning. Hear for yourself, every day, the entrepreneurs around you who are experiencing the principles of attraction and the seven phenomena of flow. If you want to make a million, meet millionaires. As Donald Trump says, "You ask a baker how he makes bread. You ask a billionaire how he makes money."

CHOOSE YOUR PLAYGROUND

Your playground will change and grow as you change and grow. Begin by seeing how you can add value to those already creating flow around you. See what resonates with you: what fits your six internal values, from your passions to your purpose.

Once you have found a group that you want to work with, work with them, meet with them, begin the journey and begin your learning cycles. Continuously question what you and those around you are doing each day to gain clarity on the wealth equation in action: value x leverage; innovation and timing; multiplying and magnifying. Focus how you are building your luck each day by improving your location, understanding, connections and knowledge

PLAY YOUR GAME

When you are in an environment you can see yourself playing in – you are in a country, an industry, a niche, a capability level, where you are truly comfortable, begin to play the game. Understand your Wealth Dynamics profile, and learn from the role models in this book and the ones you find around you. Understand the strengths, weaknesses, successes and failures within your profile, and understand the six-step strategy to creating your flow: build your wealth foundation; maximize your moment of wealth creation; focus on your value creation; ensure your value ownership; execute your leverage; and secure your cash flow.

As your value is someone else's leverage, and your leverage is someone else's value, understand the other seven profiles. Learn their winning formulas and losing formulas, their strengths and weaknesses, and their own wealth strategy. The more you are able to effectively give to support the wealth of others, the more your wealth will flow back in return. Your greatest wealth will not come from your own personal flow, but from group flow – the magic of momentum.

As you play the game, focus on your traction and your dynamic balance. Be aware of what gear you are in through the ten levels of value. Be aware of what gear your company is in through the eight stages of enterprise growth. As your level of the fifth element grows with your learning cycles, and as your cycles ebb and flow, play the game with a clear sense of the cycles around you – and the people around you. Whenever you begin to lose flow, reassess yourself and your teams – where are you at in your team cycle? Your business cycle? Your industry cycle?

LEAVE YOUR LEGACY

The most important standard you need to keep is the standard of pursuing a worthy cause. Effective giving is not something that happens tomorrow. It happens today. Effective giving is about understanding how you are delivering value to others. Worthy giving is when effective giving occurs without any the need for any return. When the river gives to the sea, through tomorrow's rain it has a way of returning in the most remarkable way.

As you go, feel your flow: feel it by the luck you receive, your experience of time, the power you access, and the gratitude you feel. Enjoy the journey! I wish you good luck, and good fortune.

THANK YOU

This book was in progress for two years and as I traveled, different parts were written in twelve different countries. The draft had clocked about 300,000 miles in one form or another. During this time, the XL Group continued to grow. It takes a great team to make it all tick, and I am proud to be surrounded by an awesome team. They have worked hard to help me get out of their way!

Thanks to my senior XL Management Team, Dave Rogers, Margaret Loh, Irene Millar, Ian Grundy and Daryl Bisset. Thanks also to the many people without whom XL wouldn't be where it is today – to Floyd Cowan at XL Magazine, Rebecca Bisset at EL Magazine, Debbie Law at Expat Rentals, Lisa McCarthy at Achievers International, Wayan Suarma at XL Vision Villas, Sony Vasandani at XL Preschool, Justyn Barakat at XL Cafes and the XL team: Shah, Penny, Melody, Khan, Faith, Louella, Suhana, Shahira, Felicia, Andri, Azlin, Susan, Fannie, Pei Fang, Sock Yee, Suriah, Siew Lee and Irene. And thank you to Khevitha Kamal, for always making sure I'm at the right place, right time…

The XL country teams continue to do an incredible job, and thanks to: Paul Dunn in Australia; Gill Daldin and Kevin Heppleston in New Zealand; Vito Montone in USA; Daniel Priestley and Glen Carlson in UK; Carlos Rios in Singapore; Alex Tamilvanan and Yap Keong Foon in India; Veronica Ho and the team in China; Poonam Sagar in Indonesia; Steven and Jackie Khong and Lilian Lim in Malaysia; Callum Laing in Thailand; Matthew Faid and Michelle Kruger in Dubai; Merrin and Louise Pearse in Hong Kong; Bob Urichuck in Canada; Christophe Poizat in France and Masami Sato and Tamami Ushiki in Japan. When you read this, hop on your chairs and have a surf, because you're unbelievable.

Thanks to all our Life Members for making this journey so special and to Susan Gallagher and Philippa Barr for the editing.

I've saved the best to last. Thank YOU, Renate, and my little sugarplums, Kathleen, Theresa and Luke. You are my fortune.

ABOUT ROGER

Roger is a social entrepreneur and Chairman of XL Group. Roger and the XL Group are driven by the concept of World Wide Wealth: Empowering social enterprise and global change by increasing our collective ability to create and contribute wealth.

Born in Hong Kong and educated at Trinity College, Cambridge University, he became an entrepreneur soon after getting his degree, experiencing many failures before achieving success. He now owns and runs businesses in publishing, property, financing, franchising, event management, resort management, training, coaching, technology, membership, retail and education.

Roger is the creator of the Wealth Dynamics profiling system and presenter of the Wealth Dynamics Weekend. For the last five years he has traveled globally conducting workshops and private coaching sessions for successful entrepreneurs. Roger's previous book, "Wink and Grow Rich", was an international bestseller throughout Asia Pacific.

Roger lives in Bali with his wife, Renate, and three children, Kathleen, Theresa and Luke.

ABOUT XL

XL Group was founded in 2001 by Roger Hamilton and Dave Rogers to accelerate the growth of entrepreneurship and effective giving in Asia Pacific. The Mission of XL Group is to facilitate and accelerate this process by providing effective training, networking and resources to entrepreneurs worldwide. "XL" stands for "Extraordinary Lives" – a life in which we maximize our power to create and our power to contribute. In 2005, XL published "2020 Vision", which outlines our vision of World Wide Wealth and the Billion Dollar Challenge:

Our "2020 Vision" is to reach our Billion Dollar Challenge target by 2020, when we will have 25,000 companies participating in the XL Social Enterprise Accreditation Program, donating $100 million from $1 billion in profits each year to their nominated causes. The XL SEA Program, launched in 2006, is the World's first certification program recognizing social enterprises, and has attracted over 150 registrations and over $20 million in pledges in its first six months.

XL has grown into a group of twelve companies with combined 2006 revenues of over $10M. Each company is a social enterprise with its own management team, profit centre and nominated cause:

XL Results Foundation: is the world's leading entrepreneur and social enterprise network, with 60,000 entrepreneurs and global operations in China, France, India, Indonesia, Japan, Thailand, Hong Kong, Malaysia, Canada, Singapore, Australia, New Zealand, Dubai, UK & USA. XL Results Foundation runs coaching accreditation, monthly networking events and membership programs for entrepreneurs in each country, and continues to open in a new city every month. XL Results Foundation manages the XL SEA program towards World Wide Wealth, and has a calendar of over 700 events in 2007.

XL Media: publishes XL Magazine, the first magazine dedicated to Social Enterprise. The magazine has featured entrepreneurs and leaders including Bill Gates, Warren Buffett, George Soros, Rudy Guiliani, Richard Branson, Li Ka Shing, Lee Kuan Yew, Bono and entrepreneurs the world over.

XL Events: specializes in large scale events for Asia Pacific entrepreneurs, including the Global Entrepreneur Summit, the Entrepreneur Business School in Bali, and the Wealth Dynamics Weekend (The world's widest reaching wealth creation seminar).

XL Network: is the online network for entrepreneurs, accessed via mobile and web. XL also actively utilizes Ecademy & LinkedIn, the World's largest online business forum and directory.

XLTV: produces TV interviews of entrepreneurs for distribution in the network, both broadcast and online.

XL Finance: provides loan financing to entrepreneurs and micro-financing in India and China.

XL Vision Villas: XL's first resort in Bali, providing a workshop retreat for trainers and small businesses and a personal development library and workshop facilities.

XL Preschool: was launched in 2007 to provide the extraordinary level of accelerated learning and expertise within the network to the next generation, through a series of international schools.

XL Cafe: Launched in March 2007, XL Cafe provided the XL Group with its first 'on-the-street' presence. Launched in Auckland, New Zealand, XL Cafes operate as venues catering to entrepreneurs and professionals looking for a meeting place to connect with others both locally and globally.

XL Properties: was introduced to source property investments for XL Life Members across a broad range of commercial interests that also link to other XL businesses.

XL Institute: holds all of Roger Hamilton's Wealth Dynamics material and governs its use for commercial purposes by XL Life Members and others. XL coaches and speakers also belong to the XL Institute.

The companies in the XL Group are certified Social Enterprises as part of the XL Social Enterprise Accreditation Program, with at least 10% of annual net profits donated to nominated causes.

Become a certified social enterprise at: www.worldwidewealth.org
Join the XL Entrepreneur Network at: www.resultsfoundation.com
Take the Wealth Dynamics test at: www.wealthdynamics.org

ABOUT THE HUNGER PROJECT

All profits from this book are being donated to:

www.thp.org

Every day, 20,000 people die as a result of chronic hunger. The Hunger Projects is a charity dedicated to change this, working in more than 10,000 villages across 13 developing countries in Africa, South Asia and Latin America. It carries out proven strategies that are empowering millions of people to achieve lasting progress in health, education, nutrition and family income.

The Hunger Project's board includes: President, Joan Holmes; Queen Noor of Jordan; Javier Perez de Cuellar, Former UN Secretary General; and Amartya Sen, Nobel Laureate, Former Dean, Trinity College, Cambridge and present Professor of Economics and Philosophy, Harvard University. The Hunger Project's vision is the end of world hunger.

We are alive at a time when humanity can achieve the final milestone for the end of hunger. All profits from this book are being donated to the Hunger Project. By buying this book, you are already making a difference. Thank you.

"Like slavery and apartheid, poverty is not natural. It is man-made and can be overcome and eradicated by the actions of human beings. Overcoming poverty is not a gesture of charity. It is an act of justice."

\- Nelson Mandela

WHAT PEOPLE SAY ABOUT WEALTH DYNAMICS

"Every now and again I get lucky. Meeting Roger was one of those moments. Wealth Dynamics gives me clarity on where I need to receive my flow as well as to where and to whom I should pass it on."

- Joanne Flinn, Director, Shelton, Singapore

"Wealth Dynamics is a system everyone should know. My life as a banker from Malaysia changed the moment I knew my Supporter Profile. Today I have built a wide network in India with multiple business interests. Wealth Dynamics has brought out the best in me and set me on a path to live life to the fullest!"

- Alex Tamilvanan, Entrepreneur, Bangalore, India

"By doing my wealth profile I gained a whole new insight about myself and how I relate to other people. As a Creator I now understand for me to be effective I need to build a team to support me and to avoid being caught up in the detail. Understanding my wife and children's profiles has had a dramatic impact on my relationships with my family."

- Kevin Heppleston, Action Int Business Coach of the Year, New Zealand

"What Roger Hamilton is doing is amazing. After using the Wealth Dynamics system to my team, the level of excellence in the team just flows!"

- Menno Siebinga, Owner, 6 Star, The Netherlands

"Wealth Dynamics and Roger Hamilton has unlocked doorways of opportunities to me. I have been able to expand my business internationally, step out of operations and reignite my passion. Wealth Dynamics has enabled me to find more of myself to be able to give away."

- Daniel Priestley, Chairman & CEO, Triumphant Events, UK

"I am no longer struggling to operate multiple business entities. After Wealth Dynamics I have more diverse business interests than before, which are operating more smoothly and I am enjoying myself more. Love it."

- Amanda Hosburgh, Director, Zhenith Group, Australia

"Wealth Dynamics has helped me make choices not only in my best interest but in the interest of others – for in the end it is often the latter that are the best for me anyway."

- Stuart Fraser, Founder, Foundations For Life, Australia

"Wealth Dynamics profiling has transformed my life on many levels. Knowing I am a Star profile has liberated me to me, and I now have the tools to manifest it. Understanding other profiles has moved my relationship with others to a deeper level, leading to far less conflict."

- Cynthia Kirk, Director, Deva Ltd, New Zealand

"The Wealth Dynamics system took me to another level. It made me realize what I knew deep down but had neglected – that I could have fun, be the creative person I am, make more money and contribute more that I ever have before."

- Thuy-Ai Nguyn, MD, Visonpreneur Pty Ltd, Australia

"Discovering wealth profiling and then having our staff complete their profiles has had a massive shift in our company moving forward. Now, our staff interacts with so much more passion and trust. Letting go has let us move forward."

- Tom Anderson, Country Director, ALME Alliance, Australia

"Roger combines Eastern Wisdom with Western Wisdom to produce a magical synergy. Wealth Dynamics is the key to unlocking the potential of your life and business."

- Paul Wetton, Founder, Paul Wetton & Associates, Australia

"The Wealth Profiling system is so simple yet so profound. It changed the way I do business dramatically. I now recognize what my strengths are and anything that I'm not great at I delegate. Best of all, I recognize that it's okay to be the way I am. I don't need to me the master of everything."
- Kristina Mills, Creative Director, Imaginicity, Australia

"Understanding and using my wealth profile has not only allowed me to dramatically increase my personal wealth. It has allowed me to create an everlasting difference in education."
- Karen Boyes, Entrepreneur, Spectrum Education, New Zealand

"Wealth Dynamics has been the key to unlocking my past and my future. With my past I now have an understanding of why my life has evolved to what it is now. With my future I now know who I am becoming and how I am going to get there. Thank you, Roger. Another seed has started to grow."
- Ken Hawkins, Founder, Natural Wealth Pty Ltd, Australia

"I had spent so much time truing to be everything to everybody. Now I have my focus and my life is in flow. I have found out who I was meant to be before it was too late. Wealth Dynamics has given me my life."
- Samantha Backman, CEO, Revivalife & Health Solutions Pty Ltd, Australia

"This is the most profound business wisdom available."
- Iain Mackenzie, Founder, Results Insight, Australia

"Because of Wealth Dynamics, I now fit my shoes."
- Adeline Long, Director, Unison Childcare Services, New Zealand

"This is the system that will change the world – and in the direction that it needs to go."
- Dennis Page, Manager, Vibration Consultants Ltd, New Zealand

WHAT PEOPLE SAY ABOUT THE AUTHOR

"Roger has got closer to understanding the spirit and essence of wealth creation than any other thought leader in the twenty-first century. He is a gifted and generous teacher who is changing the fortunes of many, many people."

- Adrian Gilpin, Chairman, Institute of Human Development, UK

"As a Board Member on major educational bourads in India I would like to endorse that the greatest learning I have received in my whole life is from Roger Hamilton."

- Maya Shahini, Chairperson, Sage Foundation, India

"In one evening session I realised that the business model I was creating was 100% wrong for me. Roger showed me the business model I needed to succeed. He saved me 10 years of stress and heartache!"

- Ann Andrews, Immediate Past National President of NSANZ, New Zealand

"Roger is a true magician. Roger's passion and love for people is extraordinary, the energy he emits and gives to others is awesome. He really can change the world bit-by-bit! Thank you Roger for the magic you gave me."

- Penny Power, Founder, Ecademy, UK

"Roger's presence in any room, in any country, filled with people from all walks of life, illuminates the room the moment he appears and begins sharing. Roger's extremely meaningful and vital donation to SoulTalk Charity enabled us to open the first Loving Home for Women in crisis in Hong Kong. Roger, you are amazing!"

- Andrea Gutwirth, Founder, SoulTalk, Hong Kong

"Roger's depth of knowledge of being in the 'flow' is incredible. He is magnificent in his sharing and enables me to connect with the best people on this planet."

- Dr Yew Kam Keong, Founder, Mindbloom, Malaysia

"Roger is one of the shining illuminations of our generation. He has so much depth in matters of entrepreneurship and his focus on every individual's ability to succeed is uncanny! It is such a privilege to know a person of Roger's character and status. I have learnt so much from his principles of success as a person. Bravo Roger, Bravo."

- Peter Emeleogu, Partner, AW Capital, Nigeria

"Roger has taught me how to make magic happen. His ability to share his amazing gift is truly unbelievable."

- Gertrude Matshe, Africa Alive Foundation, New Zealand

"I have had the pleasure of meeting many highly successful business people in my life but Roger is by far the most impressive. Roger has this natural gift to present highly creative and intellectual principles at a level everyone can understand and use."

- Simon Warman-Freed, Founder, Xploit International Ltd, UK

"Roger exudes enthusiasm and passion for entrepreneurship and wealth building with the desire to share his knowledge and passion. I particularly like his philosophy and thoughts on everyone's ability to build wealth and more importantly share this wealth for the good of those less fortunate."

- Stuart Taylor, Owner, Asia Oil Gas, Malaysia

"Roger, your enthusiasm is contagious, your knowledge profound, your delivery astounding, your vision great and your friendship priceless."

- K.K. Ralhan, Chairman Total Energy Solutions, Indonesia

"Roger is an exceptional, high spirited individual with great vision, energy and dynamism. I commend his tireless efforts and generosity in making a valuable contribution by assisting people around the world to realise their potential, build their businesses and live their lives. I also applaud his work in helping the poor and needy and making a difference in their lives."

- Mildred Ambrose, CEO, Cornerstone International Consulting, NZ

"Roger is a unique and gifted human being sharing the most profound wisdom with the world. Roger and his insight is changing the planet. It will be a far happier place and his legacy will be profound."

- Ian Robinson, Founder, Bioglow, Australia

"Roger has touched my heart and my balance sheet – an absolute genius who walks his talk. Wealth beyond words."

- Sean Levy, Property Trader, New Zealand

"Roger is an extremely supportive person. He is a charismatic author, speaker, trainer and genuinely cares for other people's success. I am proud to know Roger, and I am grateful for all the support he has shown me. P.S: When Roger laughs, one can actually hear him a mile away."

- Aaron Goh, Standard Chartered Bank, Malaysia

"Roger is just magic. He is full of fun and wisdom – Wisdom that you will not learn from any books. His vision to help this planet is huge and unstoppable. Jump on board!"

- Rose Robinson, Director, Bioglo Pty Ltd, Melbourne, Australia

"I feel Roger is a living treasure. His gift flows out to all. Hold it. Pass it on."

- Alan Drayton, Director, Alan Drayton Builders Ltd, New Zealand

38 ENTREPRENEURS

Below is a list of each of the 38 entrepreneurs featured in this book:

Creators

Thomas Edison, (Feb 11, 1847 – Oct 18, 1931), Inventor, Electric Light bulb
Walt Disney, (Dec 5, 1901 – Dec 15, 1966), Founder, Walt Disney Company
Bill Gates, (Oct 28, 1955), Co-Founder, Microsoft Corporation
Steve Jobs, (Feb 24, 1955), CEO, Apple Computer
Richard Branson, (18 Jul 1950), Founder, Virgin Group

Stars

Oprah Winfrey, (Jan 29, 1954), Star of The Oprah Winfrey Show
Martha Stewart, (Aug 3, 1941), Founder, Martha Stewart Living Omnimedia
Arnold Schwarzenegger, (Jul 30, 1947), Actor, Governor of California
Amithabh Bachan, (Oct 11, 1942), Indian Bollywood Superstar
Paul Newman, (Jan 26, 1925), Actor & Co-founder of Newmans Own

Supporters

Jack Welch, (Nov 19, 1935), CEO, General Electric
Michael Eisner, (Mar 7, 1942), CEO, The Walt Disney Company
Steve Case, (Aug 21, 1958), Co-founder, AOL, CEO of AOL Time Warner
Meg Whitman, (Aug 4, 1956), CEO, eBay

Deal Makers

Donald Trump, (Jun 14, 1946), Founder, Trump Organization
David Geffen, (Feb 21, 1943), Founder, Geffen Records, Dreamworks SKG
Masayoshi Son, (Aug 11, 1957), Richest in Japan, Founder, Softbank
Henry Kravis, (Jan 6, 1944), Co-founder, Kohlberg, Kravis, Roberts
Rupert Murdoch, (Mar 11, 1931), Founder, News Corporation

Traders

George Soros, (Aug 12, 1930), Co-Founder, the Quantum Fund
Peter Lynch, (Jan 19, 1944), Head of the Magellan Fund
John Templeton, (Nov 29, 1912), Founder, the Templeton Growth Fund
Jim Rogers, (Oct 19, 1942), Co-Founder, the Quantum Fund

Accumulators

Benjamin Graham, (May 8, 1894 – Sep 21, 1976), Graham Newman Corp
Warren Buffett, (Aug 30, 1930), CEO, Berkshire Hathaway
Li Ka Shing, (July 29, 1928), Richest in Asia, Founder, Cheung Kong Holdings
Sandy Weill, (Mar 16, 1933), CEO & Chairman, Citigroup
Paul Allen, (Jan 21, 1953), Co-founder, Microsoft, founder of Vulcan Inc

Lords

Andrew Carnegie, (Nov 25, 1835 – Aug 11, 1919), Carnegie Steel Company
John D Rockefeller, (Jul 8, 1839 – May 23, 1937), Founder, Standard Oil
Jean Paul Getty, (Dec 15, 1892 – Jun 6, 1976), Founder, Getty Oil
Lakshmi Mittal, (Jun 15, 1950), Richest in UK, Founder, Mittal Steel
Sergei Brin, (Aug 21, 1973), Co-founder, Google

Mechanics

Henry Ford, (Jul 30, 1863 – Apr 7, 1947), Founder, Ford Motor Company
Ray Kroc, (Oct 5, 1902 – Jan 14, 1984), Founder, McDonalds Corporation
Sam Walton, (Mar 29, 1918 – Apr 6, 1992), Founder, Wal-Mart
Ingvar Kamprad, (Mar 30, 1926), Richest in Europe, Founder of IKEA
Michael Dell, (Feb 23, 1965), Founder, Dell Inc

READING LIST

The stories and quotations in this book are from the following sources. All are highly recommended reading to get a far greater insight into the lives of the entrepreneurs and pioneers covered:

Creators

Edison: A Biography, *by Matthew Josephson*
Edison: A Life of Invention, *by Paul Israel*
Edison: Inventing the Century, *by Neil Baldwin*
Edison and the Business of Innovation, *by Andre Millard*
Deconstructing Disney, *by Eleanor Byrne, Martin McQuillan*
Disney's World: A Biography, *by Leonard Mosley*
The Art of Walt Disney; From Mickey Mouse to the Magic Kingdoms, *by Christopher Finch*
Walt Disney: An American Original, *by Bob Thomas*
Business @ the Speed of Thought, *by Bill Gates*
Business the Bill Gates Way, *by Des Dearlove*
Hard Drive: Bill Gates and the Making of the Microsoft Empire, *by James Wallace, Jim Erickson*
iCon: Steve Jobs, The Greatest Second Act in the History of Business, *by Jeffrey Young, William Simon*
Insanely Great: The Life and Times of Macintosh, *by Steven Levy*
The Second Coming of Steve Jobs, *by Alan Deutschman*
Losing My Virginity: How I've Survived, Had Fun, and Made a Fortune Doing Business My Way, *by Richard Branson*
Screw it, Let's do it: Lessons in Life, *by Richard Branson*

Stars

Oprah Winfrey: A Biography *by Helen S. Garson*
Oprah Winfrey: I Don't Believe In Failure, *by Robin Westen*
The Uncommon Wisdom of Oprah Winfrey: A Portrait in Her Own Words *by Oprah Winfrey and Bill Adler*
Martha Inc: The Incredible Story of Martha Stewart Living Omnimedia, *by Christopher Byron*
The Martha Rules: 10 Essentials for Achieving Success as You Start, Grow, or Manage a Business, *by Martha Stewart*
Arnold: The Education of a Bodybuilder *by Arnold Schwarzenegger*
Fantastic: The Life of Arnold Schwarzenegger *by Laurence Leamer*
The People's Machine: Arnold Schwarzenegger And the Rise of Blockbuster Democracy, *by Joe Mathews*
Paul Newman, *by Daniel O'Brien*

Paul Newman: a Biography, *by Eric Lax*
Shameless Exploitation in Pursuit of the Common Good,
by Paul Newman and A. E. Hotchner

Supporters

Business the Jack Welch Way, by *Stuart Crainer*
Jack: Straight from the Gut, *by Jack Welch, John A Byrne*
Jack Welch & The GE Way: Management Insights and Leadership Secrets of
the Legendary CEO, *by Robert Slater, Vince Lombardi*
Winning, *by Jack Welch and Suzy Welch*
Disney War, *by James B. Stewart*
Prince of the Magic Kingdom: Michael Eisner and the Re-making of Disney,
by Joe Flower
Work In Progress, *by Michael D Eisner, Tony Schwartz*
AOL.com, *by Kara Swisher*
Fools Rush In: Steve Case, Jerry Levin, and the Unmaking of AOL Time Warner,
by Nina Munk
The Perfect Store: Inside eBay, *by Adam Cohen*

Deal Makers

Trump: How to Get Rich, *by Donald J. Trump and Meredith McIver*
Trump: The Art of the Comeback, *by Donald J. Trump*
Trump: The Art of the Deal, *by Donald Trump, Tony Schwartz*
Trump: The Way to the Top: The Best Business Advice I Ever Received,
by Donald J. Trump
Trump: Think Like a Billionaire: Everything You Need to Know About Success,
Real Estate, and Life, *by Donald J. Trump and Meredith McIver*
TrumpNation : The Art of Being The Donald, *by Timothy L. O'Brien*
The Operator: David Geffen Builds, Buys, and Sells the New Hollywood,
by Tom King
The Rise and Rise of David Geffen, *by Stephen Singular*
Barbarians at the Gate: The Fall of RJR Nabisco,
by Bryan Burrough and John Helyar
Merchants of Debt: KKR and the Mortgaging of American Business,
by George Anders
The New Financial Capitalists: Kohlberg Kravis Roberts and the Creation of
Corporate Value, *by George P Baker, George David Smith*
Business the Rupert Murdoch Way, *by Stuart Crainer*
Murdoch, *by William Shawcross*
Rupert Murdoch: The Untold Story of the World's Greatest Media Wizard,
by Neil Chenoweth
Rupert Murdoch: Creator of a Worldwide Media Empire, *by Jerome Tuccille*

Traders

George Soros on Globalization, *by George Soros*
Soros: The Life and Times of a Messianic Billionaire, *by Michael T. Kaufman*
Soros on Soros: Staying Ahead of the Curve, *by George Soros*
The Alchemy of Finance, *by George Soros and Paul A. Volcker*
Beating the Street, *by Peter Lynch, John Rothchild*
One Up On Wall Street, *by Peter Lynch, John Rothchild*
Faithful Finances 101: From the Poverty of Fear and Greed to the Riches of
Spiritual Golden Nuggets from Sir John Templeton, *by John Templeton*
Investing, *by Gary D. Moore and John Templeton*
Worldwide Laws of Life: 200 Eternal Spiritual Principles,
by John Marks Templeton
Adventure Capitalist: The Ultimate Road Trip, *by Jim Rogers*
Hot Commodities: How Anyone Can Invest Profitably in the World's Best Market,
by Jim Rogers
Investment Biker: Around the World with Jim Rogers, *by Jim Rogers*

Accumulators

Buffett: The Making of an American Capitalist, *by Roger Lowenstein*
The Essays of Warren Buffett : Lessons for Corporate America,
by Warren E. Buffett and Lawrence A. Cunningham
The Real Warren Buffett: Managing Capital, Leading People,
by James O'Loughlin
The Warren Buffett Way: Investment Strategies of the World's Greatest Investor,
by Robert G Hagstrom
Of Permanent Value: The Story of Warren Buffett, 2006 Literary Edition,
by Andrew Kilpatrick
Security Analysis, *by Benjamin Graham*
The Intelligent Investor, *by Benjamin Graham*
Benjamin Graham: Memoirs of the Dean of Wall Street,
by Benjamin Graham, Marjorie G Janis
Value Investing: From Graham to Buffett and Beyond,
by Bruce Greenwald, Judd Kahn, Paul Sonkin, Michael van Biema
Tearing Down the Walls: How Sandy Weill Fought His Way to the Top of the
Financial World and Then Nearly Lost It All, *by Monica Langley*
The King of Capital: Sandy Weill and the Making of Citigroup,
by Amey Stone and Mike Brewster
The Real Deal: My Life in Business and Philanthropy,
by Sandy Weill and Judah S. Kraushaar
The Accidental Zillionaire: Demystifying Paul Allen, *by Laura Rich*

Lords

Andrew Carnegie, *by Joseph Frazier Wall*
Andrew Carnegie, *by David Nasaw*
Carnegie, *by Peter Krass*
Gospel of Wealth, *by Andrew Carnegie*
The Autobiography of Andrew Carnegie, *by Andrew Carnegie*
Titan: The Life of John D Rockefeller, Snr, *by Ron Chernow*
Giants of American Industry - John D. Rockefeller, *by Ellen Greenman Coffey*
John D. Rockefeller: Anointed with Oil, *by Grant Segall*
As I See It: The Autobiography of J Paul Getty, *by Jean Paul Getty*
How to Be Rich, *by Jean Paul Getty*
John Paul Getty: Billionaire Oilman, *by Bruce S. Glassman*
The Google Story, *by David Vise and Mark Malseed*
The Search: How Google and Its Rivals Rewrote the Rules of Business and Transformed Our Culture, *by John Battelle*

Mechanics

Ford: The Times, the Man, the Company, *by Alan Nevins*
My Life and Work, *by Henry Ford and Samuel Crowther*
The People's Tycoon: Henry Ford and the American Century, *by Steven Watts*
Wheels for the World: Henry Ford, His Company, and a Century of Progress, *by Douglas G. Brinkley*
Grinding it Out: The Making of McDonalds, *by Ray Kroc, Robert Anderson*
McDonald's: Behind the Arches, *by John F Love*
In Sam We Trust: The Untold Story of Sam Walton and Wal-Mart, the World's Most Powerful Retailer, *by Bob Ortega*
Made in America, My Story, *by Sam Walton*
Sam Walton & Wal-Mart, *by Sam Walton*
The Wal-Mart Triumph: Inside the World's #1 Company, *by Robert Slater*
The Wal-Mart Way: The Inside Story of the Success of the World's Largest Company, *by Don Soderquist*
IKEA Magic: 20 Business Lessons, *by John Grant*
Leading by Design: The IKEA Story, *by Bertil Torekull*
Direct from Dell: Strategies that Revolutionized an Industry, *by Michael Dell, Catherine Fredman*
How Dell Does It, *by Steven Holzner*

General Entrepreneur Sources

Forbes Greatest Business Stories of All Time, *by Daniel Gross*
Forbes Great Success Stories: 12 Tales of Victory Wrested from Defeat, *by Alan Farnham*
Forbes Greatest Investing Stories, *by Richard Phalon*

Good Business: Leadership, Flow, and the Making of Meaning,
by Mihaly Csikszentmihalyi
How to be a Billionaire: Proven Strategies from the Titans of Wealth,
by Martin S Fridson
Lessons from the Legends of Wall Street: How Warren Buffett, Benjamin
Graham, Phil Fisher, T. Rowe Price, and John Templeton Can Help You Grow
Rich, *by Nikki Ross*
Lessons from the Top: In Search of the Best Business Leaders,
by Thomas Neff and James Citrin
Movers and Shakers, The People Behind Business Today,
ultimatebusinessresource.com
The Change Makers: How the Great Entrepreneurs Transformed Ideas into
Industries, *by Maury Klein*
The Prize : The Epic Quest for Oil, Money & Power, *by Daniel Yergin*

History of Flow Sources

The I Ching or Book of Changes,
by C. G. Jung, Hellmut Wilhelm, Richard Wilhelm, Cary F. Baynes
The Complete I Ching: The Definitive Translation by the Taoist Master Alfred
Huang, *by Taoist Master Alfred Huang*
The Taoist I Ching, *by Lui I-Ming and Thomas Cleary*
Understanding the I Ching,
by Hellmut Wilhelm, Richard Wilhelm, Cary F. Baynes, and Irene Eber
Tao Te Ching, 25th-Anniversary Edition,
by Lao Tsu, Gia-Fu Feng, and Jane English
Tao Te Ching, *by Lao Tsu, Jonathan Star*
The Secret of the Golden Flower: A Chinese Book of Life,
by Tung-Pin Lu and Richard Wilhelm
Five Elements, Six Conditions: A Taoist Approach to Emotional Healing,
Psychology, and Internal Alchemy, *by Gilles Marin*
A History of Chinese Civilization,
by Jacques Gernet, J. R. Foster, and Charles Hartman
A Short History of Chinese Philosophy,
by Yu-lan Fung and Derk Bodde
The Shape of Ancient Thought: Comparative Studies in Greek and Indian
Philosophies, *by Thomas McEvilley*
Study of Time in Indian Philosophy, *by Anindita Niyogi Balslev*
The Philosopher's Stone: A Quest for the Secrets of Alchemy, *by Peter Marshall*
Alchemy: An Introduction to the Symbolism and the Psycholog (Studies in
Jungian Psychology), *by Marie-Louise Von Franz*
The Forge and the Crucible: The Origins and Structure of Alchemy,
by Mircea Eliade
An Alchemy of Mind: The Marvel and Mystery of the Brain, *by Diane Ackerman*
A History of Western Philosophy, *by Bertrand Russell*
Science: A History 1534-2001, *by John Gribbin*

The Scientists: A History of Science Told Through the Lives of Its Greatest Inventors, *by John Gribbin*
The Metaphysics, *by Aristotle and Hugh Lawson-Tancred*
Galileo Galilei: Inventor, Astronomer, and Rebel, *by Michael White*
Dialogue Concerning the Two Chief World Systems,
by Galileo, Albert Einstein, John Heilbron, and Stillman Drake
Leonardo da Vinci: Flights of the Mind, A Biography, *by Charles Nicholl*
Isaac Newton, *by James Gleick*
Isaac Newton: The Last Sorcerer, *by Michael White*
Principia (On the Shoulders of Giants),
by Sir Isaac Newton and Stephen W. Hawking
The Man Who Changed Everything: The Life of James Clerk Maxwell,
by Basil Mahon
E = mc2: A Biography of the World's Most Famous Equation, *by David Bodanis*
About Time: Einstein's Unfinished Revolution, *by Paul Davies*
Man and His Symbols, *by Carl Gustav Jung*
Memories, Dreams, Reflections, *by C.G. Jung, Aniela Jaffe, Clara Winston, Richard Winston*
The Archetypes and The Collective Unconscious,
by C. G. Jung, Gerhard Adler, and R.F.C. Hull
The Portable Jung, *by Carl G. Jung, Joseph Campbell, and R.F.C. Hull*
Synchronicity: An Acausal Connecting Principle, *by C. G. Jung and R.F.C. Hull*
Synchronicity: The Promise Of Coincidence, *by Deike Begg*
John Maynard Keynes: 1883-1946: Economist, Philosopher, Statesman,
by Robert Skidelsky
The International Monetary System,
by Peter B. Kenen, Francesco Papadia, Fabrizio Saccomanni
Unholy Trinity: The IMF, World Bank and WTO, *by Richard Peet*
Beyond the Atom: The Philosophical Thought of Wolfgang Pauli,
by K. V. Laurikainen
Atom and Archetype: The Pauli/Jung Letters, 1932-1958,
by C. G. Jung, Wolfgang Pauli, C.A. Meier, and Beverley Zabriskie
The Hero with a Thousand Faces, *by Joseph Campbell*
The Power of Myth, *by Joseph Campbell and Bill Moyers*
Synchrodestiny: Harnessing the Infinite Power of Coincidence to Create Miracles, *by Deepak Chopra*
The Tao of Physics, *by Fritjof Capra*
Causality and Chance in Modern Physics, *by David Bohm*
Causality: Models, Reasoning, and Inference, *by Judea Pearl*
Causality, Electromagnetic Induction, and Gravitation, *by Oleg D. Jefimenko*
Symmetry, Causality, Mind, *by Michael Leyton*
The Power of Flow: Practical Ways to Transform Your Life with Meaningful Coincidence, *by Charlene Belitz and Meg Lundstrom*
Flow: The Psychology of Optimal Experience, *by Mihaly Csikszentmihalyi*
Finding Flow: The Psychology of Engagement with Everyday Life,
by Mihaly Csikszentmihalyi

Online Sources

The following websites have been the source of excellent reports, interviews and data on the entrepreneurs and companies covered in this book:

Economist Magazine: www.economist.com
Financial Times: www.ft.com
Forbes Magazine: www.forbes.com
Fortune Magazine: www.cnn.com/fortune
Hollywood Reporter: www.hollywoodreporter.com
New Scientist: www.newscientist.com
Press Gazette: www.pressgazette.co.uk
Public Broadcasting Service: www.pbs.org
Smart Money: www.smartmoney.com
Wikipedia: www.wikipedia.org
XL Magazine: www.resultsfoundation.com/xlmagazine

Visit the websites for more information and research.

All the books listed in this reading list are available on the XL Online Store, on Amazon.com, and can be borrowed subject to availability from the XL Vision Villas library in Bali, Indonesia.

INDEX